Privilege of Parenting

On Becoming Our Best Selves Through Raising Children

By

Bruce Dolin, Psy.D.

PoP The World Publishing

PoP the World Publishing
462 N. Linden Drive
Beverly Hills, California 90212

Published by PoP the World/Bruce Dolin, Psy.D.

ISBN: 0984625755
ISBN-13: 9780984625758

Library of Congress: TXu1-717-887

A catalogue record for this book is available from the Library of Congress.

For Andy, Nate & Will—

Blessings beyond all words.

Acknowledgements

I could write a book simply thanking the many people who I love and appreciate, who have taught and inspired me.

Nevertheless, beyond dedicating this book to Andy, Nate and Will I must also thank them for teaching me—Andy for teaching me how parenting, loving and living is really done, and my boys who I adore each for their unique spirits, and who gave up some of our potential time together so that this book might help other children (I look forward to fun times ahead with all three of you).

I also want to thank my family from Chicago to northern California and my dear friends in Los Angeles, Seattle, New York, Atlanta and my blogging friends who have helped me to refine my voice and find community in an unexpected place.

My hat is also off to Dr. Marvin Spiegelman whose guidance has been of inestimable importance on the journey of individuation—a kindred spirit.

Given that parenting *is* yoga, I must thank my yoga teachers, Marie Besso, Matt Schwartz, Jenny Brill, Shawn Bracha and Dr. Raphael Gunner—all dear to me in their own way. Namaste.

I thank my clients, from the kids in the group home who I carry always in my heart and thoughts, and for whom I deeply wish to raise consciousness about the peril we create for ourselves when we allow children to suffer in the shadows of our collective psyche.

But no less do I thank the clients who have bravely sat with me on Sawtelle and on Linden Drive, teaching me every step of the way in the netherworld of what is possible between two human beings if they are open to it—ever deepening my love and respect for the resiliency and transcendence nascent in our collective situation.

I thank my agent, Jessica Papin, whose belief in this book, even though she could not sell it to an industry busy falling off a cliff, gave me the faith to publish it anyway; and I thank my editor, Susan Salter Reynolds, who took the baton when I was out of juice, and deftly brought it to light with love and compassion.

Finally, I would like to thank this book itself, for it represents my best effort to get out of my own way and be of use—expressing not what "I" cared to say, but what my best and deepest Self was inspired to offer in the service of a more compassionate and conscious world.

Contents

Introduction

All Parents Love Their Children

I have never met a parent who didn't love his or her child. As a psychologist I have worked with some terrible situations, but there is always love somewhere in every parent's heart. Some parents are virtually oblivious to the needs of their children or unable to care for them, and still we ought not to judge them (there but for the grace of God go any one of us) but instead consider that perhaps they too love their children and are unable to actualize that love. In this book we set our sights on the parent who is doing well enough to choose to read a book about parenting, but who still knows—like every one of us—that he or she could do better. The intention of this book is to help you transform the abiding love and appreciation that you already have for your child into a more consistently lived reality.

This book strives to empower you to think more deeply about your relationship with your child or children; to help you curb endless seeking and begin your own authentic search for courage and wisdom—not in my words, not in any self-help book— but in your own Self. [Note that in this book I use the word "self" to mean something akin to the ego, and the capitalized "Self" as more akin to the deeper spirit, or soul, within us.] As subversive as it might sound (or even duplicitous, as I am an author) my wish is to cure you of reading self-help books—so long as it helps you to be your best Self. The sooner you're ready to toss this book into the trash or the fire the better.

I am proud to say that this book took me years to write because I tried my best not to work on it when I could spend time with my children. I am also proud to say that this is a self-published work; while I have a wonderful literary agent, the economic climate in which I launch this book has left me no other option—esteemed publishing houses have expressed praise and the promise to publish *Privilege of Parenting* if only I could "raise my profile," but alas I am both an introvert and someone who stands for pretty much the opposite of building a "platform" (in fact my blog at www.privilegeofparenting.com began as sweat-beading-on-my-forehead "platform building" and turned out to be a lovely and liberating way to directly connect with readers; that experience has empowered me to trust that my book might reach, and help, some parents without me having to become the "next Dr. Phil").

The following pages represent my effort to communicate some of the things I've learned through my experiences as a psychologist in the trenches of non-profit mental health, in private practice and as a parent.

The Title is the Core Message

Children are a gift, sacred beings entrusted to us to facilitate their growth and development. But parenting can also be transformative for the parent. No one is fully formed when they choose to parent, no matter how good a planner they are. Parenting is a perfect arena for our own growth and enlightenment because it takes us beyond our self and demands we use our highest power—the power to love. In parenting we are challenged to love someone more than our own self.

Beyond being nice for our children, being our best Self as a parent is actually a way to become happy. Ideal parenting is not a super-human feat. It is the cumulative effect of countless small moments well-handled. Such moments add up to good parenting just as they add up to a life well-lived.

Once we grasp that parenting truly is a privilege and a gift (try to imagine life without your child) parenting ceases to be a burden or a worry. Parenting is not so much something we have to do; it is something we *get* to do. When we parent with the clear understanding that it is a privilege, we actually receive its gift and we find ourselves getting something we have always wanted (but which had failed to come to us via money, achievement, pleasures or thrills): a feeling of being right with ourselves and the world, a grown-up and bittersweet sort of happiness I like to call, "good feelings that last."

Right Action

If we distill this book down to a guiding principal it would be that every decision, every potential action or non-action, can be put through the filter of two questions: 1) Will this choice, action or response lead toward, or away from, good feelings that last? and, 2) If I already had everything I could ever need and want and felt completely loved and free of longing, fear, anxiety and sorrow, what would be the loving thing to do or say in the situation at hand? If you could consistently consider these two questions and behave according to your own wisdom you would need very little else, if anything, in this book. The art of parenting is not so much knowing what to do, as it is consistently doing it.

The intention of this book is to help you find good feelings that last *through* being a better parent. Good parenting is mindful and conscious without being overly self-conscious or self-involved. Good parenting is rife with paradox—it must be accepting, non-judgmental and non-shaming. It must also be firm, limit-setting and structured. Sometimes as parents it seems as if everything we do is wrong—and often that is actually when we are getting it right; sometimes we think we're doing great and are blind-sided by a crisis. We wonder, "What should I do?" and the answer is inevitably, "It depends..." as so many factors are always at play. In the end, it is our hearts that choose, guide and act when we are parenting well.

Right action leads to right thinking. Use this book as encouragement to right (i.e. compassionate, patient, kind, wise, caring) action. Use its ideas not to find the right answer but to embrace the right attitude.

Relationship Is Everything

I love my own parents very much and have worked hard to build an adult relationship with them that I can enjoy (even if they still make me crazy now and then, as I am sure I do to them). I love my children with all my heart, and through the privilege of parenting them I have found the greatest happiness I have known. Yet the truth remains that my own childhood was not one to which I long to return. One result of this is that I never particularly yearned for children. I had only the vague sense that if I didn't have them I might want them later and find myself too old to take care of them. My own personal emotional adjustment to parenthood was something akin to being trampled by horses. I fell immediately in love with both of my children upon their arrival, but as any mother can attest, that is a far cry from actually "getting it"—from thinking about what has to be done and then doing it. It took many trials and painful conflicts to get into the flow of parenting, to appreciate its beauty, its richness and its healing potential.

As a psychologist I work to help people confront "reality" and take responsibility for themselves, but I also work to help people get out of their own way, to let go of resistance to success, happiness and the simple (but by no means simplistic) pleasures of loving and being. This book seeks to help you unlock your creativity and envision the sort of relationship you wish to have with your child (and the sort of life you want to live as a parent) and, with new attitudes and approaches, find your way to living, loving and relating in a way that really works for you and your child.

Understanding is the root of all real, and thus sacred, relationships, (as opposed to relationships of use where the other is seen and treated as an "object," even a beloved object). Relationship, whether it is with children, friends, Self or the transcendent source of all things, is the catalyst of healing and transformation. The right relationships can activate your natural inner healing and growth—and in turn nourish your children and activate healing and transformation in them. As a writer I seek to create a relationship with you, the reader. This book offers camaraderie in the trenches, as well as support, encouragement and validation for your efforts to serve your children. If our writer-reader relationship provokes you to come up with your own more clearly defined opinions (and the resolve to follow them as a parent) I would consider that successful.

In the context of relationships, I would be horribly remiss if I didn't admit from the start that the real expert parent in our household is my wife, Andy. Like many men before me, I pondered and pontificated at times when I should have been parenting—she is as a good a writer as me, and a better parent.

Spirituality

Whether things in your family are only partly cloudy or an outright hurricane at the moment, something has compelled you to reach for these words at this particular time. My best guess is that you need some sort of love, healing and understanding; who doesn't? Perhaps if you allow it, the parenting journey can heal you. I have found that often the cure for our alienation, isolation and despair lies largely in getting out of ourselves and giving to others, particularly when we don't much feel like it. If there is truth in this then parenting—a situation where we, with our own unmet needs, are chronically confronted with the needs and demands of our children—is a perfect opportunity for transformation and healing.

The pain of what is going wrong for us can be viewed as guidance. If we "kill" our pain with pills and distractions we kill the messenger of potential change and redirection. When we espouse and live an attitude of appreciation and gratitude for what is, we foster within ourselves a softness bred of strength and a surrender bred of free-will; then the universe seems to open and carry us along toward our deepest wishes. Parenting is a naturally spiritual endeavor; we host and care for, but are not the ultimate source of, our children. You may have a religion that you follow, you may believe in nothing beyond yourself, but we all have some sense of soul—of sacredness at our core that needs to be nourished and honored. Parenting is a spiritual path, a practical cure for the psychic wounds we carry and a balm for the fear and dread that block us from savoring the blessing that is our life and our children (all our collective children, in fact).

Children connect us to the eternal. Our children are ambassadors of spirit who re-introduce us to what we once were and could be again— authentic, true, alive... they bring us to the ultimate and only prayer we really need: Thank You. Over the years as a practicing psychologist I find myself repeating certain core ideas to struggling parents that have proven useful and it is in this same spirit that I write. My hope is that my words will help direct you toward your true Self, and empower you to turn to that true Self to guide you in your parenting, your life and your spiritual path. It serves us to ask of whatever situation we are in, "What can I learn from this? How can I grow through this?" Our task is to let go of what we no longer need and willingly embrace our children and the demands of parenting. Then magic happens, parenting takes care of itself, becomes its own self-reinforcing reward—like breathing.

The Yoga of Parenting

A challenge of this book is to bring practical spirituality to parenting. Yoga is a spiritual practice rooted in the body and the breath; the philosophy of yoga[1] teaches us to be present, to be strong and soft simultaneously, while the practice of yoga enhances our ability to bring our best Self to parenting—and to everything we do.

In recent years yoga has become increasingly popular in the United States. As a therapist I frequently encourage my clients to consider taking up yoga. It is a very effective way to relieve stress and depression. Yoga teaches us where we need to grow; it might be in balancing, it might be in opening and trusting, it might be in increasing our ability to turn inward and be quiet. Parenting *is* yoga. The word "yoga" means to yoke, inferring the harnessing of body, mind and spirit toward a singular intention (be it God, our child, or the divine between us all). Parenting, as a full-contact endeavor, can become yoga if we make it more conscious—if we "surrender to the pose" rather than flinch at the would-be torture of discomfort.

My mom introduced me to yoga when I was a small child; I would do it to a record (this was just after humans had invented the wheel), following the pictures on the album cover. As I grew older my interest in yoga was overshadowed by other pursuits and as years passed, it seemed more and more intimidating to begin again. As providence would have it, during a school fundraiser my wife had bid on some yoga lessons at a studio near my office. With the coupon dusty and about to expire and she unable to make use of it, I took my stiff knees over to the yoga studio to see what it was all about. Renting a mat and intimidated by the unfamiliar terms, I sweated and shook and barely touched my ankles, but when I left I felt rejuvenated and inspired to return. Many clients whom I have encouraged to go to one class have found themselves returning as well—and their therapy has inevitably deepened and progressed with their yoga.

If you are already a yogi you will likely find the ideas in this book highly compatible with your thinking; if you have not tried yoga, you may be inspired to give it a chance. Either way, when you dedicate an activity, be it yoga, cooking or parenting, *to* something, you give it a little boost; you introduce a spiritual element into the otherwise potentially mundane and bring more consciousness and love into whatever it is you are doing. Perhaps you might dedicate the mere reading of this book to your child— consciously setting the intention to be your best Self as a parent. If you do that, rather than just reading about parenting, in a sense you are already "doing" yoga. Yoga doesn't take us to any particular place of limberness, rather it takes us into the here and now— and in this way I hope this book can be part of your yoga.

A Scarcity of True Adults

In exploring what's really the matter with our own parenting we must consider the cultural context in which we parent, particularly the influence of our collective arrested development where an ethic of adolescent self-focus and self-indulgence (and subsequent fear, emptiness and unhappiness) runs rampant. Kids need to rebel against adult norms to test limits and form their identities, but when grown-ups are still rebelling and not setting adequate limits they can rebel against, kids have to keep upping the ante in order to try and find themselves and feel real. *Growing up in a society that mocks and devalues the very concept of growing up is one of the central challenges of becoming a better parent.*

Our world makes growing up look bad. We live in a youth-obsessed culture riddled with fears of aging and an idealization of the fat-free, wrinkle-free and thought-free. In considering where the real problems lie, we must contemplate the collective effect on children of supposed grown-ups behaving as if they were still children themselves and with as little intention of growing up as Peter Pan.

Growing up, although dreary at first if one has long avoided it, is actually fun in its own way. Many clients I have worked with initially resist growing up, but once they take the plunge they wonder why they waited so long. Becoming about something beyond meeting our own needs and pleasures typically brings increased meaning and happiness into our lives; our children are a natural incentive to do this. Whether or not we are personally keen on becoming grown-ups, "live fast, die young and leave a pretty corpse," is not much of a parenting motto. It is essential for our kids' well-being (and our own long-term happiness) that we let our children be the kids and that we give up that role and rise to our potential capacity to care-give.

America is poised to come out of its long and awkward adolescence, not just in its dealings with the rest of the world, but in its emerging willingness to take better care of its own children. Even if big social programs *do* leave kids behind, we all personally love our kids and I see us stepping up more and more at the individual level, which will have huge long-term positive effects. We are becoming less arrogant and more willing to question our own parenting and in this way we are growing up together.

This book is not a lament on social conditions and the lack of good role-models for us as parents. Those things represent the past. Even if our culture still struggles with self-involvement and emptiness, it is our task as parents to look around and find figures who inspire us as caregivers. This could be our own grandmother or it could be Oprah Winfrey who, in starting a school for disadvantaged girls to promote leadership, refers to all the students as her "daughters."

By acknowledging that there has been a scarcity of true grown-ups for us to look to we can deepen our compassion for ourselves and each other in the service of becoming our best Selves as parents. We can also dig deeper within that best Self for our faith, love, courage and optimism to look harder for our personal heroes and mentors. Being against things does not make them better—figuring out what we are *for* empowers us to lead by example, inspire and educate our children about how to live, love and participate in a better world. When we personally intuit that all children are our children we overcome the mistaken ideas that separate us from others and which sets the stage for neglect, poverty and oppression.

Too many of our children are living in poverty without access to good education and their problems are easy enough to grasp, albeit hard to ameliorate in a context of cultural indifference, but even privileged children are often quite unhappy: too often spoiled, entitled, mean and just plain rude, not to mention glassy-eyed and numb from all the electronic games they play. These are signs of low-self-esteem, lack of purpose and general lostness. All the music lessons, riding lessons, art lessons and accelerated paths to wealth and prominence do not make up for the influence of us parents if we are miserable within ourselves and rotten to each other. If we really want to help our children, we have to take a hard look at how we ourselves are doing, at what we choose to buy and do, and at how it is, or is not, working for us.

Productive Suffering— Sometimes Worry is an Act of Love

Chances are you're worried about a child. Good for you. That's a huge part of our job as parents and caregivers: we worry about children. The problems often start when they (the children) have to worry too much about their own safety and well being, or even worse, when they must worry about us (the would-be grown-ups). Children need to be protected from the harsh realities of the adult world until they're ready to make sense of them (i.e. that the world is not necessarily safe, that bad things happen, that the world is not fair, that we all die, etc.). For a child's development to unfold optimally, the right things should happen at the right times. In the very beginning kids learn to trust by being shielded from danger and anxiety, later they learn to be safe by recognizing and staying away from danger. A one-year-old cannot possibly conceptualize keeping him or herself safe from strangers, but a five-year-old who knows nothing about strangers is at risk. Thus you have to teach kids the things they are ready to learn—teach them too early and you overwhelm them, teach them too late and you leave them vulnerable.

Worry but don't despair. Worry to the extent that *someone* needs to worry, and then stop. It is important to keep in mind that our "best Self" also necessarily includes our worst self: aware of our darker aspects but consciously striving for the light. Parenting is not about being perfect; our best Self is balanced and human, recognizing our limitations and failures, growing where we can and bearing it gracefully where we cannot.

It helps for us parents to curb our anxiety, depression and bitterness or, at least, not spill them over onto our children. Kids want to please us and can all too easily learn to unconsciously hold whatever feelings we inadvertently give them. Holding our unwanted feelings is a tragic and crippling act of love by our children; the sort of parenting we want to facilitate reverses that flow so that we hold their feelings when they are overwhelmed and this teaches them how to "hold it together" as they develop.

Individuation, or truly growing up, calls for the integration of opposites. While we must confront the dark and the difficult, we must equally keep in mind the light, the fun and the silly. So as a parent, a sense of humor is advisable—besides, it looks good on you!

A Guide to This Book

Conceptually, this book is not so much a "how-to" book as it is "why-to." The more deeply we understand each other, ourselves and our children, the more we are able to be our best Self in parenting and all our endeavors.

Each chapter flows from questions that I myself, and the parents with whom I have worked, have struggled. Chapters are structured to frame a central question or conflict related to parenting, and then explore what might be in the way of your child or yourself with regard to this issue. All problems distill down to some form of resistance. When we embrace what is and manage to appreciate and learn from it, we are freed to proceed to our next challenge, lesson or blessing. Each chapter also offers various anecdotes drawn from my clinical experiences and from my life.

Keeping with the book's central approach of thinking deeply and working practically, each chapter offers an array of novel perspectives on the key issues ("Broadening Our Perspective"), followed by pragmatic tactics that parents can employ to enhance their effectiveness ("Strategies for Helping"). This book's ethic is that of compassionate understanding in the service of helping you love and give. It is the love you give that will heal you and bring you good feelings that last.

Finally, each chapter concludes with "Exercises to Consider," ranging from the practical, to the creative, to the off-the-wall that offer ways to shake things up and put ideas into action. Right action leads to right thinking—if you're stuck, consider acting "as if" you were your best, less frightened, less depressed Self and see if that might not lead to you discovering that you are indeed your best Self. You love your child and want to do your best—it is your noble passion. Let us work together in spirit—in a shared covenant of trying our best.

Chapter 1

Attitude Is Everything—Choose It Wisely

Lenny's War

I first met Lenny[1] unpacking his things in one of the melancholy bedrooms of the group home where I worked. He was fifteen, slight and pale, with poor hygiene, dark, greasy hair, and a furious-anxious, creepy quality that made me think of Renfield, Dracula's bug-eating assistant. He yanked a few nerd-plaid shirts from a scuffed American Tourister and crumpled them into the room's lone Salvation Army dresser with its faux-oak veneer slashed through to reveal cheap composite.

The sound of trucks passing on the busy San Fernando Valley street lined with body-shops and lumber mills rumbled through the flimsy walls, which were riddled with plaster patches where they had been punched and kicked through by the room's former occupants. The typical kid seemed to last about four months and the residential counselors the same. I introduced myself to Lenny as his new therapist. He met my gaze with darkly angry eyes and said "F-you."

I knew very little about Lenny, just that he was being transferred from another group home that had officially determined that he was ready for greater freedom and a less restricted environment, but I suspect it was more likely that they were just done with him. I had met his mother in the driveway. She was a proud woman in her mid-thirties with a thick yet vaguely erudite foreign accent. The make-up-dusted worry lines on her face made her look ten years older in the harsh light of stress, loss, sorrow and late afternoon sun. Her conservative clothes pegged her as at least trying, in stark contrast to her frumpy (and no doubt to her, embarrassing) kid. She seemed nice enough but harried and eager to drop off her son and get away in her scratched Camry. From the file, I knew that dad was not in the picture and that a more high-functioning younger brother got to live at home with the mom.

I tried another gambit, asking Lenny about his previous group home. He responded "F-you" as if it were the answer that explained everything. I tried to keep things positive, to be welcoming, but he acknowledged all of my efforts with a staccato volley of "F-you's" until after a long fifteen minutes I retreated, backing out of the heartbreakingly crappy bedroom that he had to share with an aggressive and intermittently psychotic kid who didn't want him there.

Although I was no stranger to rude behavior, having been in charge of the six-bed therapeutic home for several months by the time Lenny arrived, I had never felt such cold wrath come off a kid. The other fourteen to eighteen-year-olds were passionately heated in their disrespect, which at least tended to be triggered by something more substantial than "hello." While none of the kids were interested in talking about their feelings with a therapist, the others were at least game for sizing me up, or trying to challenge or manipulate me. Lenny was like a steel door that couldn't care less who was knocking. He wanted no solicitations, no visitors, and he most certainly did not want to be in my group home. I was there to help, but this kid was hard to like.

I was thirty-five, accruing post-doctoral hours in order to sit for the state licensure exams, written and oral. I had staggering student loans, a baby at home and another on the way, and worked (in tandem with a small private practice I was trying to build) twelve to fourteen hour days, six days a week (and then covered on-call emergencies round the clock), all the while struggling not to be overwhelmed by the despondency and inefficiency of a system which trapped Lenny and my other charges in a decrepit apartment where you might sooner expect to find some perpetrator from a 70's cop show than a troubled kid. My own little Father Flanagan group home was just one sad piece of a sorry puzzle that all came together into a sprawling non-profit agency with twelve group homes, four special needs schools and an out-patient clinic, which in turn fit into Los Angeles' vast and unwieldy network of departments of children's services, mental health, the juvenile justice system, foster homes, other group homes and abandoned kids on the streets.

As Lenny settled in to our particular little corner of bleak circumstance, it became apparent that "F-you" was his signature phrase. He was an isolate who shunned sports and music, showed low frustration tolerance and irritated the staff and the other kids. As his therapist I was responsible for giving him sixty minutes of individual psychotherapy per week. Yet when I would come into his classroom to tell him that it was time for his session, he would say "F-you," and stay where he was. Consequences, "level drops" (which meant the loss of a weekly allowance and the brief independent walks that a student earned for good behavior) and denial of otherwise coveted outings to movies and the arcade all had no impact. He was aggressively negative and rejecting at all times. It seemed impossible to work with such a boy, and one day I lamented my frustration to my supervisor, a twenty-year veteran who was great once you learned how not to piss her off (by always erring on the side of caution and thinking of every emergency in terms of its potential for screaming, worst-case-scenario, newspaper headlines that would shame the agency and get us all in trouble). She readily conceptualized Lenny's over-all problem as low self-esteem. Her counsel was to continually confront his core issue by responding to every disrespectful "F-you," with "you're feeling badly about yourself." This initially struck me as absurd, but I had no other ideas and my supervisor had a lot of experience.

It was like being cast in a play by Samuel Beckett: Therapist: "How's it going, Lenny?' Lenny: "F-you." Therapist (with empathy): "You're feeling bad about yourself." Lenny: "F-you." Therapist: "You're feeling bad about yourself, Lenny. Do you want to come to my office?" Lenny: "F-you." Therapist: "I guess you're feeling bad about yourself." Long, long silence—maybe thirty minutes. Therapist: "Okay, I'll see you next time."

Lenny: "F-you."

Therapist (exiting the classroom, but with empathic resolve): "You're feeling bad about yourself."

Lenny (to therapist's back): "F-you."

It went like this, literally, for months. No apparent progress was being made except that I discovered that Lenny liked to play chess. Eventually, by inviting him to play, I coaxed him to come to my office, a leaky trailer on the edge of a cracked asphalt yard where the lowest ranking therapists toiled in a Siberian wasteland far removed from the heat and air-conditioned offices of the supervisors—a strategy which worked so long as we did not talk about feelings. Lenny would relax during these games, and I would think "now we're ready to start real therapy," but the moment I ventured to ask a question about his life in the past, his feelings or his family, he would quickly escalate to torqued-out indignation and become extremely upset. Once he literally jumped up from the pathetic, stained plaid couch, pushed open the grimy window, and, with desperado eyes flashing and a foot on the sill, threatened to throw himself out. I wanted to laugh and cry—cry, because the terror he felt was heart-breaking, and laugh, because the drop to the tangle of dry weeds below the window was only three or four feet. For a second I thought his eyes betrayed the humor of the situation and he looked away from me, then sat back down and resumed the game, cursing me for bringing up feelings. I told him that he was feeling bad about himself but he let it go without an "F-you."

Even though we were now chess buddies, every session still began and ended as if nothing had changed; I kept up my "and you're still feeling bad about yourself." Then, one day, after four months of this, we were walking across the yard toward the cheesy, fake wood paneled trailer with its color palette of pea-soup, rotting pumpkin and decaying leaves when, in response to some attempt to make small talk, Lenny not only said "F-you," but followed it up with, "I guess I'm feeling bad about myself."

I was astounded. It was like I had dropped a pebble in a well and four months later I heard a splash.

This moment marked the turning point in our relationship. He still started and ended sessions with "F-you," but in between he began to open up about his life—and his behavior started to make much better sense to me. Between Lenny, and later his mother, I learned that he had been born in a foreign country that was swept by war. When Lenny was two or three his parents had emigrated to the U.S., but they were unable to take their son with them; the government insisted upon holding the child as collateral to assure their return. In the meantime the war escalated. When, at age four, bombs and rockets destroyed much of his neighborhood, Lenny, in the care of a grandmother, went from being a happy and playful child to totally losing the ability to use language. His parents eventually brought him to the States, but by that time he was a completely different child and had never been okay since.

As though the trauma of his early childhood were not enough, after some time Lenny told me about his father, who had been a highly educated and respected man in his native country, but who, in America, could find nothing better than a busboy job in a restaurant. One night, when Lenny was nine or ten, his father was stabbed to death in the alley behind the restaurant. Lenny's mother, immobilized by her husband's death, could no longer deal with her elder son's Tourette's-like outbursts of obscenities and insults, his anger and his defiance—all of which were really defenses against his terror and sorrow.

Despite being overwhelmed with guilt, his mother relinquished him to the state mental health system, which, to Lenny, hadn't felt like an act of love but rather echoed his original abandonment and merely consolidated feelings of being unloved and unlovable.

Once I understood Lenny's background, I was able to improvise a little on the original treatment strategy. Instead of "you're feeling bad about yourself," my new interpretation, whenever he took a risk or made some small academic or social success, became, "I hope you're feeling good about yourself." Over a couple of years his whole countenance transformed. His hygiene, grooming and interest in clothes improved and he began to make friends, and to laugh and participate in chores and activities. He even got a part-time job. He proved a rather likable guy, albeit quirky.

My supervisor had been entirely correct. Before Lenny, I could not have imagined that telling someone over and over the simple truth that his or her negative behavior was a symptom of pain and wounded self could actually facilitate that person's healing. I can't say I went on to "cure" Lenny, but then I can't say I've ever cured anyone. I can, however, say that he taught me a lot and that he remains in my heart as a courageous human being and a sacred spirit. I like to think that we helped each other figure out some things about ourselves. This mutual quest for identity, he striving to become an American kid and me striving to become a therapist, brought conflict and struggle until I stopped trying to change him and just strove to understand, keep things simple and allow him to teach me.

I share Lenny's story, and numerous other tough cases throughout this book, in the hope that it will encourage us to deepen our faith in our children's abilities to recover, to open up and to feel good about themselves no matter what they may have been through. While you may initially feel that these examples don't relate to your child's current age or issue, developmentally speaking we all start (and end) in the same place—and we all break down along similar psychological fault lines (i.e. hurt, fear, anger). Besides offering a reality check for how relatively mild many of our parenting challenges actually are (and thus encouraging patience and trust), it also serves us to be more aware of all our collective children. Challenging kids have taught me to not give up on people, and have also given me a bench-mark against which to appreciate how relatively mild most situations we face as parents are in comparison to the most extreme ones.

So, while Lenny is an extreme case, the lessons learned about dealing with self-esteem are highly applicable to ordinary parenting. It doesn't matter how smart a child is, if they're unhappy, anxious or carry low-self-esteem they need to be understood so they can grow happier and truer to their authentic natures.

I have spent many hours talking with kids about what hurts them and about what helps them heal; more than anything I have come to believe that we help children best by helping parents understand their children, develop greater patience and compassion and by supporting parents to be happy as their best and most authentic Selves.

The Search For A Sustainable Happiness

We want "happiness" for our children and ourselves, but what is happiness? The American dream is sometimes a nightmare from which we seem unable to wake up. We have a constitutional right to "the pursuit of happiness," but what we think of as happiness and what Thomas Jefferson meant by the term are two different things. The right to follow one's beliefs, to contribute, participate and live with freedom and dignity—this is synonymous with purpose, meaning and happiness. On the other hand, the manic pursuit of money, sex, thrills or material possessions is an endless jog on a treadmill to nowhere. Certainly we have the *right* to live an empty life, but we have become embroiled in a cycle of getting and spending that may actually *engender* an empty life. If we were more conscious about what really matters to us, we might spend our time, money and energy differently—and those different choices could benefit our children. They might end up with less "stuff," but with a parent who models realness and a sense of purpose rather than exhaustion, futility and a sense of being a slave to money, which may be what our parents collectively modeled for us, and might have something to do with why we so-called grown-ups are generally suspect about growing up.

A definition of happiness that I like as a therapy goal is: "Good feelings that last." I learned to think in these terms when working with emotionally disturbed teenagers who were prone to impulsively chase every thrill and pleasure they could lay their hands on, and always to their own detriment. Marijuana, being a depressant, would get depressed kids even more depressed, and mind loosening drugs would throw psychotic kids even further over the edge. Torrid romances would get abandoned girls pregnant and even more abandoned, suicide attempts would land already confined group home kids into the even stricter confinement of a psychiatric hospital.

While misguided teen behavior may seem obviously problematic, consider the more subtle behaviors we may indulge in that also bring good feelings that do not last. Our credit cards may tell the story of things we really didn't need (and often that lost their luster before they were even paid for). Our body may tell the story of the food we consumed to soothe our wounded hearts that only left us hungry for real nourishment and genuine love. Our resume may tell the story of jobs that failed to bring good feelings that last; our countless emails, texts and tweets may chart the course of good feelings that didn't last. If we haven't figured out how to live our lives in an emotionally successful way, how convincing are we when we tell our kids not to eat, watch or do certain things?

"Good feelings that last" can serve as a guiding principal in our parenting and in our life's journey. It is useful to shift our focus from "getting away from bad feelings" to "moving toward lasting good feelings." Ambition (i.e. to be a better parent) depends on the ability to emotionally tolerate the discrepancy between where we may be at the moment and where we want to be. It is essential not to focus on what we think we lack, but on appreciating the things we have while softly letting go of the mental and emotional blockages that stop us from seeing the beauty of our lives.

All actions consistent with how we would live if we were free and happy (managing debt responsibly, exercising, working at worthwhile endeavors, parenting with joy, making art, meditating, doing yoga, gardening, etc.) send powerful messages back to ourselves that we are already happy, successful and empowered and that nothing we need to be happy is missing. This attitude unlocks us to receive more good things and "spend" our good fortune wisely in the world. For example, if we are clear that we don't need more money to be happy, we bring less urgency and fear to our economic dealings and money flows more freely to us in return for goods or services we bring to the group. With a positive, pragmatic and loving attitude, we put our kids ahead of ourselves. We stop trying so hard to be happy and instead love and serve and before we know it "happiness" sneaks up on us, and that inspires happiness to grow organically in our children.

Framing Problems

To be effective in helping our children with their problems, the first thing we need to do is accurately determine what is actually wrong. The way we frame pain and conflict helps determine how we go about changing situations—and whether problems become entrenched or get resolved. For example, instead of "my child and I don't communicate" we say, "my child doesn't listen"; instead of realizing that we need to build a better relationship with our child, we declare that our child is problematic.

Relationships are of primary importance; it is in the context of them that we get wounded and it is in the context of the right relationships that we heal and develop into our best Selves. Genuine interest and expansive curiosity are at the heart of good relationships. Understanding how much it can mean to someone to simply be heard when flooded with difficult feelings can help us remember to take the time to be that person for our child when they need it.

There are no stand-alone "problems." Everything, good and bad, happens in a context—social, physical and even spiritual or meta-physical. Just as traditional Chinese medicine views illness as stuck or stagnant energy and healing as facilitating the movement and re-balancing of energy, we could view problems with our children as blockages in understanding, communication or the flow of love between us and our child. We generally cannot heal our children, but our love and connectedness with them moves stuck energy, which can activate healing—in them as well as in ourselves.

If we operate on the supposition that everyone has a right to be happy with who they are (even if they are unhappy with their circumstances and wish to improve them), we can shift our approach from problem-solving to relationship-building. If our child is unhappy we don't need to jump to conclusions and start fixing things. It might be more helpful to ask ourselves (and, probably more importantly, our child if they can answer) why they aren't happy at this present moment. If we are not asking and truly listening, this is the first thing to change.

Ask, Don't Solve

Carl, a chubby fifteen-year-old with bifocals and thin brown hair that clung tightly to his shinny forehead, was exceedingly bright and prided himself in his intelligence. He connected with adults by discussing Tolkien with the pathos of a Hobbit. But he had no friends and was a fish out of water as a good boy in a "bad boy school." He was a very feeling child but he had never learned how to manage his strong emotions of rage and longing, which would swamp him and make him feel inadequate and frightened. In sessions he would become enraged at me when I directly gave him empathy because it hurt so much. Gripped by a paroxysm of anguish, he would reach out and hit my shoe with an open palm, and then, overwhelmed with shame at his own aggression, he'd run out of my office in tears. I would usually find him sitting glumly on the nice couches in the marble school lobby donated by robber-barons-turned-philanthropists and the plaques that honored them. I would work to convince Carl that he hadn't hurt my foot (I felt his anguish much more keenly than his feeble slaps to my shoes) and, once he was calm, I would bring our inconclusive sessions to a lonely end and Carl would openly acknowledge that he was sad to say good-bye to me.

After several weeks of shoe-slapping followed by guilty tears, we were sitting once again in the mausoleum-like lobby where he looked up at me with eyes wet with shame, anger and sadness and asked us both a painfully honest question: "What's the use of being smart if I'm so unhappy?"

His question was a turning point in therapy where he let down his guard and acknowledged that intellect wasn't going to solve his loneliness. We then set to work on helping him learn how to be a friend—to himself and to others. The triumph of our work together came when he actually made a friend and had his first sleep-over, shortly after his sixteenth birthday.

Carl helped me learn how questions can deepen relationships while mere answers tend to cut them off. Sincere questions drive growth and learning which connects us to the world. Answers cut the world into pieces, which makes our relationships more static and less alive. While families need rules and codes of conduct just as societies do, these expectations must serve the group and its members, not imprison them. As parents we must notice our own contradictory impulses, such as our need for order and safety in contrast to our needs for emotional vitality and self-expression. Our children are also naturally self-contradictory beings and we must not demand consistent logic or predictability of emotion from them. Just as my lonely client needed to be emotionally rather than intellectually understood before change could occur, we need to learn about how our children are really hinged together in order to bring about more happiness in them and our families.

As parents trying to help our children, we must work to identify our true questions such as, "Why isn't our family happier?" Our children's so-called problems can be understood as eloquently honest questions. If we join them by asking ourselves not "What is wrong with my child?" but rather, "What must my child feel like and how might I better understand them and their feelings?" we connect with them and this can transform isolation, despair or negativistic behavior into melancholy shared with someone who deeply loves them. This connection is a critical interim step between pervasive sadness and lasting happiness. Accurate understanding is like a ladder one can climb down to reach a child who has fallen into a sad, lonely or otherwise difficult place. Sometimes we must climb down in order to show them the possibility of their climbing up.

Problems In Context

Before emotional questions of parenting can be contemplated we must ask basic questions of health and safety, which can also affect mood and behavior. There are times when we *do* want answers, such as when our child is sick. Still, no one expert is perfect for every child or every situation; an expert who makes us feel inadequate and intimidated, or who has an answer for us before we've even opened our mouth might not be the best person for us. Ideally, professionals work with us but they also work *for* us and we have the right to feel comfortable and respected or to seek a different professional.

When emotional or behavioral problems arise in a family, our first question can be whether something physical is going on with our child. Many things, such as too little sleep, hunger, earaches, colds, growth spurts, etc. can all cause patches of disagreeable moods and behaviors. It would be silly and annoying to interpret a child's sadness as emotional when she is actually suffering from an earache. Obviously, ideal parenting includes periodic check-ups and visits to the dentist. It also calls for common sense questions about how our child is feeling when they seem to be in distress in some way. Children (and many adults) are not always able to identify their

14

feelings and it helps enormously for them to be asked about how they feel so they learn to pay attention to their bodies and their hearts—and also learn that they are loved and that we are interested in them no matter how they feel.

When challenging behaviors arise and medical issues can be ruled out, one might then ask if anything else in a child's life has changed around the time the "problem" manifested. An example might be when a child reverts to bed-wetting or accidents at pre-school shortly after their parents have divorced. In such a case merely treating the bed-wetting misses the bigger picture. Our question might be, "What positive purpose might the child's behavior serve?" Maybe the father has moved out and the child's conscious, or unconscious wish that the father come back is being expressed as, "I am still a baby and I need you to come back." The child may alternately be saying, "You have made a mess of my life and I can't deal with it so you now have to deal with the mess that I can make." Once the right questions lead us to an accurate understanding of the child's feelings we can link with them so that at least they won't feel totally alone in their grief or fear. Often acting-out behaviors will drop away naturally once the message they carry has been received and the emotions behind them held consciously and compassionately in the parent's heart.

The Right Questions

As human beings, if we get what we need we are generally safe and happy. Our unhappiness begins in the past and perpetuates itself in the future. Our happiness can only really exist in the present moment. When we have been hurt we begin to anticipate more hurt, betrayal, rejection, etc. We try and stay safe by anticipating danger but our mind ends up like a hamster on a wheel, trying to get somewhere on a contraption that can't possibly take us anywhere other than the cage in which that wheel sits. Our fear that we won't be able to handle sad feelings blocks us from feeling, and from learning that sadness is okay.

Our children need to learn emotional courage and resilience from us. Intense emotion, even if it's painful, is better than feeling very little and is a first step to truly feeling good. Our feelings are an important tool we must use to understand our children's feelings. It is always useful to ask ourselves what might be in the way of our child feeling or behaving better? Perhaps the first thing that may be in the way is our fear of intense feelings. The ways we once had to psychologically and emotionally protect and numb ourselves can sometimes remain and block us long after the time when they formed in our own childhoods. The worldview that was once our fort can later become our prison. Considering what is in our child's, or our own, way is to peep out from our fort to see if the battlements are still needed or if we can notice that the siege is over—and that our children and everyone else we love live outside, and not within, our fort.

What's In the Way?

The first, albeit unconstructive question to we tend ask when we perceive a problem is, "Whose fault is it?" We may blame ourselves and succumb to guilt or shame, but this fails our child; when we become self-involved it cuts us off from our child, which may be the primary problem. We may blame other people for our child's unhappiness such as our spouse, the child's teacher or other children. When other people are seen as mean or bad rather than human and probably unhappy with themselves this invites passivity and a victim mentality, which do nothing to encourage better relationships.

We may despair that our child is messed up—a "problem child." This view reinforces problematic behaviors and low self-esteem. Blaming and labeling are divisive. They encourage us to view people in isolated terms rather than in the context of relationships. If we constrict the range of acceptable emotions such as fear or sadness it can lead to anxiety, depression or behavioral problems. For example, a child can be taught that tears are bad and so they become inhibited from expressing their naturally sad feelings. With no outlet for their tears they are forced into more socially sanctioned expressions of feeling, especially for males, such as anger and aggression. While this may be more comfortable than tears for some mothers or fathers, bullying often brings social ostracization and poor school performance, which only begets lower self-esteem and more cruelty, as other kids are made to feel the bully's fear and cry their tears for them.

Conversely, if anger builds up but cannot be expressed it turns against our self and results in depression. Labeling other children as mean or bad rather than encouraging a deeper understanding (such as seeing cruel behavior as reflecting insecurity) teaches a child to judge, fear and reject rather than to observe, wonder and learn how to connect with people who may be different from us. We may not want to facilitate friendships for your child with violent or problematic children, but if we are overly definitive that there are good people and bad people how can our children, with their naturally human but hidden dark sides, not secretly fear that they too may be one of the bad ones?

With low self-esteem, a child's difficult moments and frustrations seem more drastic than they are. They feel destined to continually lose or fail because of who they are; hope diminishes as sadness rises. Our natural instinct to cheer-up depressed people can backfire and make them feel misunderstood and more isolated. Being truly interested in how they came to see themselves in such a poor light bridges isolation and helps unlock stubborn negative self-images marked by shame and inadequacy. Interest, not persuasion or logic, allows a distorted sense of self to repair itself naturally.

Perhaps a child's negative self-image or sadness stems from a physical or neurological difference that does legitimately make some aspect of life harder for them than for others. We would not want to deny their differences, but we can gently challenge the erroneous generalizations they make about their core worth as human beings based on their differences. It is appropriate to feel sad about difficult situations but the more fully a child can express their feelings the more able they will be to love and accept who they are—and succeed by virtue of authenticity.

When a child's self-esteem is okay but they feel bad about life circumstances (i.e. moving) we want to ask ourselves what their life feels like to them. We as a parent may know what "the plan" is but if we don't talk to our child about it they may fear that there is no plan. Asking children about their specific concerns allows us to give them the information they need in order to feel safe or secure. If we are overwhelmed and do not have a plan, we can trust that our child will pick up on this feeling. By simply asking and listening to what our children feel we connect with them and this alone will help them feel better by being less alone and clearer about what they feel. We also want to be conscious of our own feelings so we do not ask our children to hold our fears, anxieties or sorrows for us.

Is our child getting what they need in order to grow, feel loved and be true to themselves? This is a core question. Our right questions can help us differentiate between what can, and thus should, be changed and what cannot be changed and must be managed. As parents we want to ameliorate all unnecessary suffering. After that we must help children contain and manage their pain where suffering is unavoidable.

The clearer we are on these points, the more convincing we will be when we tell our children that something is not their fault and they have nothing to be ashamed of— who they are is perfect and splendid. Where behavior can improve, the essence of who our child is still can be valued and appreciated, not criticized or condemned. We must trust that their best Self is eager to live and breathe, and we must see it even when they don't.

Maladaptive feelings and behaviors result from feeling threatened, unhappy or inadequate. Our child's feelings guide our questions; fear makes us ask what are they truly afraid of and why? Low self-esteem begs the question of what they think is not good enough about themselves and how they got that idea? Trouble letting go or making a transition calls for deeper understanding of what they feel they have lost. What could restore security and trust?

We must repeatedly ask ourselves if our relationship with our child is good. If it's not we need to figure out why and try to make it better. A good relationship doesn't mean that our child is always telling us everything they think and feel—more that we are graceful in tolerating their needs for closeness *and* for space, neither clinging nor rejecting. If we remain consistently interested in whatever they want to tell us our child will come to us eventually because we love them and they love us and they want to be understood.

Our primary problem as parents is the tendency to take our children's negative behaviors or feelings and make them about our self. Self-focus blocks relationship and we would not do this if we felt better and more secure about ourselves. We must ask ourselves, compassionately, what we are afraid of, what we secretly fear is inadequate about us so that we can get these insecurities out of the space between us and our child. We do not have to be totally secure to be good parents, but we cannot remain overly self-focused. If we can manage to put aside our questions about our self and truly focus on our child this improved parenting comes right back around to raise our self-esteem and to increase our feelings of happiness.

If we are overly self-focused our children can become emotionally neglected because we are too busy trying to get our own needs met. A more subtle presentation of self-focus appears, on its surface, as the very opposite of self-involvement. In this situation we are so over-focused on our child that they are smothered by the wrong kind of attention. Here our child's every emotion and action feels like an extension of us. In the first case we fail to notice our child's pain and in the second case we overreact to our own pain, which we see in our child's distress. It's as if our child cuts their finger and we faint. While us over-involved parents believe that our love for our child has no bounds, the truth may be that we lack psychological boundaries and have trouble differentiating our own thoughts and feelings from our child's. Over time, the selfish aspect of this sort of love becomes clearer as our child fails to develop the security to separate from us—at preschool or after college.

Our children generally tend to love us very much unless we abandon or hurt them, and even then they often cling to an ideal image of us in their minds. When we are unhappy it is very hard for our children because it is always painful to love someone who is unhappy, especially if we utterly depend on that person. If our unconscious message to our child is that their pain is our pain, sometimes our pain becomes their pain. When our child is sad over a long period of time we might want to ask ourselves if they could be picking up on our depression. When we deal with our own issues our kids no longer need to hold or express our unexpressed emotions.

Two key parental blocks to a good relationship with our child are guilt and shame. If we make use of guilt as a motivator to apologize and manage better behavior, guilt can be a guiding force; if guilt becomes pathological we beat ourselves up but do nothing to apologize or improve our behavior. This sort of guilt is another variation of an over-focus on our self.

Shame is more debilitating. Guilt makes us feel bad about our hurtful behavior, but we still sense that we are basically good. Shame brings an agonizing sense of being a bad person; then our bad behavior does not feel like a mistake so much as a reflection of who we are. When someone makes us feel guilty, or we make our child feel guilty, the message is that a positive expectation, such as kindness or generosity, has not been met; when we are shamed, or when we shame our child, the message is of disgust. As parents we do not want to shame our children, so we must consistently communicate that we have unceasing faith in their core goodness even when we

21

disapprove of their behavior. If we suffer from shame we may overreact to even constructive criticism with anger or rage because we feel that there is no way for us to do better since at core we fear we are no good. This reflects mistaken learning that can, and must, heal in order to become a better parent. Knowing this is a first step.

Broadening Our Perspective

After graduating from a doctoral program in clinical psychology, I had hoped to build a private practice working with high functioning adults. But I had very few clients and fewer still could afford to pay me. Meanwhile, student loans had to be paid, I had a child to feed and my wife had been largely supporting our little family during my studies. My panic-without-a-plan left me in a daze that was broken by a fellow graduate who called to see if I might be interested in a *paid* job. His apologetic tone was alarming: it was very low pay, but it was a chance to make a real difference in the lives of severely emotionally disturbed adolescents living in a group home. My friend was already working as a therapist for another group home within the organization. Turnover was extremely high and few people stayed longer than a year; the last therapist only lasted a couple of months.

On the plus side: there was a small salary. On the negative side: the kids were very angry and could be violent, they had to be *severely* troubled to even qualify for the program and many of them were schizophrenic, bi-polar or sociopathic. Beyond being frightening, the work was heart-breaking because it was virtually impossible to do much to help them or change their dire and unfortunate circumstances. You did individual treatment with kids who generally did not want to talk to you and you had to discipline and sanction the disgruntled house staff. You were also assigned a case load of kids who went to the school for disturbed kids but went home to their dysfunctional families each night, generally to get in more trouble and grow increasingly disturbed. The worst part of the job, "on-call," meant that every few weeks you had to be available by pager from Friday evening to Monday morning for emergencies pertaining to all ten group homes—and that, by all accounts, was a nightmare—kids going crazy, going AWOL, stealing cars, trying to kill themselves, needing to be committed to the psych hospital, etc. Whatever trouble they got in, you were the point person to deal with it. Gulp.

The job interview included a role-play where a seasoned female therapist pretended to be an angry adolescent male whose response to my every comment was to stare at me with dagger eyes while a second, equally battle-worn, woman therapist narrated the boy's imagined behavior: "He gets up and moves toward you looking threatening." Beads of sweat break out on my forehead as my inadequacy and lack of experience are laid bare. I try to sound firm and say the right thing to the still-seated would-be adolescent: "I see you're upset, but you need to sit down." The narrator continued: "He picks up a chair and brandishes it over his head while coming closer to you." I got the message that whatever I was doing was completely wrong and admitted that I might run at this point. Both women looked at me stone-faced and then thanked me for my time.

I was surprised, suspicious and in no position to say no when the call came the next day excitedly telling me I'd gotten the job. I was told that the fact that I'm male helped because these boys needed male role-models. I didn't have the heart to tell them I was still looking for a male role-model myself.

And so began the worst, best and most instructive job I've ever had. I recount this particular beginning because although the job was often hellish, my work with these kids taught me a lot about what does, and does not, work with children and adolescents and about some hard and beautiful realities of life. I have drawn constantly from my experiences there, first as a therapist and later as a clinical supervisor. In work with privileged families and private school children, I have seen that human struggles for love, self-esteem and security are universal and vary mostly in degree; severe cases reveal that the most troubled amongst us are a lot like infants stuck in bigger kids', or even adult, bodies. All kids regress under stress and to parent them kindly we must meet them at their *emotional* age and not just their chronological age.

Materialism

Although most of the group home kids I worked with were from economically disadvantaged circumstances, one of the very angriest was from an affluent family. He was keenly aware that the poverty and deprivation that affected many of the other kids was no excuse for his family. While the children whose parents were "poor," in jail or mentally ill tended to understand something about their parents' limitations, this wealthy kid was particularly bitter and hurt by what he perceived as his family's valuing material things and social appearances over love and relationship. He felt that his dad loved his car and himself more than his son, and whether or not this was accurate it is never the way we want our children to feel.

Many so-called privileged kids possess more stuff than ever before, and yet in important ways they have less than ever. As parents our confusion about what we value and how much is enough can push us off track; then we over-indulge our kids and then call them lazy, over-control them and then worry that they have no direction or neglect them and lament that they don't want to spend time with us. Our generation is approaching the peak of our powers but too many of us are unhappy. Statistically, our kids are more sedentary and unhealthy than ever before. Compared to the U.K., the richest Americans are on the whole less healthy than the poorest Brits; as a group we are obsessed with money, worried that we don't have enough and increasingly are socially isolated.

Materialism is a self-perpetuating trap that can obscure our natural human spirituality and block our non-material connections with each other. Sometimes materialism is a compensation for restless emptiness; it's the hollowness we cannot fill that keeps us chasing for more—more of what will never fill us. A cultural overemphasis on material things creates feelings of poverty and inadequacy and blocks compassion and generosity that could help those who are truly in need (and not just neurotically poor in comparison to America's *materially* wealthiest icons). Beyond growing up, our job as parents includes *waking up* and asking ourselves what we truly need. If we can realize we have enough and find contentment in our present material circumstances we may help our children learn what happiness is about.

Problems in a Marriage

Living in a home with a lot of conflict or even quiet contempt amongst the grown-ups can have a huge negative impact on a child's well-being. When parents don't get along, children suffer. Often a parent is wonderful to their child and awful to their spouse, ex-spouse or wish-they-were-ex-spouse. No matter what we may think about the other parent of our child, if our relationship with them is toxic or destructive and we sincerely want to help our child, we must espouse civility and respect. Just because we might not live with our child's other parent doesn't mean that getting along with our ex no longer matters. Our attitude toward the other parents in our children's lives influences their feelings of security and self esteem. If we cannot forgive the other parent of our child we can at least strive to *understand* their wounds and limitations. Hate binds us to the one we hate at an unconscious level. Love allows us to be together, and it also allows us to let go. Being kind and compassionate to our spouse (even if it is an ex-spouse) is an act of kindness for our child. This does not mean accepting abuse or mistreatment; people who have achieved real self-esteem don't find themselves staying in such relationships. The bigger person does not need to split hairs or be argumentative, and their best Self knows how to deal gracefully with others—even if those others are troubled. Boundaries are part of love. Leaving someone who is abusive or has a substance abuse problem and refuses to get help can be an act of love for that person and for the child who is stuck in the middle. Often what we hate in someone else is a window into what we still don't recognize, understand or accept in ourselves. For those who struggle in painful marriages, the way back in and the way out are the same: love and compassion are always freeing in the end.

The Unconscious in Parenting

The worst parenting is unconscious, by which I mean unaware. When we are oblivious to our own feelings, issues and wounds we are highly at risk of burdening our children with our own psychological baggage. Our children want to please us and they often behave just as we unconsciously "ask" them to (which can include unspoken requests to hold our shame, pain, anger, etc.). It may seem unbelievable that you would "ask" your child to be rude or oppositional; however, if they are, it's worth considering if you're not unconsciously signaling the child to behave in just such a manner. For example, the mother who hates social situations, might unconsciously prompt her child to tantrum or get sick in certain circumstances so that she herself has an excuse to leave, or not go at all.

Whatever our issues, it is important to remember *not* to talk to our child about the complexities, angst and turmoil of our own psyche. We can save that for our spouse, friends or therapist—not our child. Thinking deeply is essential, but talking to children about overly complex issues before they are ready can be equally misguided and even detrimental. Parents who are therapists are often the worst offenders, unconsciously making the child into patient, friend, spouse or even parent. Prematurely interpreting feelings for a child provokes them to be precociously intellectual rather than getting a chance to struggle and grow in the developmentally appropriate fog and mystery of childhood. If that was taken away from us as a child, it is all the more reason to protect it in our children. They will grow up fast enough, there is no need to rush them.

Envision What We Want
(Appreciate What We Have)

As we shift from conceptualizing our kids as problems to be solved, we draw on our powers of imagination and visualization to create space for happiness and success. Our kids can motivate us to break free of obsessive re-living of past hurts and anxious anticipation of future problems. It's fine to cry and be down when sad things actually happen, but vividly imagining ourselves being kind, patient and happy in the present moment paves the way for our lives to fall into this pattern of energy. Positive actions (i.e. behaving as if we were already kind, patient and happy) strongly leads to positive mood, enhanced self-esteem and increased resilience to meet our children's needs and make our lives together into what we really want.

Gratitude

An attitude of appreciation for the way things are helps us align with our deep Self and form a better relationship with it. Just as our child needs to be understood and appreciated for who they are in order to feel loved and to activate their natural growth, it is the same with our deep Self. If we see beauty, guidance or perfection in the current situation we master its lessons and are both happy now and free to proceed to something new. Take a moment and notice the many things about your child and your current situation that are not problematic. Notice as many positive things as you can.

Strategies for Helping

Put Relationship Above All Else

Sincere interest and understanding are the foundation for the sort of relationship we want to have with our child— and with the world. Recognizing the sacred in our child, the depth and richness of their spirit seen without judgment is, in and of itself, a strategy for helping. In parenting, all problems are relationship problems. Learning how to see and listen with an ethic of understanding rather than of fixing problems is the first key to being our best Self. Our ability to see our child as an already "successful" being helps coax their best Self to the surface. We don't need to fix, and cannot heal, our children, but appreciating and loving their true essence supports their optimal development, their natural unfolding.

Whatever our child must go through, feeling that we are in it with them (even if that looks like us trying and them pushing us away) makes all the difference. Heavy emotions are like heavy furniture—to move them it is a lot easier if two people work together. We are social creatures and being part of the group brings more happiness in the end than believing oneself superior to, or apart from, the group. We teach children how to have successful, respectful and authentic relationships by having such relationships with others, especially our children. Modeling positive social relationships calls for consistency between what we say, do and actually feel; authenticity means not smiling to people's faces and then talking trash about them in the car.

Use Deep Understanding To Drive Simple Interventions

Children's behavior is not always easy to understand; when we apply mere logic to situations that are really ruled by emotion we get nowhere. For example, a child might break a rule and we shout: "I've told you fifty times not to do that!" Our reasoning might be, "I wouldn't want to be yelled at and so, if I were my child, I would cut it out." Yet the child mystifies and enrages us by continuing their same behavior, which we may start to think of as "stupid," "obstinate," or "deliberately provoking." We generally do not stop and think, "What might we be missing?" If we have told them fifty times and it hasn't changed anything, why on earth would we think the fifty-first bout of shouting will solve it? If we fail to put ourselves in our child's shoes we're blocked from seeing the idiosyncratic reason why their behavior makes perfect sense in light of their situation, worldview and perceived options. Perhaps they feel ignored and the only time they get attention is when they do something wrong and are secretly gratified by the yelling because it lets them know we still care. Maybe our child feels powerless and has learned that if they "push our button" we blow-up; especially if we are all bluff and bluster anyway (and no real consequences follow our empty threats), it probably feels powerful to push that button and make us explode. If this is so, when we stop blowing up it stops being fun and they stop pushing our button.

If we ask ourselves what more could be needed to make our child feel safe, valued or encouraged we can at least make a guess. Right or wrong, we can provide what we imagine might help and see if their behavior changes. For example, if we suspect our child feels ignored, we might try lavishing attention *before* they've had a chance to do something wrong— even if that means right when they wake up. If we head off and address an underlying motivation for negative behavior at the pass, we can curtail that behavior by rendering it unnecessary.

When a child's behavior is troubling us, it may be useful to think carefully about *where* and *when* this behavior occurs. What precedes or provokes it? Let's say our child nags us to watch an inappropriate TV show and we cave-in because we are on the computer putting out a fire at work. After the show, when we thought they'd be an angel because they got what they wanted, we are vexed to find our child is misbehaving. Perhaps the overall pattern of behavior suggests that the show really is inappropriate for our child and they are unconsciously demonstrating this—in effect saying, "Look at me—I'm a mess after I watch a show like that!" If we tell them so, they will fight us tooth and nail, but if next time we hold the line they will feel that our limit shows love and they will probably calm down and behave better.

Really paying attention is a powerful component of good parenting. Of course, if we are always on the computer, just saying no to the show won't end the negative behavior, as children need positive attention, not just the absence of negative influence. Compassionate, non-critical and accurate understanding requires taking time for keen observation as well as an emotional willingness to feel our children's painful feelings right along with them. Parents must contain, understand and help our child label these feelings so they can better understand, name and cope with the intensity of their own feelings. Think deeply but work simply: if a child needs more kisses for very complex reasons, in the end we just need to give more kisses.

Grown-Ups Before Children In Therapy

On an airplane we are told that if there is an emergency we should put the oxygen mask on ourselves before placing one on our child; likewise in a family crisis, the first therapy should go to the parents. Parents' concerns about their children are often the only motivation powerful enough to get them to cross that initially scary, expensive and time-consuming threshold into the therapist's office. A child can sometimes seem to mysteriously improve if parents change and grow so that the child is liberated from taking care of their parents' emotional needs.

Sometimes, getting along better with our spouse is more meaningful to our child than giving them therapy, a place where they can merely talk about how we, their parents, don't get along while week after week nothing changes at home. Think about it from your child's point-of-view—would you want to live with a parent who is frustrated, angry or unhappy? Maybe as a child you did, but that is all the more motivation to seek help for yourself as an act of love for your child. If we choose to stay with a partner for the sake of our child we're going to have to go a little further than just not leaving—we must find a way to *love* that partner, even if it is purely platonic. If we cannot manage love and civility with our partner, sometimes the well-being of a child is better served by an amicable and respectful divorce than by an "intact family" that is locked in chronic acrimony. If it has become very hard for us to see the good in our partner we might need to figure our why we picked that person in the first place; perhaps they have come represent our own Shadow—if so, this would be a good topic to explore in therapy.

Of course there are situations where therapy for a child is called for. Sometimes a family is doing everything right, the parents are loving and attentive, they work on their issues, but a child legitimately has neurological differences or has suffered a loss or trauma and could benefit from professional help. Whether it is for ourselves or for our child, how do we find the right therapist?

Generally speaking, we are well served to get the most experienced therapist we can find who has actually helped at least one human being who we personally know. As to expense, we want the best therapy we can afford, not the cheapest therapy we can find. This doesn't mean expensive is better, just that experienced and skilled clinicians command market rates just as lawyers, accountants and personal trainers do. You don't have your transmission fixed by the kid down the block just because he says he'll do it for half what an established mechanic will charge.

One suggestion I make along with referrals for therapy is to gather the various numbers and then call them all after hours and just listen to the voice messages. While we can't draw any real conclusions from a voice message, going to therapy can feel vulnerable and intimidating to start, so it can be empowering to just listen to someone's voice and let our gut sense if this sounds like someone we could talk to. However we go about choosing, if we have doubts or questions about our therapist, keep in mind that they work for us when we are their client. We have every right to be able to discuss even our negative feelings about *them* and have our therapist be non-defensive and non-shaming toward us. In a good therapy we will tend to feel better after being honest. It is precisely the development of a good working relationship with a trusted therapist that can help us learn how to have better relationships with ourselves and our children.

Clearly Organize What You Want To Convey

As parents we must learn from our children, but we are also their teachers. In our teaching role it is important to think through what we want to impart to our child. Great teachers are clear and simple even in presenting complex material. If we know what we're talking about we can make it clear to others. If we're not sure what we want to say to our child, we can take time and think.

Sometimes an anecdote about our own experience helps create a point of connection between our child and us but sometimes it loses them—if they're tuning us out, whatever we are doing at that moment is probably not helping. We want to make what we say relevant to their experience and calibrate messages to their intellectual and emotional level. For example, if our child is feeling hurt and when we ask them what's going on they won't tell us, we cannot be sure they really know what they are feeling. If we get frustrated and angry with our child when they don't respond to our attempts to talk with, or comfort, them things can easily collapse into a power-struggle (i.e. "you must respect me").

If it feels like we're talking to a wall, consider why that wall might be there— what about our approach might create a need to defend against us, rather than receive our love or wisdom? Or could the feeling of facing an unfeeling wall be the way they feel about whatever is bothering them, but which they cannot fully realize much less articulate? In such a case it is better to understand the wall than to try and break it down. If the parent-child relationship is not good and lines of communication are blocked, even clear and concise information is useless. Keep things simple: "You seem sad, did something hurt your feelings?" If they don't want to talk right now we make that okay and do not close the door on them in case they want to talk later. Our core message is that we notice and care—even if that means noticing that they don't think that we care.

Use Your Strengths, Know Your Weaknesses

None of us is good at everything and everyone is good at something. Know your strengths and use them to help your children and others in your life. The more we give to our child from the sphere of what we love to do, the more successful we will be in deepening our relationship and in inspiring them to discover their own strengths. This does not mean making them into a competitive athlete if they have no interest in that, but perhaps using a love of sport or coaching ability as inspiration to coach them in what they love to do. Passion is energy and our love of the Cubs or the Yankees can still help us understand their love of Lego or Harry Potter (or vice-versa).

We also all have weaknesses, which we must come to recognize and accept even if we wish to change them. In these areas we must ask for help in order to learn and grow. We can view our weak areas as potential points of connection with those who compliment us in their strengths. By knowing our blind-spots we can avoid asking our children to help us with our problems. For example, if we are lonely we must try to meet our need for mature intimacy with appropriate grown-ups and not in our relationship with our child. We may be brilliant at business but need help from someone gifted at intimacy in order to improve and get more out of life in that area. By giving what we can, and seeking and accepting the help we need, we teach our children by our example to use their strengths to give and we also demonstrate to them that there is no shame in needing help.

The more we know, the more keenly aware we become of how much we do not know. Reaching for a parenting book need not be an emblem of how we are failing as parents, but can remind us that we are committed to enhancing our awareness and capacity to love. It is healthy and life-affirming to seek new ways of thinking and different strategies to enhance the lives of our children and take our parenting, and our own happiness, to the next level.

Choose Your Attitude—All Else Flows From It

If we realize that our attitude is a choice, we take responsibility for ourselves; we may then choose an attitude of humility, compassion, life-long learning and service to others. Choose this and we teach our child by example. Live this and good feelings that last are ours to be had. If we are unable to do this but wish we could, consider our child as a sublime gift that we fully receive only by giving selflessly to them. If we need more help from the world in order to fully love our child, make that child our noble cause and we might notice that there is indeed help and support available if we can soften and allow it in. Perhaps even the spirit in which this book was written can align with your own spirit to unlock and enliven your best and most authentic Self in the service of, and out of love for, your child.

Exercises To Consider

1. Brainstorm Then Focus: Make a list of your problems— those related to parenting and those that are not. Pick one problem that you would most like to improve and brainstorm ten or twenty possible solutions (when brainstorming there is no criticism or rejection of any idea—no matter how ludicrous, improbable, or irrelevant). Then put on your critic's hat and review your ideas. Pick the best five and rank them. You can try your top-rated solutions, but most importantly, take note about whether merely thinking about your problems (i.e. coming into a more aware and creative relationship with them) has any mysterious correlation with improvement in your child's mood or behavior. If their mood brightens or their behavior improves, be sure to keep thinking deeply about your child as well as dealing with your own issues.

2. Empathy Exercise: Make a list of what you think, or fear, is "wrong" with your child—their individual "problems," worrisome, or irritating behaviors. For each problem, come up with a list of perfectly logical reasons why your child might feel or act this way given all their circumstances. Make it a long list. For example, if your child refuses to do homework, possible reasons might include: they don't understand it; doing it makes them feel dumb or inadequate; maybe they get attention from you when they do the wrong thing but not when they are diligently at work; perhaps

they want to be "popular" and think doing well in class is not cool; maybe someone hurt their feelings that day at school and they're too upset or distracted to concentrate, etc. Be imaginative and empathic. This will help you be more effective in connecting with what's really going on with your child. Once in this mind-frame, ask your child if they can tell you what they feel or why they are upset—but only listen and consider their point-of-view. You may improve your relationship with your child just by trying, even if you don't come up with the "right" answer, much less the perfect solution.

3. Reminders of Intention: Consider some behavior you wish to improve on as a parent such as increasing patience, being less sarcastic, decreasing yelling or being more affectionate. Pick the one that seems most important (or maybe two) and write this down as a small note to yourself. Take the note and place it in your wallet or other place where you are likely to come across it often. Keep working on this primary intention until the note seems like old news. If that takes a week, a month or a year just keep at it. When the intention has been met, pick another intention and write a new note.

4. Read To Your Child: Think about your child and what interests them. Talk with the school librarian, friends or a local bookseller and come up with some books that seem right for their developmental level and current interests. You

can think about what emotional or maturational themes they are struggling with and seek stories that explore these themes. Then take time to read to your child—no matter how old they are (it could be Seuss or Faulkner). There is something bonding, nurturing and healing about reading and being read to. You can further make use of the story to engage them in discussing what they like, or don't like, in the story or what they might do in a similar situation to the characters. If they are too old (in their opinion) to be read to, or have too much homework to read anything else, consider reading whatever they are reading— even if they won't discuss it with you. If you keep trying and are pushed away, consider if *that* is the message—that they feel pushed away or unwanted (even if this is a distortion of how you, or others, actually feel about them). If you can engage your older child in a book for you to both read, and they are feeling left out or unwanted, consider books like, "Catcher In The Rye," "A Series Of Unfortunate Events," "The Outsiders" or "Oliver Twist.

5. Yoga: If you do yoga, dedicate a practice or two to the well-being of your child or to gaining insight into what may be off for your child or yourself; recall your intention at the end of your yoga session, and also note if you feel any improvement in your parenting that day. Make note of whatever poses you find most difficult and try to learn from them (Could tight hips relate to a need to release stored up sorrow? Could fear

of doing back-bending poses point to a need to open the heart?) If you have never done yoga, consider doing it yourself, or with your child, as an unconventional way to improve your child's life. Even if you choose not to do any yoga poses or take any classes, by setting your intention to dedicate a day, or an activity during the day (i.e. driving to work, emptying the dishwasher) to your child, you elevate the mundane by harnessing your spirit to that activity in the service of something greater. Parent as if it is yoga and it becomes yoga in the sense that "yoga" means "union with the divine."

6. Spiritual Exercise: Get up and play a game with your child, shoot baskets, or simply watch them doing whatever they are doing. Reach deeper to find something, anything, interesting about it; consider why they are doing what they're doing, what feeling they are trying to achieve (mastery, comfort, excitement?). Simply, but more fully, see your child. Pay careful note of how they respond to your burst of sincere, undivided attention by tracking mood and behavior over the next hours, day or series of days. Also, use this book sparingly; don't read it when you could be parenting.

Chapter 2

Good Feelings That Last—A Goal For Children And Parents

The Meltdown

It's late afternoon and your twelve-year-old daughter is in a mood. Her hormones are fluctuating, her body is changing; you're doing your best to make her life great but she has a report that's due tomorrow, you have to make dinner and you have an important call that has to be made right now. But your daughter also needs you to help her with something on her report, right now. You stop what you are doing, you make your call a lower priority than your child; you sit down next to her and begin to explain something that she was having trouble understanding but she gets angry and accuses you of doing her work for her. You suggest she try to work it out herself and you will make your call. You get up to walk away when she bursts into tears. Obviously, she's stressed; you hold your irritation in check and sit down beside her again to comfort her, but she's still miffed with you and wants an apology for *the way* that you were helping her. Whatever perfect parenting fuel you had in your reserve tank has just run out. You get up and walk away, but she literally drops to the floor, crying so hard you'd think she was Babar when the hunters just shot Babar's mother. In spite of the melodrama, it's your baby who's wracked by sobs and it breaks your heart. You stoop down beside her and put a loving hand on her shaking shoulder, but she looks up at you and there is hatred in her eyes mingling with her desperate sorrow, fear and shame at her own vulnerability. As her mother or father, you too feel a mix of emotions—angry, sad, vaguely guilty, resentful, inadequate as a parent, helpless, confused and overwhelmed. This cannot possibly be just about homework; she's not even a full-blown teenager and you're both drowning as some sort of meltdown has recently become a nearly daily occurrence.

Am I Messing Up My Kid?

No matter how hard we try, parenting will bring us moments where we don't know what to do. When our child is having a hard time and we are at a loss as to what to do it's good to ask ourselves if we may somehow be part of the problem. It is better to risk guilt and consider our own possible role than to be over-confident and oblivious.

Our own issues are painful and seeing them clearly (i.e. feeling them strongly) hurts. As in the meltdown example above, there may be a lot of different things going on at once when parenting finds us at a loss. Trouble with parenting most often flares up around transitions—big and small, our children's and our own. When a child is in a transition of identity, as from childhood to adolescence, they have a tendency to have a lot of inner confusion about who they are, what they need and what they want. Often they want opposite things, such as help and space to figure things out. They unconsciously draw us into their drama and make us hold one or the other of their contrary feelings. Then we find ourselves invited into a melodramatic play in which we are playing the role of our child's opposite feeling. Thus the drama of you approach and they push you away, you withdraw and they pull you back in.

This is hard enough to deal with, but if we are not entirely clear about our own identity then our child's drama can provoke us because we aren't that much clearer than they are; their pain can make us feel resentful if we did not get the patient and compassionate parenting that we now try to offer. Ironically, we have put heart and soul into forging a positive identity as a caring and compassionate parent, and when our child casts us as selfish or hurtful—and then asks us to contain their rage *and* their sorrow at the same time it can be too much and we spill over.

Containing our own feelings *and* our child's feelings when they cannot hold them is the core of our confusion. When they regress we must try to stay connected and contain their feelings much as we had to do when they were infants and waiting to nurse caused a panic. Meltdowns are transitional times of emotional crisis. Until they are calm, you cannot reason with them, you cannot explain anything at all—the only thing that helps at this point is to try to understand what they are *feeling*. You must avoid the danger of a chain reaction where you meltdown too.

Things may actually be your fault—and then again they may not. When we don't know what to do in the face of emotional intensity, it is best to keep the focus off our self and our estimation of our worth. Ideally, we need a solid self before we can relinquish our self-focus, but parenting doesn't allow such luxury. If childhood left us a little shortchanged, we can heal and grow *through* parenting—it just hurts to give what we did not get. Understanding yourself can certainly help you to be a more conscious and effective parent, but keep in mind that your child needs you to understand *them* much more than they need you to understand yourself.

We May Not Know What To Do, But Do We At Least Know What Our Child Thinks And Feels? (And Do They Know That We Know?)

If our child is experiencing a painful and confusing issue, our task at that moment is to grasp and validate what they are going through. If they say that they want us to leave them alone, it is respectful to let them be—if we do it with love. There is a huge emotional difference between storming away from our kid and remaining sullen and frosty long after they are ready to talk, and kindly telling them that you're sorry that they are so upset and not getting mad at them for getting mad at us. Try not to say, "I know how you feel." Tell your child that you can see that they are upset and you are really interested to hear more about it, if and when they want to talk. Then look for those soft moments like bedtime when they say a little something about their fears, dreams, or struggles. Don't jump on this moment and give the lecture you've been holding back; you will know you have succeeded if they tell you more than they usually do and you talk less. The best time to share information with them is when they actually ask you a question—and then it's good to try and address what they asked and not just what you want to tell them. As they develop they will be more likely to seek, and trust, your input if they feel understood.

A family is a team but the parents are the team captains. By being the grown-up no matter what your child does, staying the course through the storms of outbursts and meltdowns, you as parent keep a relationship based on loving kindness alive. If you can be this way consistently—even managing your own anger and hurt in mature and appropriately expressed ways, the family will transform. The "problems" may not go away, but the fact that you are united as a loving unit in dealing with difficulties goes a long way toward helping your child integrate their own opposite feelings and teaching them how to have a happy life.

"Bad" Behavior Vs. Raw Emotion

"Bad" behavior in children is a bit like bad acting—over the top, self-involved and unmoving to the audience. Tantrums and power struggles usually start with bad acting, but can slip over the line and become authentic meltdowns if a child gets carried away into believing their own performance. Tantrums that become meltdowns are like "The Boy Who Cried Wolf" and likewise often leave a child truly unnerved and feeling both abandoned and ashamed of the "bad" behavior that used up the parents' trust and compassion when the child didn't really need it. As parents we must do more than just not reinforce bad behavior, we must be like skilled directors to our gifted little actors and intuit what their true motivation is and better direct them to achieve their goals while keeping things real.

We will devote an entire chapter to the art of managing power struggles. For now, it is important to differentiate attempts at manipulation from emotional overload. As we become clearer about our own "buttons" it will be harder for others, including our children, to push them. Beyond that, we still must help our children deal with the intensity of their feelings.

Great parenting can take a cue from great acting, which is actually generous— interesting actors know how to listen and are compelling to watch even when they aren't "doing anything." Their stillness and realness draws us in. Similarly, our sincere and quiet interest will draw our children out. We just have to be sure that when our child is lying on the floor and screaming it is not because that is what we secretly feel like doing and they are "acting it out." In such a case they are trying, and failing, to contain our feelings when it should really be the other way around. When our child's needs for attention and true understanding are met, their propensity to tantrum calms down.

Variations on meltdowns are virtually unavoidable at certain points in childhood and they spike in frequency at developmental transitions such as three-year-old power struggles, five-year-old struggles with increasing autonomy and separation—and echoes of these themes in the transition to middle school and puberty. Some top meltdown triggers to keep in mind include transitions of all kinds, for example, after-school fussy break-downs; next day after sleep-overs when sleep deprivation and post sugar highs crash on your watch. Changing plans often causes problems; in such cases the child has been tottering on the brink and the fact that the orthodontist or the allergist was changed to today instead of tomorrow sends them over the edge. Another classic meltdown scenario is when a child does not get their way and then uses your limit to rage against, cry, pout, reject or otherwise release pent up emotional intensity. Finally, anything that is perceived as a threat to a child's identity or sense of self can provoke an emotional 911. This could be a young child losing a security blanket, a sibling spilling juice onto a treasured (maybe "lucky") sports jersey or any sort of teasing about a child's mannerisms, appearance or ability level. Anticipating when your child is heading for a meltdown and working to help them feel understood and respected can sometimes head it off or lessen the severity when it erupts.

As a general rule you cannot give in to tantrums because giving in rewards that behavior and thus reinforces it. Not only does a pattern of tantrums and giving in make family life unpleasant, giving in ill prepares them for the world where they will not generally get their way by having a tantrum. Our external boundaries slowly become their internal boundaries, which solidify their emerging identity.

One of the most important emotions that bad behavior and tantrums express in a child is their need for love in the form of limits. Testing limits ideally brings clear and loving boundaries where "no" means "no" and rules are consistent and actually make sense. It must not be "yes" one day because the parent is in a good mood and "no" the next because the parent is in a bad mood. If a sensible and kindly limit brings a tantrum or a meltdown then the limit is very likely what they are really after. Kids may wake up the next day oddly cheery or affectionate, knowing that setting limits is hard and reflects the fact that you really love them and that you are strong enough to help them feel safe.

Kids Against Kids

It's the end of a long day and your nine-year-old is struggling to finish her homework when you hear an anguished "STOP IT!" and you catch your eleven-year-old making the "loser" sign at the younger one. The younger one is also making the loser sign back, but they are doing it "the wrong way" which is allowing the older one to laugh mockingly. The sinister laughter is hitting its mark and invoking real torment. As a parent this is both infuriating and tedious. The pure silliness of being a "loser" for incorrectly making the loser sign make us feel like a loser for even having to parent at this ridiculous level.

You may manage not to lose your temper, and even remember to not reinforce bad behavior and so give extra love and attention to the younger child, but your love feels like sympathy and it doesn't raise their spirits or their self-esteem; meanwhile the older one drops back into the secret misery they were trying to fob off on their sibling and they slither into bed in a cloud of resentment and self-contempt refusing all later affection. You may have technically handled the situation correctly, but as you drop into bed exhausted you feel sad that both your kids are feeling low and powerless to make them happy and help them know how wonderful they truly are.

Teasing and tormenting are particularly hard on parents because they are about cruelty—deliberate attempts to make someone else feel bad. Cruelty reflects painfully insecure feelings within oneself. A key thing to keep in mind, and to continually remind our children, is that people who feel good about themselves are generally kind; mean behavior comes out of someone feeling bad about themselves and wanting to give these feelings to someone else. When we become more conscious that our sadness, confusion, frustration or fears of inadequacy might be feelings our kids cannot yet manage, we can suffer with a sense of purpose. Kids bounce back more quickly than adults from hurt feelings and this is something we can relearn from our children.

Are You Happy?

Much as our children lobby us for questionably healthy toys, games, foods and privileges, we grown-ups often look for good feelings that last in all the wrong places. There are different sorts of happiness but as a parent we cannot be truly happy if our child is unhappy. Very young children are quite able to be sad or angry and then brighten quickly when their immediate needs are met. We adults can learn a thing or two from them—especially the art of being sad without being depressed. As parents we can widen our view of happiness to more of a healthy feeling as opposed to the take-a-pill, have-a drink, buy-something ethic, which our culture seems to espouse.

I wonder if our children's generation, being generally better attended to and more sensitive than we parents were as a group, aren't having some problems that actually stem from dealing with the torn, tattered and too often false-faced world we are set to bequeath to them. Maybe their angst, sorrow and brooding anger is called for and it is our behavior that is wrong. If we look unflinchingly at what we do to this world, we too might have a meltdown, and then make some changes. If we are willing to feel a little more distraught, not about what we don't have, but about how we treat each other and the world, then our kids can stay kids a little while longer and not have to grow up so quickly to deal with their parents' problems. Our pain and confusion has a purpose, and we may find we are happier about our way of relating to our kids even as we continue to suffer intermittent pain and confusion about what to do.

Perhaps we do not want to make our children feel better about the world we have created, but rather support their sensitivity and even their pain so that they might bring a more relationship-based world into being rather than perpetuate the material-based world that is making so many of us grown-ups either rich but empty or poor and worried. If it were true that our kids keenly feel the sorrow of our world, we would become happier as parents by becoming more properly sad about our own disconnect with each other and with our children.

Individuation

Children begin their lives as authentic human beings. As they grow, they ask piercingly honest questions. They notice if the emperor has no clothes on and they say so. If we have drifted away from our authentic Self, our children may threaten us with their worldview. We may have been "happily" oblivious to the fact that we are not happy until a child comes along and, by virtue of their realness, confronts us with an unconscious dilemma: return to our own authentic Self but face potential conflict with the collective group that supports a materialistic, false or even violent and uncaring "normalcy"; or "teach" our child how to be "successful" by conforming to the demands of a sick culture and buying into the notion that nothing is wrong, as long as you can get your big piece of the pie. Down the former path we delve into a spiritual agony of transformation that brings realness and compassion—even if no one else seems to care; down the latter path we shape our children to be false and stuff away their own authenticity and in the end we suffer a worse agony in our soul because we've deprived, or at least delayed, our child's chance of true happiness.

One reason we parents may come to feel like we don't know what to do, is that underneath it all we don't really know who we are. While parenting calls for a primary focus on our kids' needs and feelings, they do fall asleep eventually, or go to school, or have a play-date at another kid's house. In our rare quiet moments we may be haunted by vague sadness, exhaustion or hollowness; it is important not to run away from our feelings but to take time to contemplate them and consider who we really are.

When we think about who we are we think of our "self," but often that identity is a mask that family and society have pressured and influenced us into wearing. Eventually we've worn it so long we forget it's not our true Self. For the purpose of this book, the "Self" (capitalized) is meant to denote the authentic being we might become if we have the love, support and courage. The Self is inclusive of the unconscious. It is deep, wise, powerful and ultimately in charge of us. Truly "growing up" could be thought of as bringing more and more of the Self into our lived experience as a human being and of trusting that Self to teach us how to be. This process of soul-driven growth and awakening consciousness leading ultimately to some sort of purpose, meaning or service to the world could be called "Individuation[1]."

Individuation is the momentous life task of becoming our complete, psychologically integrated, Self. Total individuation, if there were such a thing, would take at least a lifetime and probably many; it is a never-ending project. Still, to parent successfully, one does need to be at least somewhat individuated. And, conversely, since parenting involves service to someone beyond us, it potentially gets us out of the ego-self and links us to the wider world. Thus parenting and individuation are like a circle you can enter at any point; parenting helps you individuate, and individuating helps you parent.

To individuate is to differentiate oneself from the group, to become a unique, distinct individual—to discover our own identity. This allows joining the group without losing one's sense of individuality. The paradox of individuation is that we must differentiate from the group (family, religion, social class, country of origin) in order to truly join the group—to participate rather than conform. Individuation often involves separating from our family of origin, making our way in the big bad world, confronting our fears and coming to terms with our limitations; in essence, it is the development of true character.

True intimacy and nourishing relationships become more possible through individuation. In order to figure out what to do as parents, and to model independent thinking and authenticity for our children, we must learn, or re-learn, how to be authentic and think for ourselves. From our softer energy, our calmer limit-setting and our sincere interest in our children they receive our over-riding message: that we love them. When they get this, trust deepens, behavior improves and we feel better about our parenting.

Grown-Up Meltdowns

Emotional and physical breakdowns build more slowly in adults than children, but with more dire results. The realization that we need to change some aspect of our life can be prompted by powerful forces such as illness or "mid-life crises" that stop us in our tracks and function as limits that force us to deal with our own truth. Kids reach out to us as parents when they break down and need us to hold them. Protected by our relative strength they grow strong. When we break down badly enough we reach out to the unknown architect of our body and soul. Loved and protected by mysterious forces, if we are lucky we grow stronger still, more appreciative and understanding. Our own meltdowns deepen and redirect us if we accept their wisdom.

Our Self wants to be known just as our children yearn to be accurately understood. When we honor the deep Self, by paying attention to dreams for example, our conscious will comes into line with the Self and things seem to go better with us and our children. The Self is our link to cosmic forces utterly beyond us—the energy we need to reconstitute when we break down in order to grow more true to the Self. This is individuation.

Success comes with being true to our Self so we must try and listen closely to what it might be trying to tell us when the paths we think we want to take are blocked. The more earnestly we listen, the less need the Self has to "shout" with big and shocking messages—and the less frustrated we become with the way things are; this is when things change. If we listen to the faint sadness of our child it need not grow into chronic depression. If we find out how to harmonize with the true needs of our child, particularly for understanding, life's unavoidable struggles shift from the body, the checkbook or the conflicted space between our children and ourselves into the private realm of our soul. The soul is where individuation ultimately leads—parenting is where the needs of our children and those of our soul converge, and it is why we are tortured in our soul if we fail our children.

Why We Avoid Individuating

If individuation is so great, why don't more people do it? Pain. There is a melancholy tinge to individuation that mingles loss with gain. We all have an aspect that resists growing up and taking responsibility, but it is particularly strong when childhood was lacking and we are holding out as grown-ups for the childhood we never had. One of the hardest aspects of parenting is giving our children the things (emotional and/or material) that we ourselves did not get when we were children. Conversely, it can be an agony to find oneself downwardly mobile and unable to give our children the clothes, trips, luxuries, educational opportunities or lack of concern about money that we might have grown up with and then, often bitterly, seen evaporate. Many wealthy children sport contempt and flippancy regarding the money they were born into, knowing nothing else. It is easy to take for granted or even devalue wealth when one has never known struggle, but these children's emptiness and sense of entitlement may echo the unhappiness of their achieving and "successful" parents. These kids may not know what will bring them good feelings that last, but they are loathe to follow their parents' path if they see it doesn't lead to true happiness. Such children may vex their parents by failing to do well in school, but if the parent really wants the child to follow in their footsteps it generally helps to be happy by way of example.

I spent my childhood trying to escape from upper-middle class suburbia only to spend much of my adulthood trying to crawl back in—having realized that a nice home and a steady job were not the problem, and that the absence of economic security is no more a formula for happiness than is having money. We avoid individuating mainly because we have so few models for it—hardly any images of authentic and happy adults living in their integrity, generosity and loving kindness. Sure, we may be lucky enough to find one or two in our lives, but they certainly do not represent the collective energy of the last few generations.

Another reason we avoid individuation is that we are unused to emotional intensity and imagine that we cannot manage strong feelings. We then block our feelings with TV, internet, food, drink or spending, but when we block our feelings we block our individuation—and we increase the need of the Self to provoke crisis in order to get us on our soul's path. When a child is being oppositional, they are taking a war of opposites that rages within them and turning it into a battle between a parent and a child. They may want freedom *and* limits; they may want to numb out and avoid feeling *and* they may wish for understanding and help with managing feelings instead of blocking them. Out of these inner storms come family drama; when you as parent hold the battle within you the child can calm down.

If a parent cannot hold opposites within themselves, then power struggles will be extra provocative. The parent can get triggered and discharge their pain or anxiety onto the child; or they may get emotionally overwhelmed and disconnect. When children are in emotional pain, logic goes out the window. They terrorize for what they "say" they want when politely asking would actually be more effective. Of critical importance is understanding that one's need to be known and understood often trumps the need to actually have things our way. Problem behavior is not illogical if the underlying goal is to express feelings that cannot be expressed in any other way, or that are not heeded by parents without drama.

Individuation Clarifies The Parent-Child Relationship

As you come to better know your Self and its seemingly contradictory nature, your communication style and overall emotional energy will be clearer and calmer. Clarity and tranquility give birth to coherence and organic structure and this tends to calm and reassure children. True grown-ups do not treat their children as their developmental equals; they are friendly and play with their children, but they are not "friends" in the sense of reciprocal democratic equality (besides, kids and grown-ups need friends their own age). When we individuate we relinquish shameful secret roles such as dependent baby or entitled prince or prima donna. It is easy to see how letting go of such distortions and embracing the ethic of becoming nothing less than, nor more than, a regular human being can make us better parents.

Some writers on parenting have suggested that parents exert the most influence on their children's behavior up until they reach their pre-teen years or early adolescence at which point peers begin to become a dominant influence. This doesn't mean you throw in the towel when your kid turns eleven. It does mean that the younger your children still are at the moment, the greater impact your individuation will have on them. Real grown-ups trust development—they don't hate being grown-ups and manage to make it look reasonably fun. They love children without longing to *be* children again. They know there is no rush to make their kids grow up, but neither do they unconsciously instill fear of growing up through their contempt for it.

Change Is Possible!

Current research on the brain and on attachment shows that the brain keeps growing throughout the lifecycle. Dan Siegel speaks of a 92 year-old client whose whole world opened up when he was able to change his thinking, connecting and thus his very brain. So we need not give up, despair or think we're set in our stuckness and pain; we do, however we can find it, need trusting relationships in which to heal (and thus we need to make these things available to everyone who wants/needs them).

Scientists used to think that the brain was fixed early on and further change impossible. It is very much shaped by early experiences (which is one of the reasons those first years of life are absolutely critical for establishing security), but we grow new neurons throughout our lives in the part of the brain that connects everything together—and it is that deepening of integration of the different parts of the brain (i.e. traumatized and logical; fight-flight and empathic; language/logic and narrative/meaning/feeling) that helps us really heal and to be there for our kids, ourselves and each other (not to mention to flourish, express our true Selves, contribute and have fun).

And, by the way, attachment can be secure (if they are accurately understood) with any child with any sort of brain. For example autistic children may have deficits in their mirror neuron systems (which makes social relating more difficult), however if they are accurately understood and attended to they will form secure attachment (and this strongly protects them from serious mental health and life problems down the road).

What's In The Way?

What's In Our Child's Way?

While the primary focus of this chapter is our parental experience of not knowing what to do, our children also suffer from confusion and uncertainty. When children behave in confusing ways we can imagine that they are in some way confused themselves. There are three basic reasons why a child (or grown-up for that matter) would be confused and/or confusing to others.

1) <u>They have not developed the capacity to understand what is being asked of them</u>

Here we want to consider if "bad" behavior is really honest overwhelm. Trouble comes when a parent expects thoughts, words or behaviors from a child who is simply too young to understand. High expectations are good, but impossible expectations create meltdowns and erode self-esteem.

It helps to know what children can generally do at a given age, but every child varies in their development and capacity to hold things together. Roughly speaking empathy doesn't happen until six or seven; abstract thinking not before ten or twelve; and true maturity not until twenty-seven.

2) <u>They have never been taught or had examples of what to do in a similar situation</u>

Let's say your kindergartener has been upset after school and you finally figure out that it is because they never get the spot they want at naptime; when the teacher gives the cue all the children rush the mats and scramble for positions. Your sweet child (perhaps first-born or only child who has not had to fight for things) watches perplexed and then takes what is left. While it is lovely that your child is not aggressive, their disappointment is a cue that we can help them understand the situation. Next we can help *them* generate strategies for getting what they need, perhaps making more haste at the proper moment, perhaps asking the teacher for help in keeping things fair for everyone.

3) <u>Their emotions or thoughts have gotten the better of them and they are blocked from accessing (much less acting</u>

on) their own natural wisdom and trust that they can try and
fail and try again until they figure things out

A child may be emotionally swamped by the first day of
school, by having their feelings hurt, by not getting their way,
by changes in what they thought was the "plan." As parents
we draw on our empathy and work to accurately understand
what they are feeling. This must happen *before* we can teach or
explain, otherwise our words cannot be taken in as the child
remains focused on their feelings and not on our words. We
must try not to shame our children for not knowing things,
but instead view these occasions as teachable moments.

A parent who is exceedingly hardy may think their sensitive child a wimp or a crybaby because that parent has little
understanding about how intensely their child feels things—
and how different it is from their own experience of the same
noises, pains or smells. Your best Self as a parent is validating
and accommodating to your child's style rather than shaming
them for being different from you. If you consistently treat a
child with honesty and sensitivity they will have little need
for excess drama or manipulation as they get their needs met
by being straightforward. If such a child says they feel cold,
sick or hungry you can take them at their word and help comfort them rather than suspect deception.

Regressing to an earlier level of behavior can frustrate a
parent because they've seen the more advanced behavior and
know the child is capable of more. But as annoying as baby
whining behavior is in an eight, eleven or twenty-seven-year-
old, it is worth asking yourself what has caused the regres-
sion. Often the answer is that they feel overwhelmed by current circumstances, perhaps in the context of a transition (i.e.
going into middle school, dethroned by a new sibling) or a

developmental leap (i.e. a girl's first period) that has frightened them and evoked nostalgia for earlier and easier times.

Another wrinkle to consider is that they had an unsuccessful transition in the past (i.e. started school too young and had a bad time of it) and so new transitions bring back the old feelings of "I can't do it." Validate their feelings and support their efforts to differentiate the past from the present. A detailed discussion of every possible trigger is less important (as there will be hundreds along the way) than facilitating trust that while your child's behavior may be confusing to you, it makes sense to them. When you manage to understand what is going on, and communicate it back to your child, you have turned the corner on the conflict or struggle at hand. Good strategies for helping will flow from that, ideally coming from your child once they feel calm and secure again.

What's In Our Own Way?

Sometimes we might be in the dark about our child's behavior for reasons that have to do with our own issues. A child may implode in some way because we unconsciously need them to be scared, anxious, insecure, etc. Be clear with yourself and with your child that they are free to feel whatever they feel but you do not need them to emotionally take care of you. The following are some common parental feelings or defenses that, if we are not consciously aware of them, can trip up our parenting.

1) <u>We long for feeling understood and close with someone who understands us</u>

If we feel confused or alone we might unconsciously get our child to bond with us in our pain. This can occur subtly, as when our child is mildly sad for their own reasons but we then make it into something more than it is; we indulge them, inadvertently reinforce their sad mood by paying *overly* kind attention, giving them treats for comfort, etc., creating a special friendship rather than a proper parent-child relationship. Conversely, their social successes might trigger our unconscious jealousy and subtle discouragement. In this dynamic we may *inaccurately* see our child as a loner, masking the pain we felt as a loner in the past or present and projecting that pain, along with our compassion, onto our child. Here consciously taking on our own pain frees our child to confidently connect with friends and have a better childhood than we did; then at least our suffering becomes conscious and redemptive, and frees us to escape a stuck and lonely past, perhaps bonding with kindred spirits our own age.

2) <u>Our own natural limitations</u>

We all have relative weaknesses and we may be confused by our child (and the world in general) if we are not naturally analytic, organizing sorts (perhaps more feeling, creative, intuitive). Maybe in school math, logic and history left us feeling bored, dumb or both. We must be the person we were meant to be, but as a best-Self and a parent we must develop our opposite aspect in order to be a whole person and raise a whole child. Besides, we may have been told we were no good at things for unfounded stereotypical reasons (i.e. girls aren't good at math) and with a little faith in ourselves we can figure out plenty.

Here we are at risk of perpetuating our own dubiously achieved (i.e. if we were scripted into seeming inadequacy) negative traits in our child (e.g. *"we're* no good at sports in this family"). We must counter our own anxious concerns about appearing pathetic with an ethic of positive risk-taking and doing things purely for the sake of it (i.e. "it's about having fun"); lead by example and expose kids early to a variety of activities, sports, foods, etc.

3) <u>Wishing for Rescue</u>

Sometimes we unconsciously refuse to figure things out hoping that some good mother or Prince Charming will notice our lost and hapless way of being as a call for help and respond. Some of us may be chronic advice askers, the sort to talk to our parents three times a day as grown-ups and consult them on every decision major and minor. This is a sign of non-individuation where, if we aren't unconsciously trying for rescue, it might be that our parents need us to be helpless, perhaps in order to bind us to them and not have to let go of us. In the meantime, keep in mind that if we are disempowered in this apron-strings way, we may in turn have difficulty setting limits and being firm and decisive as parents. This sort of softness in parents makes children nervous and prompts limit-testing (so they can get a reassuring firm limit) and it also can engender hesitancy and uncertainty in our children that sorely tests our patience as it presses on our own buttons by mirroring our own weakness back to us.

4) <u>Anxiety</u>

Our fears can cloud our thinking and create confusion, sometimes as a defense against actually seeing our fears too clearly. If we are scared or anxious we may need help to manage it, but it must not come from our child. Being aware of anxiety is a first step, using our love for our child as motivation to confront fears and reclaim living in the moment (as anxiety is about the future and the bad thing we fear is coming). Unmanaged parental anxiety can lead to anxious children. Total presence to our child *in the moment* is a fantastic coping strategy to relinquish anxiety—it takes us out of our ego-self, which is where all the neurotic pain is anyway.

5) Denial

When who our child is does not mesh with what we wish they were or need them to be, whether that means denying their strengths because we need a weak child to boost our own self-esteem, or denying their weaknesses because we need a "successful" child to reflect our own precariously inflated ego, either way we are asking them to be who they are not and this creates confusion in them that will eventually spill back over into us. Our denial leads to cut-off relationships. We counter denial by letting our children be who they are, athlete or *not*, artist or *not*, and then seeing if they feel happier and become more receptive to us and others in their life.

6) Projection

Often the unconscious tries to hang its own unacceptable aspects or feelings on someone else. Much over-anxious parenting might be better understood as the projection of our own inner child and *their* problems onto our real child. This can make us overly critical or overly attentive, but fails to see our actual child. When parents project their problems onto their children, the children often take on the very qualities that their parents secretly possess but cannot admit—even to themselves. The child becomes the "not me" aspect of the parent, and the parent then tries to fix their secret self in the child rather than in their own Self. Thus the nipped and tucked mom has the overweight daughter (and it really bothers her), the Great Santini dad has the low self-esteem introvert of a son (and feels ashamed of him). These not-living-up-to-potential children sometimes end up expressing the split off (and seemingly unacceptable) elements of the overly achievement oriented parent. We are then confused by our children's problems because we do not realize, and cannot accept, that they are actually our own problems.

7) Idealization

When we feel compelled to be, or at least appear to be, the perfect parent of the perfect child, we tend to circle the wagons of denial around our idealized child. Now all blame, negativity, aggression and problems are to be found in the rest of the world. Other children are seen as too rough, too selfish, too spoiled, inferior, etc. This creates a self-concept in the child of being above reproach, and yet it frightens them as they know they are not perfect but don't yet realize that their parents aren't either. Idealization of the child dooms friendships as no other child is a good fit for long with our over-indulged and self-involved child—the monster we have created by anxiously blowing our child up like a balloon.

Personal growth involves examining the strategies we use for psychological protection and, hopefully, finding healthier and more effective ways to manage. Humbleness, patience and sincere curiosity in the face of confusion allow clarity to emerge. Courage to feel our feelings, and also those of our loved ones, helps render our old defenses obsolete and they drop away. Becoming less defended and less preoccupied with our ego self allows real interest in our children and the world and empowers us to take better care of both.

Broadening Our Perspective

Danny's On The Roof

Danny was staring at me with wide expressionless eyes, peering out from his impassive, pit-bull face. He was fifteen and solid muscle shabbily wrapped in a dirty white t-shirt and grimy Wranglers that had been personally distressed by Danny. He'd been sent to my sorry office in a leaky trailer because of "horseplay." There had been a lot of horseplay lately—that boys-will-be-boys sort of jocular affection that reminds one of *A Clockwork Orange*. Danny had injured a smaller boy and yet it was clearly an accident; it was always an "accident" as Danny seemed incapable of intent. In trying to do therapy with him, we talked about anger management and "triggers," or rather I talked about them as Danny stared with uncomprehending eyes as he added his dusty impression to my archeological ruin of a couch. We sat in silence as I pondered the family situation: his dad would come to visit the group home on occasional weekends, a caricature of dirty plaid and filthy fingernails; his mom was "not in the picture."

Try as I might, I was just not reaching Danny. I went deeper. I gently gave it to him straight: I told him that it had hurt him to not have his mom in his life, that he was lonely and sad inside; in fact, part of the reason for all the horseplay was his need for hugs and affection. His eyes flickered briefly. I said we needed to help him understand his need for love and support and to get these needs met constructively rather than by acting them out in destructive ways. He fidgeted. He'd had enough. I released him to the yard as the day's last moments of play were drawing to a close. Momentarily, the kids who *got* to go home each night (which did not include Danny who would spend the night in the group home) would board the busses. I leaned back satisfied that Danny and I were getting somewhere.

The phone rang. The intervention staff was on the line—their walkie-talkies crackled in the background as they told me that "my kid" was on the roof of the clinic...

I rushed out to the blacktop where kids who normally chased each other as exasperated teachers tried to herd them, like cats, onto busses, all stood in atypical order—like the crowds looking collectively up at Spiderman. Everyone was staring up at the roof where Danny, in nothing but his underwear, stood high above the parking lot. Leave it to emotionally disturbed children and adolescents to chant: "Jump! Jump! Jump!"

The beefy intervention staff, like a defensive line on a pro football team, managed to coax him away from the precipice. I met him at the bottom of the fire-escape ladder where he stood sheepish and pathetic in his Carters. Next we escorted him to the "Quiet Area," (literally a locked, carpet-padded, room) where it was my task to evaluate his level of suicidality to see if he needed to go to the psych hospital. He was not consciously suicidal. He didn't know why he had stripped off his clothes and climbed the fire escape. He sort of knew he had felt upset and just had to do it. But he was all better now. His eyes were simple and clear, he just wanted to go back to the group home so he could play a video game.

One thing I learned from Danny that day was that sometimes we might have a good understanding about what's going on inside someone, and why they behave in a certain way, but we can't necessarily tell them what they feel as it can overwhelm them. Generally speaking, if someone like Danny could contain their feelings, express them appropriately and not act them out they would do so. Thus pouring the pain or confusion that they spill over into us, right back into them tends to be ineffective, painful and provocative—it all just spills right out again and often in a bigger mess than the first time around. In hindsight it is obvious that I should have known better, but I was emotionally pulled into Danny's confusion and it was *my* need to sort it out and "help" (i.e. straighten him out) that blinded me.

Thinking deeply about our kids and trying to figure out what's going on inside them is a good idea; restraint and compassion in what we say back is also important. Even with milder levels of confusion than those of profoundly disturbed children we must still tread a balance between helping our child identify their feelings and prematurely labeling their feelings for them. A two or three-year-old is ready to know they are scared or angry, but they are not ready to know that they are ambivalent, or that their nightmare that you died is actually about their unconscious rage toward you. It will suffice to intuit this and *not* point it out to them. Parenting is not about being right, it is not about being smart or insightful so much as it is about being patient, containing, kind and compassionate—and often it is about being able to know and *not* say.

Teasing And Sarcasm

Children younger than ten or eleven are typically very literal in their thinking. Sarcasm is generally lost on them. A sarcastic, "great job" is confusingly heard as real praise, which when followed by parental exasperation (because the kid kept doing what they were doing) leaves a child feeling defeated. Teasing can be gentle and affectionate, but more often than not it makes children feel self-conscious and criticized. With kids old enough to understand sarcasm it's still a bad idea because they receive the full force of the cruelty embedded in our text. Remember, the reason we would make someone else feel bad, whether we do it consciously or unconsciously, is that we are feeling bad about ourselves at some level. Perhaps we grew up in a cynical or sardonic household and must work extra hard *not* to do to our children as was done to us. Teasing and sarcasm hurt, and as our best Selves we try to keep it to a minimum.

We're Not Sure What A Good Parent Even Is

We have internalized many stereotyped images of the archetypal Mother and Father. Think of biblically inspired Western art: God giving the spark of life to Adam on the ceiling of the Sistine Chapel; the Virgin Mother holding baby Jesus on her lap; a bereft Madonna holding her dying Son in countless paintings and sculptures of the Pieta. Images of antiquity such as angry Father God Zeus hurling thunderbolts or jealous Hera taking him to task, track along the same conventions while modern representations of parents bring to mind lurid talk shows and their parade of sensationalized dysfunction or "Family Guy" satire only slightly exaggerating the collective stupidity into which we've fallen.

As we explore these images we may get clearer on what we are trying not to be, but we are left without much inspiration for what we *do* want to be. What is an ideal "Mother" or "Father" anyway? What are we trying to become? Who can we look to for guidance and inspiration?

To find characters who embody the ideal mother or father I have to search back decades to books and movies predating our current age of narcissism.

Mary Poppins: The Idealized Mother

A quintessential incarnation of the impossible ideal of the Mother is Mary Poppins[3], a childcare Goddess who descends from the sky, travels in the guise of humble nanny, unites families and teaches them to value love and unity above all else. She models faith and humor (along with a musical sensibility) that helps parents and children get out of their own way and discover that anything can happen if you let it. Mary is a superb teacher of parenting who empowers families to function without her so that she can move on to other families who need her. She is a paragon of giving as a way of being and is thus eternally cheerful, living in her good feelings that last.

Like the Virgin Mary, Ms. Poppins is transcendent and inspiring, but like all archetypes, impossible to fully emulate. Mary Poppins is a gift to parenting because she personifies an attitude or approach that balances toughness with great fun and, as is key to success in any field, she loves her work. Mary helps us envision childcare as more than dutiful—as pulsing with humor, vitality and life-spirit. Parenting with its endless tasks is but a "jolly holiday" with Mary. Her ultimate value to us parents is that her appearance from the sky as a timeless archetype coalescing into our consciousness via the artists who write and act activates the Great Mother within our own psyche and helps us integrate her into our living experience and our parenting.

The concept of archetypal mothers and fathers is potentially confusing. These characters and images pre-exist within the deep Self from our inception, awaiting activation. We find these figures in the collective art and myth of culture, but like our expansive soul, we live and parent *within* these archetypes more than we might say that they exist within us. Mary is not a little lost piece of us so much as we are the little lost parents trying to find our way within the vastness and eternity of Mary Poppins. It is hopeless to try to ape her, or any other idealized figure, but they can inspire and guide us if we let them. Mary Poppins may not do it for you—she was irritating to me when I was younger—and you may have other ideal mother figures to draw upon for inspiration, but like the Grinch in relationship to Christmas, if we soften our hearts as a parent we can hardly help but to fall in love with the infectious life energy of the likes of Mary Poppins.

Who Is Our Ideal Daddy?

In our breast-obsessed "guys night out!" world of adolescent male sexuality, our "men" are too often merely boys intent on never growing up. Images of these Peter Pans may sell a lot of beer, and later on keep a lot of AA meetings going strong, but do very little for the children who are trying to figure out what to grow up into, or even if they should bother to grow up at all. They offer still less to us grown-up fathers trying to figure out who our best Self as a parent even is.

While men may dominate the imagery and starring roles of our collective culture, they are usually heroes, warriors and romantic comedy lovers and rarely fathers—if they have kids at all the children are more like background scenery, and if the man is actively parenting then *that* tends to be the central joke. While positive Mother figures may be scarce, ideal Father figures are as rare as Yeti sightings—we can't even be entirely sure they exist. Father no longer knows best and the dad most men long for is more like an archetype waiting to happen, one that we can't quite clearly envision yet. So we sort through the past images searching for bits and pieces we might like to build into the brave new model.

The patient, wise, kind, not-overly-sexualized male caregiver—seems to be generally insipid if and when depicted in current popular culture. Ozzie Nelson has morphed into Ozzie Ozborne. Andy Griffith, Marcus Welby and Mr. Rogers[4] are awfully nice, but dull, dull, dull, not to mention culturally pre-historic relics of the past century. By the time a child is old enough to hate Barney[5], especially a male child, he'd be hard pressed to look around and see a role model who is strong, capable, powerful AND kind, generous, sensitive and nurturing. To come up with inspiring Fathers we might have to go even further back in time—but the founding fathers like George Washington are too dusty, spiritual giants like Martin Luther King and Gandhi are too saintly and remote (not to mention busy with things other than child-care and not known for their marital fidelity). Then of course there's God—not the imageless and unfathomable source of all creation, but Father as symbolic representation of all that. Here we find Father at his most awesome: bearded, muscular—power incarnate as he reaches one finger across the ceiling of the Sistine Chapel to spark life into the primordial human. Magnificent yes, but hardly a guy with whom a child can curl up and read, *Go, Dog. Go!* As far as a man from modern culture that one might hope to emulate as an excellent Father and yet retain the core vestiges of one's own masculinity and the right to hold one's head high amongst other men (as opposed to only amongst approving, albeit sexually turned-off, women), for this the pickings are exceedingly slim. Maybe Bill Cosby is the epitome of humor, kindness, grace and humanity, a man to match Mary Poppins; but with reality interpenetrating even fiction these days, Cosby[6] as the humble man's man as father is, in reality, not only exceptionally funny, but super-rich as well. No lowly nanny is Bill Cosby, and in the end, he's as hard to emulate as Mary Poppins and her magical powers.

My vote for best heroic father image is Atticus Finch in Harper Lee's novel, *To Kill A Mockingbird*[7] as well as Gregory Peck, as Atticus, in the film[8]. In the startlingly beautiful book we see the father through the eyes of Scout, a young girl who hardly remembers the mother she has lost. Scout just sees Atticus as he is, and her non-idealizing of him allows us to idealize his kind heart, his quiet sorrow, his fear-tinged courage and his stoic integrity. Atticus is a great dad and the book is particularly worth reading as a parent. Sadly, however, Atticus is fading fast from the mainstream of collective cultural consciousness (and he was a rare bird to begin with)— and even Atticus, as ideal father, had a maid to handle most of the childcare while he worked, even if it was to defend an innocent man who was the victim of racism. To be Atticus *and* cook, drive the kids to school and participate in all the "parent-involvement" demanded of today's ideal Father is probably too much to ask of any mortal man or woman.

While idealized mother images may make women feel inadequate as would-be super-mom, the paucity of contemporary good father archetypes leaves men confused about what they're even striving for. Often men don't know what, or who, to be as fathers, and the dilemma that they face parallels the raging debate between stay-at-home and working moms. It is a time of unrealistic expectations and this may be why no role models exist—we can't even *imagine* someone who could really achieve all that the world asks of us and at the same time be a parent who is fully present to, much less patient and understanding with, one's children.

Fathers may secretly relate to Tony Soprano and his struggles as a family man, tough-guy *and* neurotic. Our culture often reinforces aggression and insensitivity in men who may fear that if they are not violent or remote they are not real men. Sensitive, caring males are for the most part devalued when depicted in mass culture. The very characteristics that most benefit children are often ridiculed if they are seen in men. This sends a confusing message about how real men are supposed to deal with emotion. For a man to be a good caring father he must develop enough self-esteem to be his own authentic Self and to know, and be able to express, not only what he feels but *that* he feels.

Knowing We Are Lost Is Better Than Wrongly Believing We Are Not

New parents sometimes quip that their kid did not come with an instruction manual, and yet they were the most complicated "equipment" they'd ever had to deal with. Just when we think we've learned the nuances of our infant's cries (the subtle difference between hungry, wet, tired), they embark on a series of three-hour inconsolable crying jags. We hesitate to label it colic, we get all manner of advice but nothing helps and soon we want to throw ourselves in front of a truck just to stop hearing that wail. There we sit: futile, sad for our child, angry at our child, sad for ourselves, angry at ourselves—overwhelmed and confused. Or maybe we get derailed when they come home from school upset, withdrawn or aggressive and we know something is wrong but they deny it (maybe not consciously realizing that they're upset) and we find ourselves completely unable to help them. We doubt ourselves, our kids, the school, the teacher, other kids. Maybe they open up to us at bedtime and we talk it through, maybe they tell us about some hurt or fear months later, maybe never. Compassionate parenting demands that we enter into painful psychic spaces with our children and learn to tolerate, and even embrace, these feelings rather than trying to "fix" or dispose of such feelings; it's more about being with our kids when they feel lost than it is providing them with so-called clarity. This is especially challenging for men, but if we are to raise compassionate sons as well as daughters, we must have compassionate fathers as well as mothers. Compassion means feeling *with*, not feeling bad for, but helping to contain, understand, map and tolerate painful emotions as part of life. If we run scared from our feelings, we teach our children to do the same; this is generally the root cause of their troubling behaviors as their feelings must be expressed somehow or other; acting out is just that—"acting" out a pantomime of the feelings that could not be verbalized, cried or otherwise expressed in a safe or constructive manner.

Childhood Is Not Just Preparation For Adulthood

When it comes to "happiness," children younger than nine or ten experience their happiness in a pure way. They are not ambivalent or conflicted about happiness, they either feel it or they do not at any given moment. A key difference between kid wishes and adult wishes is that kid wishes exude the pure joy they still know, while adult wishes are informed by life's pain. All wishes come from the perception that something is lacking while pure happiness is the realization that nothing is missing.

Very young children are also able to be deeply sad without shame or inhibition. Kids split their joy and their sorrow; they cannot do them at the same time. Grown up happiness rests on simultaneously holding opposite feelings. When we are able to feel happy and sad at the same time, we have taken a quantum leap toward good feelings that last. Any moment in which we are able to be fully present to the gift that everything potentially is (especially our children) is time that we can rightly call ourselves "happy." The world reflects us. If we change, it will reflect the kinder, more compassionate being we have unlocked from within us. That is our best Self, and our kids will appreciate being parented by it. As we evolve we may come to realize that our confusion might be re-conceptualized as the way that holding opposite ideas or emotions initially feels, we may even come to recognize the value and personal success to be found in this experience. If so, it deepens our appreciation for how parenting seems tailored in its challenges to our own needs for personal growth.

Envision Our Best Self As A Parent

Acknowledging our faults is different than obsessing on them. In order to help, we must generally get beyond ourselves. We are usually able to picture the sort of parent we would wish for if we were children once again. Let that serve as a working model for your own ideal Self as a parent.

Picturing "success" helps us get out of our own way. The act of visualizing what our deep Self has in store in the good-parent department helps us shape it in our mind so our conscious self can follow a sound plan.

In this spirit we might contemplate what our best parenting and might look like. The sentences below are invitations to imagine ourselves in various positive ways or situations. Be mindful not to read these as demands, or reprimands, but as encouragement to picture yourself, as vividly as you can, being "successful" as a parent. Try not to just plow through the list; pick one idea and spend a little time with it, make it your own. Take particular note on how you feel and behave *following* time spent seeing yourself in your best light.

GOOD PARENTING IS TRULY INTERESTED; interest creates relationship with one's child and the world.

GOOD PARENTING IS PATIENT AND KIND.

GOOD PARENTING IS CALM—it contains anxiety rather than giving it away or stirring it up.

GOOD PARENTING IS SOFT—it is free of resistance and, like water, makes its way naturally and persistently.

GOOD PARENTING IS CLEAR AND CONCISE.

GOOD PARENTING IS ABUNDANT—it trusts that we have what we need; it is generous and free of envy, jealousy and resentment.

GOOD PARENTING IS JOYFUL, free of shame and blame.

GOOD PARENTING IS CREATIVE—it honors life and finds beauty in the humble and seemingly mundane.

GOOD PARENTING IS INTUITIVE—it lets the heart inform and guide.

GOOD PARENTING IS MANY SMALL MOMENTS WELL HANDLED—not virtuosity and brilliance, but consistent right attitude and right action.

GOOD PARENTING IS SPIRITUAL—it connects us to bigger forces.

GOOD PARENTING IS ITS OWN REWARD.

Strategies For Helping

"Good Feelings That Last" As Inner Compass

Imagine an emotional compass. Instead of north, south, east and west its directions, read: Good feelings that last, Bad Feelings That Last, Good Feelings that Don't Last and Bad Feelings that Don't Last. Realize your heart is a compass. It's your conscious mind that needs to read and follow it. If you think about what good feelings have actually lasted for you, and what brought these on, you can pay more attention to your internal compass. The tricky part is remembering that good feelings must endure over time or they're just good feelings that don't really last. Bad feelings that don't last that we frequently weather for the benefit of our children, such as the initial reaction to our limit setting, can lead eventually to good feelings that last. Your own instincts and lived experience must ultimately guide you and all advice must be put through the filter of your heart's compass. If we want our kids not to choose behaviors that lead to good feelings that don't last as they develop such as drug or alcohol abuse, random and disconnected sexuality and other blind alleys we are wise to model restraint and thoughtfulness.

Use Confusion About Your Child To Intuit Their Feelings

Let's say that every time you are putting your infant down for a nap your three-year-old starts to play with the dog, bang the toys, call out for you—anything to wake the baby, which deprives you of any hope of a nap for yourself, much less any quality alone time with your three-year-old. You end up feeling confused, angry and helpless—unable to prevail on your three-year-old with the logic that he's ruining it for everyone including himself. Given that logic has been tried and failed,

77

you might consider whether the feelings of helplessness and frustration that you feel are also what your three-year-old is feeling, and communicating to you by their behavior. They don't *only* want your undivided attention—they want you to understand, even feel, their pain. This is not conscious on their part, but if you make it conscious on your part, and empathize with their pain and frustration their behavior may no longer be needed to get you the message and it may drop away, allowing better behavior to return.

It seems few modern parents lack a well-thumbed copy of *What to Expect When You're Expecting*,[9] and on through to *What to Expect on Tuesday at 6pm If It's Drizzling*. The overall deluge of help, Self-Help and unwanted help can be contradictory, confusing and overwhelming. If we embrace the notion that confusion is natural, authentic to human experience and drives learning, then confusing behavior in our child can be understood as a trap-door that drops us right next to them emotionally, smack into their world and what it actually *feels like* to be them.

When we are confused by our child and clouded in our ability to think we could be connected with them on an unconscious level. We can use our emotional experience to intuit a deeper understanding of their feelings. If we happen to get it right, even if we say nothing, suddenly our children might not feel so alone, they sense our interest and compassion and sometimes things mysteriously shift.

Accept The Negative To Deepen Your Connection With Your Child

If your child is older than five or six and has never told you what an awful parent you are, how mean you are and how much they hate you (at least at some points during the parenting experience), then they're simply not telling you the whole truth. Perhaps they fear you won't receive it with an open heart; that you will be guilty and defensive or angry and retaliate. If you are struggling with your parenting, find a quiet moment to sincerely and openly ask your child if anything about you or your parenting hurts, or has hurt, their feelings. If you open yourself to your children in this way, accept their full emotional experience and perhaps apologize if you have inadvertently hurt them, you deepen the bond between you. All real relationships have conflict; always making things smooth and nice, at the expense of honesty, leads to feelings of emptiness and alienation. Chronic bickering may reveal those who can only experience closeness through conflict or who find direct expressions of love too vulnerable or emotionally intense. Real intimacy is nourishing, healing and life affirming, but it demands a willingness to grapple with emotional and psychological pain.

Teachable Moments

When kids do the wrong thing we are often confused about why they did it and we may be equally confused as to what to do about it. There is a difference between punishment and discipline; punishment is a penalty meant as a deterrent, which may be of questionable effectiveness with children (and in society where punishment in the absence of realistic incentives has lead to our current high levels of incarceration); discipline reflects natural consequences and guides toward positive and effective behavior. As parents we must teach by example and by the thoughtful and creative use of consequences.

Good teachers are culture heroes, called to a difficult path that is given lip-service as being important to our society yet vastly underpaid given that the future of our world depends on it. The sorry state of many public schools and the staggering cost of most private schools aside, real education is about teaching children *how* to learn, not about stuffing them full of largely irrelevant "facts" which may, or may not, turn out to be true much less useful in the world they will inherit. Good teachers find teachable moments in every situation. What, to a lesser teacher, might be a "problem" (i.e. one child hurts another child's feelings), to a gifted and experienced teacher becomes a teachable moment. For example, if there were 30 children and only 29 cupcakes, how much of their cupcake would everyone need to give up for the last child to get most of a cupcake too? One way things could unfold is that everyone would have a half, then a quarter, then an eighth and finally all will be truly tasting their final bite of one sixteenth of a cupcake and have had more fun than if they'd just gobbled a whole one down. In this way the children learn about fractions, sharing and fair-minded problem solving all at once. Life is rife with frustrations, conflicts and unfair situations; since we cannot always and forever protect children from such things, we strive to teach them how to cope. Children can learn coping strategies from a gifted teacher, but they also internalize a model of a person who approaches adversity cheerfully and creatively and knows how to transform it into something useful, even wonderful. Such inspired and wonderful teachers are some of the most valuable and important members of any society.

While not possible to do at all times, we can strive toward the Mary Poppins approach to child-care (i.e., set firm limits and still manage to make virtually everything fun). In the end, you will teach your kids about true success by being successful as a person—kind, patient, and strong—and by struggling gracefully and with good humor in the face of life's challenges and difficulties. A parent, in their role as teacher, models lifelong learning and enjoys learning from, and along with, their children.

Creative discipline seeks to impart natural consequences in response to potentially harmful or problematic behavior. Natural consequences run along the tracks of reality yet shield the child from the full danger possible from risky or unhealthy behavior. Obviously, children shouldn't play with matches because they could get burned, but while actually getting burned is a natural consequence, we must find something in-between harm and talk. Taking away the Game-Boy does not relate to fire danger and is a meaningless consequence. A lesson in how to safely light matches (i.e. over the sink with parental supervision) might be a first step. If you set the rule and then they break it perhaps you give them a brief time alone to contemplate why they were not concerned about the potential danger. Maybe they can make a call to the pediatrician's office and ask the nurse if she's ever seen a child who was hurt from fire—not to freak them out but to see that it's not just you, their parent, who arbitrarily decided that this is a concern. Perhaps asking what the treatment for burns is, making the logical consequences of fire more real to them. Properly done, they will come to respect things like knives and matches and eventually learn to use them safely. Safety must come first; after that, if they break the rules they might just be asking for more limits because they do not feel safe in an emotional sense. Limits help them know you love them and this often helps them calm down and eliminates the need for acting out and limit-testing.

Coming up with natural consequences is a challenge that asks us to imagine what would happen in "real life" if a child persisted in any given problem behavior until they got hurt or sanctioned by the world. It helps to 1) make consequences echo reality, and 2) have the consequence occur as quickly as possible following behavior to reinforce the natural connection between the behavior and the consequence (one's finger in the fire hurts right away). But, it is better to delay consequences if you are either too angry to give them in a neutral manner, or you can't think of a logical consequence. Explain the concern you have and the expectation for behavior and let your child know there will be consequences. It helps to anticipate your child's behavior and think about consequences in advance. Your effective use of consequences will give your future warnings more weight and, over time, reduce the actual need for consequences. It must be clear that we are rooting for our kids to stay safe and do well, and that we expect them to succeed.

Negative consequences employ small but logical discomfort in order to avoid larger pain for the child later. For example, if a child hits other children some "cool-down" time away from the group does reflect reality; if we are cruel and aggressive, others (especially kind others with good self-esteem) will shun us and we will lack the sorts of friends we really need. Spanking a child for hitting another child basically teaches that it is the prerogative of the biggest and strongest to use violence. This may stop a child in his or her tracks when bigger people are around to threaten, but as they

get older a bully nature may emerge when they find themselves the bigger one in relationship to others.

Consequences such as having a child apologize when
they've hurt someone, or even facilitating a positive activity
to teach that one can mend things teaches being powerful
through being kind. Take both kids out for a treat to reinforce the idea that good things and feelings come out of kind
behavior. Taking away TV privileges (which is, ironically,
probably a *positive* consequence in the long run) is lazy and
irrelevant because TV has little to do with aggression (other
than possibly encouraging it by example)—in fact in "reality" the more socially maladapted and isolated you become
the more TV you will probably end up watching.

Exercises To Consider

When you face decisions, temptations or
challenges consider your options and ask yourself
which course of action best leads toward your
good feelings that last.

1. Calibrate your good feelings that last compass:
If you use your imagination to think about what you
would feel like if all your dreams came true, you
can get a good idea of the feeling your deepest
heart is after. Imagine whatever comes to your
mind as happiness, success and abundance.
Try and envision the fantasy in as much detail as
possible: how it smells, tastes, sounds, looks and
even what it feels like on your skin. Don't just
passively long for it—make it real in your mind and

in your soul. This is your current conscious best guess of good feelings that last; the feeling that is the biggest clue.

Now use this feeling of yourself as happy and successful as "north" on your heart's compass Re-envision your life. Think about your own life as if it were a novel or movie and imagine how you would continue it from here. Feel free to make it more dramatic or interesting than the current facts might seem to warrant. Consider where your life story is now, with all its obstacles, pains, and frustrations and then picture your most desired "Hollywood Ending" (or brilliant novel ending, or art-house film ending—the ending at which you truly wish to arrive). Make that ending vivid in your mind; taste it, see it, feel it—want it. Make being a great parent part of the fantasy. Now imagine some fantastical, creative, heroic or unexpected way in which your current situation could transform into your desired ending. See if your inner author can take dictation from the true Self and see if things start to slowly transform in reality.

2. Feelings maps and art projects: If your child is younger than six or seven, help your child make a "map" of their different feelings, using different colors to represent different emotions. You can then encourage them to navigate "roads" or "paths" of color from different feelings—such as from angry to calm, or from frustrated to happy. Let them teach you what their feelings look like

and what it looks like when they are stuck, lost, hurt or confused. Encourage them to draw their way back to safe, calm and happy.

3. Watch closely and learn from your child: For older children they might be willing to write or make art. Invite them to share it with you if they like, and respect their privacy if they prefer it. Even if your child is a teenager or older, you can get them a diary or a nice pad and some art supplies. With no other instructions you communicate that Self-expression is important and that you value it in your child.

4. Walk in search of guidance: If totally confused, take a walk and ask the universe for any sign or guidance. Notice odd scraps of paper, clouds, numbers, animals, people you pass, street names and billboards. Pretend it all has meaning: be playful, and try to decipher the subtle world's code. Be skeptical, but admit that the approach of logic and reason has not always brought the results you wanted. Stay open and see what you get from this non-logical, not linear, non-intellectual approach. Let mysterious inklings and sensations be your guide. If you don't tell anyone what you're up to, no one will think you're crazy. Don't go off the deep end and eschew logic, just bring in a bit of the mystical.

5. Google your current dilemma: Go on line and Google some words that reflect your stuckness, confusion or simply your desire to be a better

parent. Trust your intuition and the collective nature of pain, struggle and desire. Notice the potential brilliance, as well as the potential dumbness, of the group as a pulsing and alive entity—the whole of which we are part whether we like it or not. The main point is that when you are lost, try a different way, perhaps more random, less logical.

6. Yoga: If you don't do yoga, take a yoga class to clear confusion and bring more tranquility to your life. If you are a yogi already, when confused, don't wait for the next class—do down-dog or child's pose—feel your hands and feet (and your forehead in child's pose) grounding into the earth. See if it helps your parenting in the hours that follow.

7. Watch *Mary Poppins*: Watch with your kids or without them. Dedicate it to being your best Self as a parent and let it lift your spirits and shift your mood.

Chapter 3

Seeing Without Judging

The Ugly Duckling In Red Pumps

The only reason that I knew that Derrick, a four-year-old in my son's preschool class with bird-like features, dirty blonde hair and large anime eyes, liked to wear high heels was because he had stepped on my kid's foot one day and it was still hurting that evening. The bruise (and not Derrick's fashion choice) prompted my child to describe, quite without judgment, how Derrick would wait until his dad left after dropping him off before going to the dress-up box and donning a pair of red pumps and a tutu which he'd wear all day until clean-up. The boy's dad was a sturdy Irish-American athletic sort with ruddy skin and a zero-tolerance for emotional displays or clinging children. The dad was an actor and Derrick was ultimately a chip off the old block, drawn as he was to the family business in his love of dress-up.

One Friday I was in the midst of picking up my child as Derrick's father strode into the land of wood blocks and play-dough to find Derrick still in full costume. The look on the man's face remains seared into my inner hall-of-shame portrait gallery: shock, anger, contempt, disgust and embarrassment displayed in equal parts. This dad was not a bad fellow and he loved his son, he just could not see his son's splendid and unique beauty at that particular moment because its expression was so far a field from the father's expectations—as well as obscured by the man's own insecurities. We too may have envisioned a fireman or a choreographer, but if our child surprises us with the opposite of our expectations it is we who must adjust our world-view and realize that sometimes a so-called "ugly" duckling is not *going* to be beautiful when it turns into something else—it is beautiful right now, in heels and a tutu.

There are moments in every parent's experience when one's child appears wrong or ugly to us. It may be when they're newly born and covered with monkey-like hair and one secretly wonders if something hasn't gone terribly wrong—perhaps having expected a radiant Gerber baby and not a mini Winston Churchill. Our child may look ugly to us when savaging a younger sibling or when fiercely pitching a public tantrum designed to relentlessly embarrass for the sake of personal gain. We may be guilty about our negative feelings and try to hide them but kids pick up on them all the same. We may be openly shaming, critical or teasing about our child's *perceived* shortcomings; we may even come to pervasively see our child in a negative manner. When we lose sight of or children's intrinsic beauty we lose sight of them altogether.

The Importance Of Appreciation

One reason we lose sight of our child's innate brilliance is that we fail to find the sacred in our own self and in the world around us. Our child introduces us to the sacred—that is, if we haven't found it before having children in endeavors such as art, spiritual practice or romantic love. When we trip over our own insecurities and start to see ugliness instead of beauty in our child this uncomfortable feeling can be a cue to slow down and wonder, "What's gone wrong?"

By looking with our hearts, with our whole Self, we *relate* to our child; our soul *participates* with their soul in a shared experience of grace and transcendence. This is the essence of love and the foundation of good feelings that last. Although our humanity may render us limited, confused, sad or lonely we are also capable, creative and connected with each other in loving-kindness. Life is tragic *and* it is joyous; we love our kids *and* they knock us off our center and provoke us to find another, deeper center. When we are able to see spirit in each other we all feel more alive, more treasured and treasuring. When we parent from our gratitude everything goes better.

The challenge is to see things as they are and go beyond, "Do I like what I see?" beyond "Is there something I can get from what I see" and beyond "Will what I see hurt me?" Then we might quiet our fears and desires and find the patience and tranquility to simply gaze without judgment until the magnificence of the living world opens to us. When this happens between you and your child you transform the very nature of your relationship, more of your full Self comes into conscious awareness and what is actually needed will be clearer to you. Our negative judgments are really just learned responses that must be questioned as we learn to think, feel and non-judge for ourselves.

Try to see your child with eyes that are seeing for the first time, free of preconceived criticisms and open to the joy and wonder of seeing and feeling—reclaiming seeing itself as a privilege. Deeper than romantic love, parenting is based on gratitude and not desire. By loving as a parent we are initiated into a spirituality of giving. This lets us consciously participate in the mysterious force that is our source, destiny and ultimate love.

Good Grief: The Triumph Of The Losers

We may conceal our foibles and shortcomings at all costs or we may feel that we disproportionately represent awkwardness. To some extent we are all geeks, nerds and losers—and so are our children, each and every one from the star athlete to the friendless sad-sack. The task is to love our archetypal inner loser rather than trying to deny that it exists at all or, on the opposite end of the spectrum, over-identifying with it and believing that we are a total loser. The most insidious manifestation of the archetypal dweeb comes when we unconsciously project our inner loser onto our child, shaming them and making them feel bad about who they are while underneath it all telling them to *be* a loser by seeing them as one. Acting the loser ourselves is not a solution to anything either, as it offers a pathetic role model for our child and denies us the full experience of life in which everyone is both a winner and a loser.

From Charlie Chaplin's Little Tramp to Charlie Brown and Napoleon Dynamite[2] we relate to the misfit and we root for underdogs to succeed. Charlie Brown is always going to pick that dinky little Christmas tree for the school play and at some point, maybe our twentieth viewing, we stop wishing he would choose differently and, like the rest of his friends in the end, come to see that he chose perfectly. Just as the meager tree can convey the authentic spirit of Christmas and stand in counter-point to commercialism— when truly seen, loved and celebrated—our children elevate us and our lives to the *authentically* cool; then our relationships are resonant rather than hollow, and we have Self and community. Parenting is a two-way mirror; our children see their luminescence reflected in our eyes, but we might also come to see spirit in ourselves reflected in the pure beauty of our children.

Where's Jonas?

Jonas was seventeen, tall and lanky with a sullen expressionless face. He lived in the group home like a ghost, saying little and making no real trouble. I knew little more than his name and conducted polite, dull, monosyllabic therapy with him once a week; beyond that he hardly registered amongst the angry, defiant, demanding and colorful rule-breakers. The staff didn't much care for him and considered him "sneaky" because he was suspected of having stolen sometimes from roommates. However, all the kids did *that*, even though none of them had much to take in the first place. Jonas was just there and not much more.

My first strong impression of Jonas came one afternoon when the staff was loading the boys onto the van for an outing. Therapists did not go on outings—I was hanging out at the group home trying to wrap up my Friday by catching up with children who had been absent from class, (usually because they were truant and up to no good). The kids liked outings and the staff was perplexed because they could not find Jonas. The others boys were already in the van despite its emblazoned clinic logo, which they felt announced to everyone that they were losers. Today they were just happy the van wasn't broken down. Jonas was holding up the show.

I could see that the staff was mildly concerned but mostly irritated. The movie would start with or without them and they had been looking forward to a couple of hours in the dark watching something mindless. Had Jonas run away? Many kids went AWOL, but never Jonas. He had no friends or family to run to, no drug or alcohol problem to feed, no troubled girlfriend waiting to hook up with him in some abandoned house. Seconds began to stretch out in that surreal way they do when really bad things happen, when fear and dread creep up on us. This was at the core of the stressful nature of this job where the upside of things was infinitesimal and the downside was horrible and ever-present. Bad things happened a lot around a place like this. Horrible pasts and bleak futures always crushed heavy on the present moment and everyone, from the kids to the staff, mostly wished they were somewhere else. A lot of kids had tried to hurt themselves on the way to qualifying for state funding as "severely emotionally disturbed" children.

Jonas would soon turn eighteen at which point the funding would end and he would be forced out onto the street with no prospects. Had Jonas gone and done something stupid—so stupid that we could all understand it and probably strongly consider doing it ourselves if we were Jonas? Our guts collectively tightened, fueling each other with fear and guilt.

I found him in his room, standing stock still against a corner easily overlooked from the door. He had the faintest trace of a smile on his large-featured face. Hadn't he heard us calling? He had no explanation and offered no excuses.

Perhaps he had been trying to steal something from his roommate, maybe money for the outing (but that turned out not to be the case). Maybe he was having a psychotic break, which would typically onset at about his age. Jonas' biological mother was schizophrenic and had "conceived" him in a state mental hospital. As to the father, all we knew was that he was someone who thought that raping a heavily drugged mental patient was an okay thing to do. Jonas wasn't psychotic. He was just terribly sad. His reason for hiding in his room was utterly simple: Jonas just wanted to know we cared enough to even notice if he were missing and bother to look for him. His ability to ask for this was at a very young level, but at least he was coming out of his shell and communicating.

After that day we all started to take more of an interest in Jonas. The kids took to teasing Jonas and I that we were father and son. To them, especially the white kids and the African American kids, Jonas' Latino features and my own Semitic features made us virtual ringers. They would say to me, "Do you know what your son did today?" or tell Jonas, "Hey, your dad's here!" when I walked in. What was meant as a mutual insult brought Jonas and I closer together. We were both introverts, so our relationship naturally built more slowly and took more time than with the in-your-face kids.

We worked on Jonas' "life skills," doing a resume and practicing for job interviews. When he got his first real job beyond chores in the group home it didn't matter to me or to Jonas that it was as an entry-level custodian position. It was the first thing he'd ever let himself want and he had gotten it! His triumphant smile of pride and blatant joy is still happily emblazoned in my mind. Wherever he is now, I think of Jonas with great affection and appreciate how much he taught me about seeing beauty.

What Blocks Our View Of Beauty?

What Keeps Our Children From Seeing Their Own Beauty?

Our children rely on us as caregivers to serve as mirrors in which they can discover their beauty both inside and out;

if they do not see themselves as wonderful we must ask if our blindness has left them with eyes unopened to their own splendor. Not being truly and lovingly gazed upon, heard, felt and sensed causes a failure in the development of the individual self. If a child seems hollow or joyless, like Jonas, we can't just *tell* them they are wonderful, we must be able to see it—to fully see *them* so they can see themselves.

While the world can be a cruel and critical place, if a child knows that they really matter and thus that they truly exist and are real, all other development will rest on a more solid foundation. Better still, if they learn that they are wonderful as their first and most enduring impression they will seek, and be better at, relationships throughout their life. When a child knows who they are it is not up to the self-involved world to define them or tell them whether they are beautiful or not. Once freed from the question of their own adequacy they are free to eventually get beyond their narrow ego-self and truly engage and influence the world.

If our child is still so young that they are not yet sure who they are, we potentially have a lot of power to show them their wonderfulness by simply but truly seeing it ourselves. To have maximum impact this must be done consistently and repeatedly. This benefits both you, in teaching you how to truly love, and your child in teaching them that they are lovable. If a child in your care has come, for whatever reason, to believe that they are not wonderful, special and sacred at least you can hold it clearly in your own mind that this is a matter of distortion that they have learned, perhaps from you, perhaps from others who they depended on in the past. We will explore the issue of how self-esteem forms and how to help raise it in the next chapter, but for now the main tool to employ is that of paying non-judgmental attention to your child and holding firm in the belief that if they don't see their own beauty they really have no idea yet who they truly are.

What Keeps Us From Seeing Our Child's Beauty?

Seeing beauty is much more than finding someone pleasing, it is seeing to the very essence, the soul of everyone and everything. If one can accept the assertion that every child is sacred and beautiful, then when we see our child as less than that something has clouded our view. Our own blockages are like sunglasses, dark lenses that we can take off whether we are passing through a dark night of the soul in relationship with our child or just a cloudy afternoon. Such blockages might include the following:

1) <u>Preoccupation With Our Own Self</u>

The key to better parenting is to be found neither in yourself nor in your child but in the relationship between you and your child. If we, as parents, are overly concerned about our adequacy we fail to see our children's beauty, as well as their needs, because we're too busy looking at ourselves in the mirror. Our tendencies toward self-focus are never really about vanity but rather reflect negative feelings and insecurities about our worth, appearance, adequacy, etc. Such doubts often stem from our own lack of having been seen and appreciated for who we were when we were children. When we use our hearts more than our eyes to see our children we get out of our heads and the negative chatter there that keeps us from fully seeing the world in all its glory and possibility.

2) <u>Our Own Low Self-Esteem</u>

Sometimes we project the "negative" aspects that we judge to be wrong in ourselves (but cannot fully accept and

95

acknowledge) onto our children. In such cases we find our child's "faults" irritating or even personally embarrassing. Here we are not seeing our child in a clear light. This may relate to a physical aspect such as a body size or shape out of line with the parent's ideal. It could manifest in a trait such as gentleness or sensitivity if it goes against the parent's ideal of toughness (as equated with aggression or insensitivity). On the other hand, it could be assertive behavior that is seen as bad (if the parents' ideal is gentle or sensitive). Preconceived ideas of what is appropriate may be important for socialization, but everything has a shadow side that must also be expressed for us to feel whole. Good self-esteem in a parent creates greater acceptance and appreciation for a full range of feelings and behaviors natural to one's child. By accepting and embracing wholeness one can socialize a child to joyfully join the group rather than shame them into a narrow box of "appropriate" feelings and behaviors.

If we doubt that all that is good already exists in us, then how can we convincingly see and cultivate soul in our child? By just realizing that our own low self-esteem could be in the way of seeing our child's innate excellence, we can begin the process of bracketing off our own anxieties and putting more energy into beholding beauty in our child.

3) <u>Culturally Learned Ideals of Beauty</u>

Our own self-esteem may be okay, perhaps partly because we are lucky or hardworking, or have somehow found ourselves in line with culturally approved looks, jobs, lifestyles or are luckier still to have seen through that and not care. Then along come children, and we find that we are not nearly as together as we had thought. At least at first, when they are still their pure self, children are generally lacking in the sort of drive and discipline that we may have banked on to succeed.

Being more consciously aware of whatever, sometimes dubious, values a culture may prize (i.e. celebrity) can help us think more independently and appreciate our children just the way they are. This supports kids to make choices that actually nourish them (i.e. being kind), rather than just seeking approval from others in ways that ultimately lower their own self-esteem (i.e. acting cruelly in order to fit in with a certain group).

4) <u>Fear Of Feelings</u>

If we are afraid of strong emotions such as sadness or anger we may become preoccupied with trying to avoid negative feelings. Ironically, we then get depressed or anxious about what we might feel if such and such were to happen. Instead of feeling sad about a sad situation, such as a loss, we get emotionally blocked anticipating overwhelming feelings. Our fear and lack of confidence in our emotional resiliency traps us into a narrow and emotionally constricted way of being. Relationships are emotional. If we fear strong feelings we tend to fear intimacy and our relationships are unable to nourish and soothe us. Relationship is at the center of good parenting. If we fear powerful emotions we are blocked from being our best Self as a parent.

Children do not block their feelings when they are very young. They cannot help but feel life very strongly. If our child loses touch with what they feel they are at risk for being told what to think, feel, buy and do. This sweeps them farther and farther from their authentic Self. Such a child is at greater risk to be bullied, to succumb to peer pressure about drugs, drinking and sex and be more inclined to participate in cruelty to others. Conversely, our children can reconnect us with our own truth and beauty, if we do not judge or criticize, and instead see and appreciate our children as they brilliantly are. A lot of acting out, in children and adults, boils down to an inability to contain and manage strong emotions. The better we deal with our own emotions the better our children are likely to do with theirs.

Broadening Our Perspective

Oscar Wilde said that if you haven't seen the beauty in something you haven't really seen it.[3] Whether it pertains to our own child or to other children who may suffer from poverty, illness, neglect or abuse we sometimes turn away, not because we don't care but because it is too painful to bear witness—particularly if we feel powerless to change things. The troubled 'tweens and teens I've worked with were often quite hurt by the perception that no one really wanted to see them, much less take care of them. Often they would be sent away from the school during fund raising events and they were painfully aware that they were not considered a plus in the clinic's attempts to coax large checks from wealthy donors. Younger, more innocent children, and kids who could sing pretty songs, were chosen to tug the heartstrings and loosen the purse strings. Whether or not wealthy donors would have cared to mix with the wounded and unruly souls suffering unseen in their midst remains an open question, but our general society as a whole does seem to turn away.

It hurts to see pain, but if we look and do not turn away we will also see vitality and authentic emotion, truths that may languish unexpressed in our own selves and which bind us across all lines of age, race, wealth, giftedness and wellness.

To see without judging, without condescension and with the courage to feel is in itself an act of love and it is potentially transformative. Our children do not need our pity—they need our interest.

The Beauty Of Orphan Stories

While we grown-ups may prefer to look away from sad and troubling things, or be morbidly fixated on the soul-numbing local and world news tragedies that fuel our anxiety but typically fail to empower us to care or help more, there is inspiring and redemptive beauty to be found in children's natural love of orphan stories.

Whether it's *Bambi, Babar, Oliver Twist,* or *Harry Potter*, the common thread is that the central character experiences a catastrophic loss of parents and is orphaned when small and vulnerable. The hapless little hero is seemingly unwanted, mistreated, suffers greatly and appears to be a loser in life's lottery. But alas, they are destined for greatness—to lead, love and prosper. They learn from their trials and tribulations and come to realize their inherent value. They inherit natural gifts and rise to take on the mantle of responsibility: Oliver Twist ends up sitting pretty, Babar and Bambi become kings of their respective herds and Harry Potter becomes a wizard able to face ultimate evil in "he who can't be named."

What inspires and encourages children in these tales is the young orphan succeeding against all odds and triumphing despite seemingly insurmountable obstacles. These stories are of particular interest to children because they fear, at least unconsciously, becoming orphaned as they are not yet ready to fend for themselves and losing their family is more than sad. In their child-mind it is a virtual death sentence.

The child listens to these stories and identifies with the lost and vulnerable child. This type of story provides a container into which children can project their own frightening fears and fantasies. The child allows herself to imagine losing everything, being unwanted or abandoned and then making their way out of despair to end happily ever after. These stories are important for children's development because they build tolerance for bad things happening and suggest a paradigm of resilience and hope. They teach making the best of our circumstances whatever they may be. Actual orphans also find hope and redemption in these stories as roadmaps of possibility.

As long as a story ends well, children can generally handle dark situations. I remember reading Babar with my child and being horrified when Babar's mom dies on page two. I had forgotten how tragically the story began, remembering more about Babar and Celeste happy in a hot air balloon. My first instinct was to skip the death scene, but I have come to trust that the writers of these beloved stories such as Laurent de Brunhoff, Charles Dickens, The Brothers Grimm and J.K. Rowling know what they are doing. As adults we know that things in this life do not always end happily ever after, yet these stories remind us that sometimes things can start badly and still end happily.

If we do not turn the page on the moments with our children that make us sad or fearful, but stay with them to instill hope and confidence by letting them know that every aspect of them is human, valid and lovable we too unlock our love, creativity, prosperity and whatever else currently eludes us.

It's Cool To Be Kind

While orphan stories encourage perseverance in the face of hardship, fairytales teach the paramount importance of kindness, especially toward the seemingly ugly or misshapen.

In *The Hunchback of Notre Dame*, Esmerelda's truest beauty (her soul) is revealed in her kindness to Quasimodo. Shrek's true love, Fiona, is equally beautiful to him at night when she is an ogre and not a pretty princess. Many Grimm's fairy tales contain a supposed ne'er-do-well younger brother or sister who is kind to a dwarf, beast or hag—in contrast to their haughty older siblings who are cruel and dismissive in their haste for worldly success and treasure. Frequently an overlooked and rejected character holds a secret key that allows the younger child to succeed and rule the kingdom. They become the winner, after having been considered the loser, by virtue not of obvious intelligence or boldness, but by virtue of non-judgmental *kindness* that reveals a true and good heart.

If we are contemptuous of seeming losers or outcasts we will never learn to see true beauty and get the keys to real success. Children start out small and unable to do many things that they later master. It is right and good for us to be kind and compassionate to them when they need us, as they will soon be responsible for taking care of our world. If children learn to treasure the world by our example they will act with love when it's their turn to tend it.

Envision What We Want

There is a parable I heard as a child in which someone is given the opportunity to visit hell and see what goes on there. They are taken to a world teeming with abundant and fantastic foods of all sorts but everyone is miserable because their arms are bound to long boards so that they cannot bend them. They can touch the food but they cannot bring it to their mouths. Then the observer is asked if they would like to see heaven and they are taken to a world that, at first glance looks exactly the same as hell, until they notice that in heaven everyone works to feed each other so all are happy and none go hungry.

When we envision the way we wish things would be with our children we might envision a situation where we work together in loving kindness no matter what obstacles confront us. Try and envision a relationship with your child where you see their exquisiteness. Visualize yourself sustaining affectionate interest as your child basks in your attention. Watch them, in your mind's eye, find their way to social connections, generosity, perseverance, pride in their accomplishments and the deep well-being that comes from feeling loved and cared about. Envision yourself succeeding in relating to a loved and happy child and you may notice that you too are happy.

Strategies For Helping

Model Kindness

In parenting, as well as in many other relationships and endeavors, kindness turns out to be the highest value. It is amongst our most powerful tools for spiritual growth and one of the fastest routes to good feelings that last. It serves us well to seek and value kindness above intelligence, wealth and power; we can facilitate kindness in our children by being kind to them, to others and to ourselves.

Let Kids Be Who They Truly Are

Let your children excel in their own unique manner. Help them discover what they love to do, and help them not despair in the things at which they are terrible. For example, if you help a child have joy in sport for its own sake they may have better long term potential than if they are coached to play only to win; especially if they have talent, they soon come to expect to win, to always be the best. Those children might excel in peewee soccer or t-ball, but when they come up against the other "winners" from the next town, they might lack the heart to keep playing for the love of sport. Love of the game is the winning formula, and losing is part of developing character and becoming one's true Self. It is the same with academics; your little genius gets to Harvard or Princeton and is met with the rude fact that there are a significant number of brilliant people in this world. If they feel blessed to be amongst stimulating minds they will flourish. If they only want to be top of the class, to prove they are better than the lot of them, they may even succeed at that, but with such a hyper-competitive attitude will reap little but lonely misery in the end. So be brilliant at whatever nature made you brilliant, and model this for your children by struggling to lend heart, depth and soul to your natural gifts, and by knowing that there are countless things at which each of us are not brilliant. Be this way so that your children can, without necessarily knowing how it happened, learn to be true to their deepest gifts and yet remain humble before all that which is beyond us (be it calculus, poetry or the divine).

Let Yourself Feel

Since fear of our own emotions can be a block to seeing the full range of our child's wonderfulness, a powerful strategy for helping our child is to allow ourselves to simply feel our own feelings. We can improve our emotional awareness and tolerance for intensity by paying closer attention to our bodies and its messages—we might notice where our sadness, fear, anger or jealousy reside. Typically we might hold fear in our belly and lower GI tract, we tend to carry repressed sorrow in the lungs and sinuses, but everyone is different and we must listen to what our bodies are telling us. While it is easier said than done, we can surrender to feelings and let them flow through us. A good cry can make a grown-up feel better just as it can a child. Our fear of feeling blocks us and is much more toxic than the feelings themselves, even if those feelings are painful. If we surrender to our emotions and let them run their course, free of judgment and criticism, this could embolden us to let our child have their feelings and also liberate them from us unconsciously trying to give them our unwanted feelings.

If feelings are not appreciated and lovingly accepted in us by our caregivers we tend to develop false masks to get approval. If we can't feel we cannot really care about anyone or anything; in falseness we cannot tend to ourselves properly and we are hobbled as parents. If we have not yet learned to manage our feelings and let them guide us we may try to escape them by using sex, drugs, food or work as numbing and avoiding strategies. If we rely on our brains to keep feelings at bay we may find ourselves running exhausted on the hamster wheels of our obsessive, negative and inevitably circular thoughts. Hiding out in our brain can bring chronic headaches and sinus problems. Sadness gets imprisoned in our heads or languishes in a rib-cage dungeon we make of our hearts and lungs that can invite ailments there. Not all illness is emotional, but feeling our feelings can free the body and the heart to love, connect and be better parents.

Love And Encouragement For You

When we get stuck in life, we sometimes need *relationship* with another human being in order to bring the healing process to life within our Self. Faint as my influence may be, I wrote this book to encourage you to hang in there. Trust that in some way we all know each other somewhere in our collective soul; in this remote way, you the reader, and I the writer are united in wishing all the best for your beautiful child—and for, and from, your beautiful Self as well. Be present to the love that is around you, and to the love that is within you. We can invite this love into our consciousness, and into our lives by giving love freely, especially to our children via non-judgmental interest and by trying to see into the subtle heart of things—including our own pain or limitations. Love heals us, softens our bitter edges and flows to our children who can thrive like flowers in sunshine.

Exercises To Consider

1. Structure time to pay attention to your child: Dedicate an hour, or even fifteen minutes, to giving yourself freely to your child or children. In that time don't do anything, just pay attention to them—watch them play, create, even just hang with them as they do their homework or chores. Think of your role as elevating observation to an art, not of keen scrutiny but of softness and openness. Find your sincere interest and lavish it on your child. Do not evaluate them in your mind, certainly do not criticize them—don't even praise them. Only seek to see them, love, adore

and appreciate them for who they are. Imagine that your sincere interest in gazing at your child functions like light and water to a plant. Pay attention to how seeing in this way nourishes your own soul. If it helps, strive to do this exercise consistently and often.

2. Look at your child when they are sleeping: Go into your child's room tonight when they are sleeping and really look at them. Truly see their beauty, grace and poetry of spirit. Gaze down at your sleeping child and see their innocence, vulnerability and the yearning they possess for your love, attention and approval. Kiss their soft cheek and take in the fleeting tenderness of it all, allow your heart to be full and know that even though we may lose our patience with them five times before breakfast the next day, they are our greatest gift, a treasure of infinite value. Honor the gift of their existence and the opportunity for us to love them, which in return rewards and transforms us.

3. Surrender to your own feelings: Find a quiet moment to be alone (whenever you can steal the time) and ask yourself what you feel. Pay attention to your body and your emotions. Don't try to analyze why you feel, just feel and notice what occurs, what is hard about this or what is pleasurable about that. Let your heart teach you how to listen to it, then try to use what you are learning to listen more fully to your child. Quiet your mind, if you can, and trust that your heart will realign and renew your energy.

4. Feelings journals: Make "Feeling Journals" with your child. Get a notebook or sketchbook and provide art supplies. Suggest that the journal will be a place to write or draw feelings when you aren't available to talk about things right at that moment when they need you, or when they want someplace to put overflowing emotion. Consider making one for yourself. See what they do with their journal and take a real interest in anything they are willing to share with you. Let them choose not to show you. Do not evaluate as an art critic, but simply allow yourself to experience whatever they share, create or feel. This is about building your relationship through sincere interest and shared experience, not about teaching them, or yourself, to be creative. You are both already "creative." What you want is to be more fully Self-expressed in your natural creativity, and more connected with each other in your shared experience of being alive. Being interested in your child's feelings brings you closer to the core of who they are; seeing the splendor of their inner essence would probably be illuminating for both of you.

5. Appreciation exercise: Look around and find something you can appreciate—a cloud, a building, a pet— and put your attention on that positive thing. Make it a game; work your way up to finding beauty in less and less obvious things or situations. See that flower pushing its way up through the cracked parking lot; actually taste your food; notice the song the birds are singing and find yourself living in a world that is increasingly lovely.

6. Portrait of a so-called loser: Draw a picture of your personal loser, or make a collage from magazine images, or make it a mixture of characters from films or TV. Make it a narrative description as in a short story, sculpt it out of play-dough or trace it on the water of your bath. The healing aspect is to give this "Charlie Brown" self a little compassion, a little love (or at least know that you're giving him/her a little attention). Keep in mind they are only a loser to the extent that this is how you see them. If you bother to actually do this exercise you may find that the work you create evokes your affection and helps soften the critical eye that falls on your child.

7. Yoga: If you do yoga, consider dedicating your practice one day to the beauty of the world as it is, perhaps to the glory of your child as they are right now. Ultimately, the yoga exercises and positions are preparation for final mediation, the culmination of any true yoga practice. Since emptying the mind completely is very challenging, consider meditating on a simple object of your choosing—a leaf, an orange, a flower, a rock, etc. Nothing fancy, just take some time to deeply look at something. Breathe and fix your attention and appreciation on your chosen object, let it teach you and trust that your deep Self aligns in this way. See if this helps bring forth your best Self as a parent.

Chapter 4

Building Self And Self-Esteem

The Mean Girl

After five years at the group home and later supervising other therapists working with special needs children I became a consulting psychologist at a private elementary school in West L.A. When I balked at leaving the at-risk kids, the director of the private school argued that these students needed, and deserved, the help just as much as any other child. To be honest, I also needed to make more money to support my own kids.

It was in my new position that I stepped into my charming and well-lit office one morning to find eleven-year-old Allison, darkly weeping on my couch between two solemnly watery-eyed friends. Allison's big blue eyes were filled with tears of betrayal over not being invited to Erin's, the reigning cool girl, sleepover party. Allison had been included in Erin's past parties but this one had a theme inspired by a popular book of the moment. There had to be the same number of friends at the sleepover as there were in the special circle of friends in the book—and Allison hadn't made the cut. Allison, a truly nice kid, was devastated and unable to understand how such a good friend could be so mean. Yet Erin had systematically excluded practically every girl in the class at some point. This included the very friends who were comforting

Allison at the moment (and who were both immensely relieved that they were not left out this time).

Although Erin held sway over the other girls, she generally presented as remote and subdued. Erin's teacher told me that she had been sweet and enthusiastic in years past, but had become increasingly sour since her parents' divorce. Her dad was hardly involved in her life, and although the family had a lot of money, Erin and her older sister (who could herself be quite cruel and dismissive) were often with nannies. Erin seemed to be socially dominant mainly because she had decided that that was what she wanted to be; now she was using her power to make others feel bad. Perhaps Erin secretly felt neglected, excluded and angry at home and the feelings she could neither acknowledge nor contain were spilling over and into her friends. One could say that she was the most popular girl in her class, but she was fast becoming feared more than liked and was on the verge of becoming disliked by her friends.

Although it was Allison who came crying to my office, it was Erin who was suffering from low self-esteem. Erin was bottled up with pain and ashamed of her feelings while Allison was healthy enough to feel her sadness, express it and quickly bounce back. The other children might not have guessed it, but Erin's mean and manipulative behavior reflected a distorted belief that she could not get her needs met with kindness and honesty.

The teachers and I encouraged all the children in that class to understand that unkind behavior comes from low self-esteem. We worked to encourage an ethic of inclusion and kindness that addressed Erin's pain without directly confronting her, or her behavior. By more deeply realizing the root motivation for excluding and meanness, all the girls in that class became just a little bit kinder to each other. Allison realized that she was an excellent friend, and that even Erin still liked her—and might have been acting out of jealousy of Allison's friendships with other girls. Eleven and twelve-year-old girls can be mean creatures... and so need extra compassion and understanding.

When we wonder whether or not a child has positive self-esteem a rough measure is how generally kind they are to others. People who feel good about themselves are typically nice. As parents, this underscores the importance of being warm and thoughtful to our children, ourselves and everyone else in our lives whenever possible. Through kindness, even when others are less kind, we can bolster or maintain our own positive self-esteem and help facilitate it in our children.

Self Before Self-Esteem

It is not possible to have truly good self-*esteem* until we have a clear and solid sense of self to begin with. Much of what passes for self-esteem problems would be better understood as problems owing to the lack of a cohesive self. Boastful and flashy behavior that irritates people and creates rejection and isolation in the end is generally an insecure person's attempt to compensate for an underlying sense of inadequacy—it is a mask that hides a weak, unformed or damaged real self. Chronic self-defeating behaviors, dejection and negativity are likewise better understood as reflecting a wobbly, wounded or shattered underlying self than as mere low self-esteem.

As parents it is important to be aware that helping to form and cultivate a solid self in our child is a fundamental task that precedes building self-esteem. As a psychologist working across the life-cycle, most of the problems I deal with seem to have at least one thing in common: a disruption in one's sense of self. The severity of this problem can range from mild to extreme, but is often the core, underlying, problem upon which all other problems rest. Every diagnosis, from substance abuse to bi-polar or eating disorders, are at the very least made worse by an absent or tattered self, a condition which also impedes work, love and care-giving relationships. Helping form and/or repair the self is often a central task in psychotherapy.

Children come to know who they are by what their caregivers reflect back to them, and through this interest come to believe not just that they are interesting, but that they fully *exist*—that they have a self. Seeing a child for who they are builds their sense of self. Neglect can be debilitating as it renders a child starved for attention and thus vulnerable to the wrong sort of attention.

When a child is abused they are used as a receptacle for unwanted feelings. Treating a child badly is far worse than mistreating a grown-up because while the grown-up may be hurt by mistreatment, a child is more likely to be *defined* by it.

There is no substitute for the development of the self. A solid self is one's most treasured psychological asset. In the right circumstances the self develops naturally, like language. And as with language, there are critical times when a person's self readily forms; if we miss the window it is much harder to set things right later on. The foundation of the self is laid in the first few years of life; and like a house with a poor foundation, problems with the core self later show up as cracks and fissures in the structure of our personality. We parents may be playing catch-up in our own self-development, or hobbling along on psychological crutches, but no matter what else we must strive to give our children the right mix of compassion, understanding and limits to allow them to develop a sturdy self that will serve them all their lives.

Without A Bowl, Soup For The Soul Is Just A Mess

"The Tao is like an empty bowl." Tao-te Ching

In a self-help world where we clamor for soup for the soul, we may overlook the importance of a bowl to hold whatever soup we may receive.

Imagine your conscious ego-self as a bowl. A healthy self would be a nice sturdy bowl. A problematic self could be thought of as a cracked bowl that leaks, or a shattered vessel. If our self is more like a colander than a bowl, no matter how much love, support, or encouragement we pour into it, moments later it will be as empty as if nothing had ever been put in. When we say that a person is "draining" this expresses what we feel when we give and give to someone who continually wants more and acts as if they've gotten nothing.

The fear and shame of being unmasked when there is little or no self behind our facade can trigger rage, withdrawal or depression in a parent. Anything that rubs our nose in the fact that our self may be lacking is likely to unleash our worst parenting moments.

Therapy is not the only way to make a self, but if we suffer for lack of a strong self it may be worth considering. It is very hard to develop a self without another person to see and understand us in a non-critical and non-judgmental way. Even if we skip therapy, if we can manage to parent well it builds the bowl of self for us as well as our children. Selfless giving strengthens the self of the giver, and at the same time the loving attention nourishes the child's self.

Even in the best of circumstances the development of a solid bowl in our child's psyche takes time, consistent love and sincere attention. Self-building in our child also demands that we parents tolerate and contain emotional intensity. We psychologically hold our children's fears and frustrations within our selves the way a nest holds baby birds.

To Feel Loved We Must Feel Known

If no one knows the real us, we cannot feel truly loved. The love our mask-self receives ends up leaving the real self feeling lonely and unlovable. This deepens our shame about our negative aspects and our tendency to split them off and hide them away where no one can see them. As parents, knowing our own dark and pathetic corners makes us more complete and empowers us to consciously choose love and compassion without needing to deny or project our Shadow aspects (from cruelty, to weakness, to feeling like a loser) onto others, especially our children.

We must take an interest in every aspect of our children in order to imbue them with the abiding knowledge that they are loved. We must not say, "that is the grouchy you, come back when you are the nice you." It is better to say, "You are grouchy and I love you no matter what mood you are in." This tends to cheer them faster and allows them to take in an attitude that is accepting of all aspects of self into their minds where it will eventually be ready to speak up even when we are not there. Good parenting requires that we know our children. At times we must critically evaluate, reward and punish their *behaviors* in order to guide and protect them. Yet we must not judge their *character*. By striving to understand without judgment, trust becomes a bridge to our child; being more fully known, they develop a fuller sense of self. Our children's core essence must be perceived as sacred, and beyond judgment, in order for us to gently awaken them to fully inhabit their lives.

What "The Three Little Pigs" Says About The Self

The well-known tale of *The Three Little Pigs,* especially if unabridged, is virtually a self-development manual. Most children past the age of two or three know this story, yet most grown-ups don't know the *whole* story. In America we sanitize our fairy tales lest they be too disturbing for children, but by snipping this yarn we refine away its secret nourishment.

As you may recall, the tale begins when the kindly mommy pig informs her three darling boys that they are old enough to live on their own and so it's time to hit the road. They show no indications of feeling rejected or angry and promptly set forth on their life journey. There are psychological implications in the fact that the big bad wolf shows up immediately after the pigs leave home. Here, the pigs might be imagined to "split" the mother into the good mom who only wants to facilitate their growth and development, and her Shadow, the mom who kicks them out into the cold cruel world where they are potential wolf-food. In this context the wolf can be seen to function as a stand-in for the big, bad, rejecting mother. The young pigs can understand big and bad, but not good *and* bad. The wolf as symbolic of devouring persecution can be understood as a primitive and unconscious defense against an even more frightening idea to a child: abandonment. In other words, we prefer to be chased and even eaten than to be unwanted, unseen and forgotten; if we lack a self, we are more comfortable inside even a "bad" bowl (wolf, witch, giant) than blowing away like dust in a windy world.

The three pigs each represent a different philosophy of life and a corresponding work ethic. The first pig chooses to make a house of straw so he can get it done and set to playing; the second makes a compromise between work and play in choosing to build with sticks; and the third, and exemplary pig, chooses to delay gratification and build all day with bricks. While few people consciously yearn for a bowl, a house is also an apt symbol of the self. In *The Three Little Pigs*, the wolf is easily able to blow down the straw house-self, a wispy self that cannot withstand the hot air of someone who has no respect for the crudely constructed self of a naive pig. The first pig runs and joins the second in a stick house-self, somewhat more formed but still so precarious that it is easily blown down by the wolf. The self-shattered pigs seek refuge with the third pig in his newly completed brick house where the three pig selves (fragile, transitional and solid) merge into a unified cohesive consciousness: a modern, urban, sophisticated self that could stand proud in the country, or become a piece of a great collective city: a self which the archaic primitive wolf-self cannot blow down with unbridled hungry rage.

This may be where you thought the story ends, but the Grimm's[1] original continues with the wolf climbing onto the roof and down the chimney while the pigs quickly throw a big pot on the boil in the fireplace. The wolf goes into the pot where the pigs trap, stew and eat it. Only after the pigs have literally incorporated and digested the wolf (i.e. their own Shadow aspect—which is uncivilized, ruled by appetite, lacking in kindness and easily found in any preschool playground, and also in too many grown-up office building) do the pigs get to live happily ever after.

Now, maybe a wolf is just a wolf and it doesn't symbolize anything; still, this story seems to make it into the imagined world of virtually every boy and girl in the western world so it must be saying something to somebody. Even if we simply take it at its face value, we are still left with enduring moral instruction on how to succeed in life: build things sturdily and be wary of impulsive fun at the expense of long-term results. Still, the fact that the wolf is not simply shut out, or even killed and forgotten, but rather stewed and eaten must be more than just a macabre detail. If the story is a timeworn guide to living happily ever after, we must give the importance of ingestion its due.

The pigs actually honor the wolf by cooking him (or her) in their stew pot and eating him. If he were merely garbage they would not take the time to cook him and they certainly would not eat him. When asked if he liked children, W.C. Fields quipped, "I do if they're prepared right." Perhaps the same is true of wolf. Slowly stewing wolf no doubt breaks it down and makes it more possible to metabolize. This is true for the "big bad" parts of us—we cannot just take them into our consciousness in one gulp, but rather we must break them down through slow and careful psychological "cooking." So, before we can be our best Self as a parent, maybe we need to find a good recipe for our worst self and hit the kitchen.

Why Don't We Feel Better About Ourselves?

What's In Our Child's Way?

Where self-esteem is poor, some of the likely culprits include:

1) <u>Lack of a Solid Underlying Self</u>

Without a self in the first place there is little possibility to have good (or even bad) esteem about that self. If the self is unformed, fragmented or leaky this is the primary problem and we parents must support self building (see below).

Where the self is lacking, the child we see sulking grumpily around is more a mask than an embodiment of authentic spirit. It is good to keep this in mind and not limit our own perception of our child to the flimsy straw house of a self that they may be living in for the time being.

2) <u>Not Enough Hugs and Kisses</u>

Our first sense of self comes, in part, from our skin. As infants we need touch to soothe us when we are upset and to help us gain clarity about the boundaries of our physical being. This supports us to then develop a psychological sense of self. The "Head, Shoulders, Knees and Toes" sorts of songs taught in preschool do more than teach labels for body parts, they help ground children in their bodies. The repeated lesson that children exist as individuals, and as part of a group of children, sets a foundation for them to learn other things from letter and number recognition to playing and working with others.

We are never too old for affection. Yes, kids get self-conscious and even rejecting at certain points, but we parents must find the right times and ways to keep giving whatever affection our child will tolerate. This affection should not be a covert way of getting children to give *us* love and affection, no matter how badly we may we need it. Children's self-development, and our own individuation as parents, both largely depend on us caregivers giving. Teens in particular may no longer want hugs from mom and dad, but they are often desperately seeking each other for much-needed affection to help them know who they are, and *that they are* during the turbulent challenges to identity that come with adolescence. Adolescence presents us with kids who are babies and little grown-ups at the same time, and we should not stop giving affection just because they rebuff us a few hundred times.

3) <u>Failure to Work Through Healthy Grandiosity</u>

Kids need to puff up into super-heroes and fairy princesses as part of natural healthy development. If a child doesn't get their chance to be wonderfully grandiose and *then* calm down, they can later end up either sad and suppressed in their life-spirit, believing that they are less worthwhile than other people, or they can become arrogant and live in a childishly puffed-up way to compensate for an underlying sense of inadequacy. If a child needs to imagine themselves as a pro skateboarder or rock star we need to keep in mind how precarious the underlying self may be when the fantasies are all about power. Avoid even gentle teasing or being overly "realistic" (i.e. "hardly anybody makes it to the pros so do your math") to burst their big dreams. They'll probably figure out they're not a professional athlete in good time, but they may have a strong enough self by then to realize that isn't the only way for them to feel good about themselves. If it feels like we are walking on eggshells with our child those shells may be a clue to the fragile state of their developing self.

4) <u>Lack of Success Experiences</u>

A frequent contributing factor in flagging self-esteem is a lack of success experiences. When we do things well our personal victories, large and small, demonstrate our effectiveness, skills, and attributes back to us. These moments make us feel good and build confidence to take more risks, confront harder challenges and continue to build our self-esteem.

While we are all bad at many things, everyone is good at *something*. A child needs success experiences to build joy in their lives. As to what a "success experience" is, early in life it is framed by parents; if we are thrilled at the wanna-be block tower, the scribbled drawing, the almost thrown ball, etc. confidence evolves in a child that what they try, they can do—that their efforts have impact. Over time this builds skills as well as self-esteem in a child.

If our child seems to suffer low self-esteem, anything that can pass for success is a start. Making one basket, reading one book (or sentence, or word), "cooking" toast, planting a flower can all become a success experience; as the parent, if we set our mind to it (and we are willing to be modest in our initial expectations) we can usually help architect a success experience for our child.

5) Critical Inner Voices

When a child tries something, even if it falls short, they tend to look to their parents for a word or facial expression to help them frame their experience. If our message is "good try," our child is validated for effort and, over time, develops an encouraging parent figure within their mind. If we are disgusted by our child's poor performance and express exasperation or mock them, they internalize these negative sounds and images. Critical inner parent figures then hover and haunt our child, depressing self-esteem long after we have left the room, the sports field or even the planet.

6) Lack of Hope

Negativity and low self-esteem have a way of becoming entrenched and spiraling down. Even if children do not yet have a clear vision of themselves as happy, positive or valued, we as parents must hold a positive vision clear and strong. Often the biggest obstacle to success of any kind is a person's own firm belief that they are not capable of success. Anything is *possible*, but if we parents don't believe that this is true for our children then our own narrow minds might be in our children's way of cultivating their true genius and natural exuberance. If we can see our child succeeding (not at what *we* need from them but at what they desire to become) our mind helps pave the way for possibility. A kind, hard-working, positive attitude, in and of itself, is success—it can move mountains and bring happiness when achievement and material possessions do not.

7) Insecurity

To truly succeed we have to be willing to risk falling on our faces sometimes— and to see this as part of authentic self-esteem. As parents we can encourage appropriate risk-taking and make "failure" an acceptable outcome; we can redefine success as earnest effort and hold the ability to laugh at ourselves in high esteem. A good sense of humor about our own foibles is part of a secure sense of self. If our child does feel insecure we can strive to let them tell us all about it and not just puff them up or talk them out of it.

By connecting with them in their areas of weakness, fear or shame we help them to accept themselves as they are and strengthen them to move forward because they are not so alone. Skills and talents do not guarantee security as a human being; after all, some people are terrible at things but secure within them-selves while others are brilliant and gifted yet remain insecure.

What's In Our Way?

If we want to help our kids with their self-esteem it makes sense to check-in with ourselves to see if any of the following concerns might be in *our* way.

1) <u>Feelings of Inadequacy</u>

If we lack a solid self it makes it hard to facilitate one in our child; hard, but not impossible. Giving love to our children and others in our lives can do a lot to help us build a healthy self. Self-building, after the window of early childhood has shut for us and we still lack a secure self, rests on expanding our capacity to love and make a difference, even in small ways.

2) <u>Unconscious Need For a Low Self-Esteem Child</u>

Our obvious feelings of inadequacy can directly model low self-esteem for our child. More insidious is when we *think* that we are secure but act in ways that reveal insecurity (i.e. shaming others or tending to make them feel inadequate or envious), or when we manage to appear solid to some people such as our child, but it is actually a mask. The Shadow of our secret parental insecurity can fall across our child who may then carry our inadequacy and lack of self for us. The pain and shame of this dynamic for us as a parent can prevent us from acknowledging it and so our child remains limited in their potential for happiness and achievement. The antidote is to not rule this possibility out before we've contemplated it, even if it makes us queasy—and to consciously embrace the ethic that we wish to carry and heal our own pain, and even that of our children, but never the other way around. If we need help and support we should seek it, but not from our kids (and probably not from our parents either).

3) <u>Grandiosity</u>

If our own grandiosity remains untamed this can make us overly demanding of, and needy for, "success" and achievement in our children. While high expectations are good, impossible expectations of perfection create anxiety and feelings of impossibility in a child. Here a child may feel like, "what's the use anyway?" and avoid frustration by giving up on things before they begin. If we can handle the fact that we are a little bit ordinary, we free children to be extraordinary in being true to themselves.

4) Our Own Self-Involvement

Parental self-involvement also comes from having a less than solid self and therefore a natural preoccupation with our own adequacy, comfort, gratification, validation, etc. Obviously this compromises our ability to be fully present to our child and shades their experience of us as a mirror for them. Think of the parent who is answering our questions while talking on the phone or reading the paper; we feel only marginally important at best and often, deep down, come to believe that this is all that we deserve. Self-involvement as a parent is a symptom of our problem, not a solution to it. We can end up going to countless yoga retreats, healers and therapists but unless we come to see that our children need us to be involved with them much more than they need us to perfect ourselves we remain trapped in a closed loop of self-improvement

5) Lack of Support as Parent

Since it takes a village to raise a child, we must reach out and allow support to the extent that we consciously realize it is available. And if we believe there is little or no support we must open new ways of thinking. Taking care of our children, collectively as a world in which every child is our child, is a sacred task, an honor and a true path. If we allow ourselves to believe that sincere attempts to be present and to serve our children draws support from the deep Self, we discover resources within ourselves that we didn't realize we had and, often, the world seems to magically open and support us in our efforts. The world is mysterious, but when we are blocked or thwarted from being our best Self despite sincere effort we are sure to learn *something,* and perhaps find odd comfort emerging out of dark despair. The more we use our mind as a tool to assert that we *are* our best Self, the more easily we discover that we are blessed to live in the world, and that our deepest joy comes from taking good care of it.

Broadening Our Perspective

Why More Sense Of Self Is Needed Now Than Ever Before

We, the in-your-face-intensely-interested-in-our-kids'-every-movement sort of parents, may wonder how children ever managed to survive, much less feel good about themselves, back in the days of "children should be seen and not heard." In past generations even privileged children were not nearly as indulged or paid attention to as today's lucky few. As to life in previous centuries kids might have been working in factories or tilling the land by age ten.

In prior times there was less choice about who we might choose to become, and the world probably seemed more solid and predictable. We generally knew who we were, and stayed where we were. We didn't trouble ourselves so much with bettering ourselves or with changing the world. There were always some occasional visionaries or conquerors, but the prevailing ethic was more grounded and less obsessed with an entitled sense of personal destiny.

Because the world is so challenging, we need more of a solid self than ever before. We need to cultivate a strong self in our children, in part, *so* that they can enjoy their childhood and not just experience it as a time to prepare for their destiny as adults. Even as the most privileged parents are going full-court press to help their kids develop the self that they will need to survive and thrive in the world we will be bequeathing to them, all the manic preparing for the future might make us take pause and realize that this increasingly global driven-ness is a vicious cycle, demanding ever more self for our kids to manage it all. At some point we might wake up and use the blessing of having a coherent and connected self to think about ourselves a little more like kin in a global village than like contestants in some ultra competitive "reality show" that passes for modern life.

Envision Our Child's Healthy Self First And Good Self-Esteem Second

If we imagine ourselves, and our child, having a solid self and positive self-esteem, we create a picture of abundance, confidence, well-being and gratitude. If we can vividly hold this picture and *then* imagine confronting today's challenges, we would very likely find ourselves parenting more in line with our ideal.

The ethic here is not to fake it 'til we make it, but to honestly consider, and thus discover, what our best Self would do if it were free of fear, doubt and judgment.

Strategies For Helping

How To Help A Child Build A True Self

Two of the most important forces in self-development are sincere, non-judgmental attention and "holding opposites" (i.e. tolerating two opposite things being true at the same time). Holding opposites occurs in childhood (i.e. mom is loving *and* she's "mean" or limit-setting) but is increasingly central to individuation in adulthood; as we develop, the opposites become ever more complex and challenging (i.e. that we are good *and* evil, that we must find self-expression *and* give selfless love). Children need parents to help hold the opposites that they cannot contain, and so spill over into us.

Paying Attention Shapes The Self

When my younger son was four, he gazed deeply into my wife's eyes and said dreamily, "Mama, I see myself in your eyes." While he literally meant that he saw his reflection in her pupils, something profound was also expressed: because she was there to look at him, he could see himself. My wife also got a glimpse of her Self in that moment, delivered on the wings of the child who sees himself in her. When we parents are seen, even as a mirror in which our child is able to see their self, we too more fully, consciously and mindfully exist. When our child sees us, hugs us or tells us that they love us we cannot help but feel validated as parents and to be deeply affected and alive in the current of this love. While we must be able to parent for long stretches without much reinforcement or validation, the validating and encouraging power that a mere drop of our child's love has on us adults is dwarfed by the gigantic and life-shaping power that our love has on our developing children. The newer our child is in this world, the more powerful and essential our attention is to their developing a healthy self; and where our child regresses or struggles in their self-development the quintessential thing we can give them is our compassionate, undivided and non-judging attention.

We help our child build their self when we watch them play, when we sit with them as they struggle with homework (resisting the urge to do it for them) and when we patiently watch them shakily pour a cup of milk or labor to write their name. The parents I admire most tend to be patient and allow for messes, but also include the child in cleaning up. We lead busy lives that too often mask a hollowness that we fear to slow down and confront; carving out time that is solely about our child makes space to be present to them and helps allay our own anxieties. If our child seems to be lacking in self-esteem and natural exuberance our primary strategy for helping is to spend more time paying sincere attention to them. Sometimes paying attention means just watching or listening, and sometimes it calls for joining our child in their tasks or in their imaginative play. If our young child wants to roll on the floor, we can watch them roll on the floor, or we can roll along with them and see what it is like to have the kitchen spin all around us. When we thought playing catch would be fun and build skills but they want to jump up and down on the ball we can let them jump up and down on the ball and notice how they are able to make things fun. When they want to play fantasy games, build with blocks or have us watch them play electronic games we try and stretch beyond what personally interests us to understand what it is like to be our child and be interested in what they are interested in.

Sometimes we can't get our child to tell us much about their day, and then they are ready to tell us all kinds of things when we are on the phone, or in the middle of making dinner. Limits and manners about respect and interrupting are important, but we should be aware that our non-interest when they are ready to talk might reflect how we are missing them by trying to have things on our terms and time frames. If our child comes to believe that we are not really interested in them, even if this is not how we really feel, this can mistakenly teach them to believe that they are not interesting. It is helpful to communicate that we are interested in what our children have to tell us, even if we are not always available at the exact moment when they need us. If when we are ready to hear them they act like they could take or leave our interest, we should trust that they are ravenous for it whether or not they show it—and maintain sincere interest in the face of grunts, eye-rolling and stoic reticence.

Holding Opposites Strengthens The Self

Beyond sincere attention, holding opposites is the other key ingredient in self-building. In parenting, holding opposites means emotionally and psychologically containing whatever our children cannot. Children are a primordial sea of opposites in need of a psychological cauldron. As a holder of opposites we serve as overflow bowl for the unruly emotional conflicts that roil within our children. We catch what our kids cannot manage, but they eventually come back for everything they cast off, every drop of rage, fear and vitriol, drawn like a magnet to "big bad wolf" pieces that are needed to complete them as an authentic self.

When a child passionately, angrily or desperately wants something and we hold a limit, if we do it with kindness and grace we are helping hold an opposite: the "no" to their "yes." Limits counter-balance the unconditional love of non-judgmental seeing. Being our best Self as a parent means simultaneously bringing love *and* limits—our challenge is about making this into a unified whole rather than a battle against our child within our self.

If we want to strengthen our ability to hold opposites we can consciously reach for whatever we *don't* feel or believe at any given moment and add it to what we *do* feel and believe. The two opposites together offer a more complete understanding than either one alone. We don't necessarily *want* to fill our pockets with stones and shells when our child hands them to us at the beach, but when we are in a kind and generous mood we do. Children hand us the feelings that they cannot manage to hold—those that are too intensely angry, frightening or sad; at our best we recognize this and help them hold it together by intuiting, feeling, caring—and often *carrying*—these overwhelming feelings until they get an emotional pail or some pockets of their own.

Success Experiences Facilitate Good Self-Esteem

Once the self grows solid, enhancing self-esteem becomes a realistic goal. We can, and should, tell our children that they are wonderful, but to help them have good self-esteem they must come to believe that they are wonderful by their own estimation and not just in our eyes as their parents. A key way this occurs is through the positive effects of having success experiences.

Once a child comes to have a psychological bowl, they need to use it to discover their strengths and weaknesses and achieve a new sense of mastery at each developmental level. Every child has a genius for *something*; the art of parenting includes making a wide variety of experiences available to a child to help them discover their inherent giftedness. We can learn self-esteem by being a good sport and *trying* even if we are lacking in skills in a certain area. I'll always remember a boy at my summer camp who had severe cerebral palsy and set a personal goal of making 2,000 basketball points. Countless afternoons he stood at the hoop struggling to loft the ball through the net. When he reached his goal it was announced in the mess hall and the whole camp erupted in wild cheering. Decades later, his beaming smile of accomplishment still resonates in my soul.

Where kids struggle, whether socially, academically or developmentally, it is crucial to protect a fragile sense of self while seeking arenas where they can succeed in ways that are true to them. Particularly with late bloomers, we need to protect self-esteem as they catch up to the group on their own time-frame. For example, if a child is highly gifted in a narrow range of intellectual interest, but does not like sports, does not easily make friends and shows little interest in art or music, trying to make them into the kid that they are not will lower self-esteem and reinforce the self-concept that they lack skills and are a misfit. Making a child play Little League if they consistently hate it will do less good for their self-esteem than computer camp if that is where they feel interested or at home. The more a child comes to feel like a weirdo or a loser because they don't fit in with expected areas of success the more they tend to withdraw from all areas of life. If a child can keep their joy and exuberance intact until they can get to MIT, the Culinary Institute or off-off-off Broadway and eventually find their "people" they may well live happily ever after—and probably in a more authentic and original way than the prom king and queen.

Cultivate Self-Esteem

In facilitating good self-esteem we are gardeners more than sculptors—and definitely not machine operators; we don't *make* self-esteem grow in our children, we cultivate it. We work to protect our children from the pervading ethic that we must be a certain way in order to be a winner and if not we are a loser. When we see our child's self-esteem failing to come into full blossom we can ask ourselves if it is getting enough sincerely interested attention, which is like light to a plant, or if they need more structure or limits, which are like a stake that supports a sapling. If our children believe that people who feel good about themselves are kind, and if they themselves are treated with kindness, they will generally strive for kindness in their behavior and know that those who are mean are not nearly so cool, confident or truly happy as they would have us believe. Good parenting includes knowing which kid needs more structure and which one needs more freedom; it means checking frequently, but not anxiously, to ensure optimal growth. Dandelions grow overnight (and are beautiful in their own right), but trees ultimately rule the garden and, like good self-esteem, take time to grow.

"I Hope You Feel Good About Yourself"

When our children have their shining moments we want to help them take optimal benefit from them. "I'm Proud Of You" is not the same as "I Hope You're Proud Of Yourself." "I'm proud of you" is a nice thing to say and our child wants us to be proud, but it also conveys that what matters is what we think. When we say, "I hope you are proud of yourself," we coach our child that as far as we're concerned they have every right to be proud of themselves, but what matters most is what *they* think about their self. This also encourages taking responsibility for oneself and not being blindly led by others. Emphasizing our child's taking pride in their own efforts and achievements supports them to be more confident, more properly assertive and more trusting of their instincts; it also leaves them less vulnerable to peer pressure and group think.

True self-esteem is the foundation of originality, leadership and vision; it is the "right stuff" that makes authentic success possible and spares a person from the dead end of conforming and conventional so-called success (i.e. money from a job one loathes; fame for its own sake). Success is hollow if it is without heart and soul. When we support our children to be real, authentic and caring we help make the world a better place... and that's good for our own self-esteem.

Exercises To Consider

1. Do something for which you have no talent: Make a list of the things you are terrible at—then pick one and do it; while doing this thing badly, note the ways you feel and deepen empathy for how it feels for your child when they confront things that are hard for them; practice being a good sport and laughing at yourself. The ultimate would be to do something with your kid at which they are better than you.

2. Let your kids win: Play games with your children and let them win. Don't be patronizing or obvious; if you win, accept that and try again; just play until you lose. Let the losing feelings be yours, let your child triumph and win while you hold the loser position and model grace and being a good sport.

3. Make bowls: Consider a bowl-making art project using modeling clay, carving wood or decorating found or bought bowls. You can playfully suggest that you are making sacred vessels. Have fun with these self-made Holy Grails, Genie Lamps and Harry Potteresque Goblets of Fire—make up stories of how your bowls came to be, where they've been and what powers they have. Let yours and your children's imaginations create real magic. Meditate on the bowl your child creates or chooses in the context of the ideas in this chapter about the self. Really listen to whatever your kids share with you as if you yourself were a bowl sacredly holding whatever they pour out. Contemplate the bowl you make or choose as a symbol of support for you to be a better, more serene and more tranquil parent. When parenting gets rough, take a moment to contemplate your bowl.

4. Play with bowls: spilling and containing. Play with your kindergarten or younger-aged kids using different food coloring-dyed water. Provide bowls and cups and a place to make a mess—the sink or the yard, or put them in the tub with bath color tablets and bowls. Watch them combine colors, pour out, refill—notice how it fascinates and delights them. Pretend they are magic potions and ask your child what the potions can do. Listen and learn. (First and second graders may still enjoy this one).

5. Dream house: Our dream house is one way of envisioning our best Self. Such a house frequently has many rooms for different parts of us to work on different things: learning, resting, enjoying life, love and friends... and space to work on our great, unrealized projects. If we take our dreams seriously they guide us out of deprivation, fear and longing and into the splendid lodgings that are custom made by the deep Self. Think about your dream house as a clue to the self that exists within you as a potentiality that is not yet manifest but could be. Imagine where the house would be, what surrounds it, what the inside is like; fantasize the life you would lead there, who would come over, what you would do, learn, give, create. Clip pictures from magazines, download images from the web, find bits of fabric, start a folder or make a collage until your dream house takes more and more vivid shape.

Parent as if you *already live there*—move in to the abode of good feelings that last; often if we can move our psyche in, our body miraculously finds itself living in the reality we had somehow been blocking with our fear and our chronic wishing that reinforces the notion that we are lacking. If we get the feeling we are truly after, the need for a particular house, car or pair of shoes etc. tends to drop away. The attitude of abundance and gratitude enhances our ability to manifest our best parenting and it helps other dreams come true as well.

6. Mentors can be mythical: Sometimes we feel like we could use a mentor, a wise old man or woman to advise and console. Many great artists and scientists have had imaginary relationships with admired greats of past eras. Imagine your ideal parent, confidante, therapist, sage or friend who could be available to you whenever you needed. Such a relationship is not crazy, just creative. If it helps, that's what counts.

7. Build your yoga poses like you are building your Self: If you do not practice yoga you can still simply dedicate a day with all its normal activities to your child. At the day's end take a moment to recall your intention and take note if it seemed to have any effect on your parenting or your child's mood or behavior. If you are a yogi you might dedicate a practice to your child's having a solid self or good self-esteem. Pay particular attention to Mountain Pose (Tadasana), as standing with proper alignment helps us stand strong and true in all sorts of ways. Just as the self is our basis for self-esteem, proper mountain pose is the basis for all other poses— inverted, twisting, standing or seated.

Having dedicated our practice to our child's self, we build our poses from the ground up, rooting in the earth, drawing strength from it; we breathe in spirit and let it infuse our physical body and our subtle body with energy. Extend this attitude into the poses of Warrior I & II (Virabhadrasana) especially Warrior II where we embody the image of the noble warrior; also bring ideas of balance, rooting down into the earth and growing up toward the sky to Tree Pose (Virksasana). Be sure to take some time in Savasana at the end to allow the nourishing effects of the poses to restore you and enhance your parenting, as was your wish in dedicating your practice to your child at the outset. Take note of the effects of this on your parenting.

Chapter 5

Helping Sad Kids Feel Better

The Brownie Intervention

It was well past midnight when I was awakened by a call from the group home staff informing me that Kenneth was having suicidal thoughts. They put him on the phone and he answered my questions with his tentative, almost apologetic voice. He had tried all the coping strategies we had talked about in the past; reading, listening to music, talking with staff, taking a walk, writing in his journal, etc. But he still didn't feel safe. Bleary eyed, I pictured him standing there holding the phone in the tiny staff office, shoulders hunched over his sad frame, his perpetually startled blue eyes staring vacantly. Typically at this point I would try to get a kid in this frame of mind to make "a contract" with me to not hurt themselves until we could meet in the morning and see if they still felt suicidal. Meanwhile, we might have one of the staff shadow the child at all times to keep them safe.

The psychiatric hospital was sometimes necessary, but we generally tried to make it work without that. With Kenneth I was on the fence, and you never want to make the wrong decision in this sort of situation. I told the staff to hang tight and called my supervisor. Obviously I had woken her, yet she never seemed irritated by pre-dawn calls—she had accepted that this came with the job; she was like a kind doctor from a bygone era, the sort who made house-calls and knew families well.

Kenneth had been in the group home a year or two longer than I'd worked there and my supervisor knew just what to do: "Brownie Intervention." "Excuse me?" I replied, not familiar with this technique from any of my schooling. "He'll talk to you for hours and still not feel safe. Have the staff take him to Ralphs, buy brownie mix and help him make them. He can eat a couple but tell him to bring a tray of brownies to my office in the morning. Call me if there's a problem." She hung up.

I was sitting in her office the next morning when Kenneth trudged in with a tray of burnt brownies and set them down on her coffee table. She looked at him kindly and asked, "You okay?" He nodded sheepishly and trudged out—crisis over.

My supervisor had been there for years and she's still there as I write this. When things are hard, relationship is virtually everything. Kenneth had a relationship with her; when he heard he was supposed to make brownies he knew the order had come from her, and so he also knew that she was aware that he was hurting. More than anything else it was the image of her, as chief mother figure in our shared world caring and waiting for him, that gave him the ability to make it through that night.

Understanding Is Containing

Part of the beauty of the brownie intervention is its simplicity. When our children are feeling overwhelmed or sad we want to keep things as simple as possible. When our child is sad we don't want to deny their feelings but neither do we want to overreact. If our child suffers from depression we still want to see them as a whole human being and depression as just one aspect of them. When our child needs our help managing difficult feelings we will be more effective to the extent we have become comfortable with our own sad feelings and have learned how to feel sad without becoming depressed. Individuation calls for accepting sadness as part of true happiness.

The preceding chapter dealt with the importance of the development of the self, which is like a bowl that can hold thoughts and feelings. As parents we invariably need to be present to our children, as a psychological bowl, to help hold whatever they cannot—such as intense sadness. One way to think about depression is as sadness without a bowl to contain it, so that even a small amount of sorrow can become overwhelming.

If we tend to get swamped by painful feelings we may avoid life, withdraw, lose self-esteem and find ourselves depressed. Depression can feel like being trapped at the bottom of a well with no apparent way out. Paying sincere attention to our child and their feelings offers a way out; being understood helps a child form a self and this empowers them to contain their own sadness rather than feeling engulfed by it, which is like drowning in fear and isolation. Usually, long before a kid ends up like Kenneth, making brownies to fend off suicide, there have been many, many missed opportunities where potential caregivers might have connected and helped that child by understanding, and thus containing, painful feelings. Dealing with sadness in those we love, especially children, can be emotionally very hard but is also very rewarding when we see their spirits lift again, and when we see them grow strong and solid through years of being understood and loved.

Eeyore Is Not Just In A Bad Mood

Gloomy sadness pretty much defines Eeyore in A. A. Milne's *Winnie-The-Pooh*.[1] A donkey filled with sawdust whose tail keeps falling off and whose house is ever falling down, Eeyore is an archetypal representation of sadness. While we each have some sort of Eeyore in the hundred-acre wood of our personal psyches, it is important to appreciate sadness but not over-identify with it. We can love our inner Eeyore but we do not want our children or ourselves to go through life *as* Eeyore.

Our children will certainly be sad and moody through the course of childhood and as parents we are first-line responders to their emotional rough patches. Eeyore is stuck being a pervasively depressive character; children don't go from happy to depressed in one moment. They may quickly vary from happy to sad or angry, but it is only if they get *stuck* in a mood of hopelessness or sadness that it becomes depression.

Differentiating sadness from depression raises two key questions: 1) For how long has the child been sad? and 2) How sad are they? If a kid is sad for a couple of days we want to be present to them and trust that moods come and go—and all the more quickly if understood and shown love. If days become weeks, however, we want to pay close attention, check with teachers, question if anything else in their life has changed, etc. Whether we know what is bothering them or not, sadness that does not go away is a cue that *something* more is needed. Likewise about intensity of sadness—if a child is sad for a day or so we want to keep an eye on it, but if they start talking about hurting themselves, seem frighteningly sad or aren't able to function we must compassionately work to understand what has gone wrong (i.e. trauma, drug use they've been hiding, changes in brain chemistry, etc.) and take action to keep them safe. If and when things do get bleak, denial is our worst parenting strategy.

Behavior can also be how mood gets expressed. It is normal for kids to sometimes not want to go to school, but if they staunchly refuse or cut classes repeatedly something is off and trouble is brewing if we don't intervene quickly. Teens don't always want to talk to us, but a consistent pattern of monosyllabic grunts and persistent contempt for parents is not necessarily what all kids do. If our kid shuts down, it could be that they don't believe that we really care or understand them. If we reject our children in response to their dismissive or avoidant behavior (maybe because we feel hurt) we perpetuate a cycle of alienation that is a formula for depression. Love, compassion and feelings of connection have great anti-depressant effects. If we are present to, and aware of, our child's feelings, and they become terribly (or consistently) sad, it is good practice to consult with a pediatrician, school counselor or our own therapist, if we have one. An excellent first therapy step for helping a depressed child is for the parents to go to therapy and see if the child does not spontaneously improve. Before sending a child to therapy it is a good use of a family's resources to work to ensure that the parents are generally happy and effective, that the house is emotionally warm and safe and that there are appropriate limits and supervision for the children.

Depression Is The Belief That Nothing Good Is Going To Happen

Anxiety and depression are really two sides of the same coin. Depression boils down to the internal belief (rational or otherwise) that "nothing good is going to happen," while anxiety is the internal belief that "something bad is going to happen."

The opposite of depression is not so much happiness as ambition. Happiness, for grown-ups, is more akin to a balance of joy and sorrow and all other feelings. Grown-up happiness is about finding tranquility in what we have learned, loved, lost, striven for and acquired and being cool with what actually is. This empowers us to help kids with kid happiness, which is mostly about enjoying being a kid, and partly about reaching for things beyond their grasp so they can love, learn, grow and pursue their true path toward authentic grown-up happiness.

If a child falls into a depressive cycle, be it in sports, academics, social situations or any other arena, they will lose confidence in their own ability to confront challenges and succeed. This is when they start to withdraw and avoid situations that they expect will make them feel inadequate. The more they tune out or avoid, the farther behind they fall and the more firmly set their expectation of failure becomes. For this reason, it is important to stay closely attuned to our children's moods and struggles as small interventions early on can save much pain later.

If there is a small learning difficulty that shows up in elementary school, a bit of tutoring can do more than keep a child reading at grade level—it can protect their developing sense of competency and teach them that they can confront difficulty and succeed even when things do not come easily. In the long run this can be a more valuable lesson than the dubious blessing of everything coming easily to a child.

Ambition is the opposite of depression insofar as it calls for a vision of something that is desired, but not yet manifest, in our lives *and* the determination to work to make it happen. Ambition requires frustration tolerance, because we must confront the fact that we do not have what we want and yet remain confident that we can close the gap with our own efforts. This could relate to getting a new job or building a block tower. Confronting what is not yet there requires enough self-esteem to believe that we have the capability to succeed. Our children rely on ambition in order to learn, since learning means confronting and mastering concepts and skills that we lack. If something is easy, we are not learning, we're simply reviewing what we already know.

It is wise to keep in mind that kid happiness and adult happiness are quite different. Many adults quest all their lives for various goals, and while such ambition is better than hopeless despair or apathy, true happiness for grown-ups is all about being present to the moment. Parenting well can help us achieve that, and at the same time support our kids to confront challenges and cultivate healthy ambition. Children are also happiest when they are present to the moment, but becoming socialized means they must learn to strive and grow and hopefully enjoy the process of becoming educated.

As our children grow, we parents cannot help but notice that life is slipping by; this can make us depressed and provoke questions about what really matters, what happiness really is and if we are living true to our full Self. We may set higher and higher goals... or we may start to live more in the moment. Children are easily bored and time often passes slowly for them; as parents, if we can learn to be patient and happy in the moments of driving, helping with homework, listening, etc. we support our kids to grow calm and confident. This is like a vaccine against depression.

Transition Is Hard

One of the key maxims of parenting is that transition is hard. Most "problems" tend to occur during some sort of transition. If a transition such as starting a new school, entering puberty or parents getting divorced brings on sadness, fear or overwhelm, and these feelings are not worked through, a child can become stuck in them and end up depressed.

Viewing emotions in context helps normalize feelings. Finding ways to get our child to express what's in their heart helps keep them flowing along, so they do not get trapped in negative feelings. Anticipating that transitions, from the birth of a new sibling to the death of a loved one or even a pet, often evoke sorrow reminds us to be there to catch our child before they fall.

When our child is suffering we want to ask ourselves if this could partly be due to some sort of transition. It may seem obvious to us, like it's a kid's first week of middle school, but it can be calming for them to be reassured that everyone is anxious and they will feel better in a few weeks when they get used to things. When we work to help break a transition down into manageable pieces (i.e. organize their back-pack, remember their locker combination) and help with coping strategies (i.e. only carry home books they have homework in, write the locker combination down and keep it in their pocket until it's memorized) they more quickly return to the comfortable position of not needing our help... until they need it again.

When a child is preparing to make a developmental transition it is common to regress to a less mature level just prior to their leap forward to new maturity. Much as we take a few steps back before leaping over a creek, as parents we can re-frame our child's regressive moments as impending maturation. Maybe this idea will better help us cope with twelve-year-olds mumbling requests in barely intelligible baby talk.

Up As Defense Against Down

If Eeyore is a representation of depression, Tigger is mania incarnate; while he may seem delightful as a character to children who revel in his hyper-active accidental trouble-making, if he would ever stop bouncing he is probably more depressed than Eeyore. Like a movie star jumping up and down on a talk-show hosts' couch declaring how happy he is, if something doesn't seem quite altogether right we want to take a compassionate view of things—and if it is our child who seems to be bouncing off the walls we need to catch them *before* they crash.

For example, if our kid comes home from elementary school and is atypically bent on raising hell, tormenting their siblings, chasing the dog with a fork and insisting that nothing is bothering them they probably feel unconsciously driven to act-out until they get a limit, at which point the floodgate of tears will be thrown open. It is important to try and remember that our child is probably feeling like they have fallen from the grace of happiness when they choose to put on the devil horns.

The general level of kids getting keyed up when they are upset has to be differentiated from true manic behavior. In rarer circumstances children will show rageful outbursts that are so intense that they are frightening (for parents, and for the kids who are inevitably terrified themselves). Other children may be markedly over-energetic (in a way that is disturbing and makes others feel exhausted to be around it) or particularly irritable for prolonged periods (or in bursts of increasing frequency). These signs that something more significant than a passing mood is bothering a child is our cue to consult with the experts. It could be a mood disorder or it could be something medical that is influencing their behavior, but early intervention (even if it just to rule out serious problems) is advisable. It is better to ask the doctor and be told it's normal than to ignore concerns and later be asked why we didn't do something sooner.

Loss, Grief And Mourning

Sad feelings that last a relatively long time are a natural reaction to loss. Big losses, such as a death in the family, can take a long time to heal, and viewing our child's level of sadness in the context of their losses can help us know when to patiently and compassionately treat their sadness as normal and even healthy.

In helping our child with losses it is useful to differentiate grief from mourning. Grief is very intense, it is what we feel in the first stages of loss; it can include shock, anger, denial, etc. but it feels like hell—it is when we want to throw ourselves into the grave rather than go on living without the one we have lost. For a small child that loved one can be a pet hermit crab. It is alternately sad and beautiful that very young children have a very immediate perspective on life. We need to help them through the acute grief of seemingly small losses and accept that big losses are not always truly comprehensible. A child can seem callous when things are beyond their level of understanding (i.e. wondering if they are still going to get a toy we promised when we are trying to explain how a loved-one is in the hospital).

Mourning is more melancholy and protracted than grief, this is what we feel as we miss, dream about and seek ways to find meaning, purpose and pleasure in the weeks, months and years after a loss. If we lose someone we love it can easily take a year to feel anything like normal again, but that doesn't mean we are depressed. When a child loses a caregiver or a sibling (which often means having devastated parents) they wrestle with feelings of fear as well as sadness. Just when they need our presence most of all, we may be compromised in our ability to be there for them. On the other hand, the need to take care of our children can be life-saving in dealing with losses such as the death of our own parents.

In mourning, time truly does heal. To mourn is to slowly let go of what was lost (be it childhood, a person, a dashed hope or dream). Mourning is how we work through loss. Grief is a transitory stage of loss unless we cannot find our way into a mourning process. As parents, just being aware of the natural emotional currents of grief and loss might help us better navigate them for ourselves and for our children when sad times occur. In the face of loss and/or trauma, a key thing children need to be reassured of is that they themselves will be okay—safe, fed, protected, cared for and loved.

Anger, Irritability And Oppositionality

While loss makes us sad, things that threaten us, by scarring or making us feel weak or powerless, often provoke anger. If we are angry but cannot express it (i.e. we fear harm or retaliation) we may turn that anger against ourselves, and that can lead to depression. If our child cannot show their anger, perhaps it is because they are scared to provoke our rage or risk the loss of our love if they hurt our feelings.

Although anger turned inward can lead to depression, anger turned outward does not mean someone is not depressed. Sometimes depression manifests as irritability, anger or contrariness. This is particularly true for young boys and adolescent males. They may not appear sad. They will almost certainly deny that they feel sad—often believing that "sadness" is a weak emotion and that tears are for sissies.

Given that children and adults who feel good about themselves are generally kind, a child who is consistently negativistic most likely feels bad about themselves. If our child acts out aggressively or opposes us just for the sake of being contrary we need to consider the possibility that they are depressed. When a child's underlying depression comes out as irritability or negativistic behavior it can help for them to recognize that they do not feel good about themselves and that their behavior reveals this. They will generally be more able to tolerate this message if we also convey a picture of how they might behave if they did feel good about themselves as well as a strategy for how they could get there (i.e. breaking behavior change into smaller steps, offering rewards for better behavior in the initial stages of change). Even though they will initially gripe and grumble, if we truly believe that our child ought to feel good about who they are, and that their negative self-image is a distortion, and their "bad" behavior a defense and an emblem of hurt, with truer self-understanding they can come to see themselves as the beautiful soul we know them to be.

Always Take Suicidality Seriously

Children and teenagers do kill themselves and we never want to under-estimate that possibility when a child tells us they feel unsafe or are thinking about hurting themselves. Children have child-minds and can miscalculate, for example, by running into traffic in a moment of despair. Children and adolescents do not always have the best judgment about what is safe even when they are not feeling depressed, so when they are struggling they especially need our guidance and supervision to help them stay out of harm's way. A depressed and isolated child or teen can be vulnerable to the wrong sort of attention from strangers, or fall victim to sexual advances that they misread as sincere interest. Obviously, bad or traumatic experiences could threaten to push someone over the edge (especially if they were already depressed), which underscores the importance of helping children process traumas (i.e. talk it out) to minimize the potential for shame-driven, or angst-ridden, acts of self-harm.

Sometimes a very depressed person doesn't even have enough energy to bother with suicide, but when they start to get better their energy lifts, along with their mood, and they can temporarily be at increased risk of suicide. If a child gives any indication of thoughts of self-harm we want them to feel safe and welcome to tell us more about it. The more they talk about it the less alone they will feel and the less urgently they will need to do something rash just to escape their awful feelings. We never want to minimize their pain or treat them as if they are bluffing. If we suspect our child might be thinking of suicide, based on indirect statements (i.e. "my life sucks," or "I don't know why I was born"), we can draw them out in order to discover if it is momentary frustration or deeper despair. No one commits suicide because they are asked about it and it gives them the idea.

If a child wants to, or fears they will, harm themselves we need to keep them under our watchful eye until we are sure they are safe. If a child is suicidal we should remove things such as pills or sharp objects from their reach. Suicide prevention is not a power-struggle to keep someone alive; we work to align with the part of them that wants to live and needs help managing the pain of life at that moment. If suicide has entered the picture it is important to find a mental health professional to help the family deal with whatever has lead up to this point, to heal underlying depression and strive toward happier times.

Sometimes a suicidal child needs to be in a psychiatric hospital; in such cases they will often be quite angry at everyone involved, but that is far better than harming themselves. Suicide generally has a lot of rage in it. The hospital (and/or therapy) is often a place where anger can come out in a safe way. If depression is anger turned inward, suicidal thoughts and behaviors are the pinnacle of self-hatred. If a child is self-destructive the antidote is loving themselves and our job, as their caregiver, is to keep them alive so they can have a chance to learn and honor the truth: that they are wonderful and lovable and it is heartbreakingly wrong for them to think otherwise.

Even if we suspect that a child is seeking attention, this is never a time to ignore them. By taking such talk seriously a child will get needed help, or else realize that this is not the way to get what they actually need. A trip to the emergency room will typically get a suicidal child admitted to the hospital, and help an overly dramatic child learn not to "cry wolf." As annoying as drama-queen behavior can be, talk of suicide is not likely to come from a happy child. If a child

needs to call 911 to get our attention we parents need to contemplate what's going on. A "cry for help" needs to be heard
and helped, otherwise behaviors will continue to escalate and
can one day go too far.

Sunday Blues

Many of us have a lot of difficulty being in the moment—
and this can be even harder as a family. We love our family
and treasure time together, at least in our minds. Then Sunday arrives and all too often we are grumpy, no one can agree
on one thing we all want to do, we end up quarreling and
feeling discouraged, alone and misunderstood. We may look
forward all year to our vacation only to get sick on the plane
and by the time we finally recover find ourselves counting the
scant remaining days until we must return to an exhausting
or unhappy life. We may even look forward to retirement,
alternately worrying that we will not have enough and imagining the joy not having to work. But then one day the future
comes and it may leave us mostly reminiscing about all the
years of relatively good health and nice times that have past,
but which we did not fully savor at the time.

Happiness is something that will elude us if we always
plan for it (and in effect postpone it). Good feelings that last
are about being present to a succession of present moments.
Thanksgiving through Christmas and New Year are difficult
for people, and busy for therapists, partly because we imagine
that everyone else is having an ideal time and that we, by
comparison, must be pathetic. We open presents in a frenzy,
eat meals in minutes that took hours to cook, and find ourselves blanketed by a depressing lull which comes creeping
up the moment there is nothing that must be manically done.

Kids get sad on Sunday night, just as adults do—if they don't love their life. It is understandable that the weekend is more fun than school, but some people manage to enjoy each day for what it is. If we can do this as a parent, our children will see first hand that it is possible. In our terror-infused world we can all think of terrible scenarios that would quickly leave us yearning for the life we have right now. We can always try to savor the beauty of our lives and the subtle pleasures of what we do have. We can set goals based on what we *can* do (i.e. at least *search* for work, or maintain a good attitude) and in this way discover our adult, bitter-sweet happiness and trust that this happiness can exert subtle positive influence on those we love.

Why Aren't We Happier?

What's In Our Child's Way?

If we want our child to be happy, asking the question, "Why aren't they happy?" is a good place to start. Some issues to consider that might cause or contribute to depression include:

1) Lack of a Self

Without a solid self, seemingly small things can be overwhelming. Normal sadness can then swamp us and become depression. Self-development is one of the key tasks of childhood and until the self develops, we parents need to be there to catch and contain the feelings our child cannot.

2) Low Self-Esteem

Low self-esteem is practically synonymous with depression. If a child is in need of some personal victory to bolster flagging self-esteem we help them discover something they are good at, or even just like to do. Supporting them to feel seen and effective at *something* will often broaden to other areas in their lives.

3) <u>Deprivation</u>

When a child is sad it makes sense to ask ourselves (and our child) if there are things they *truly* need that they do not get (i.e. not a bigger TV). Even if we are tragically unable to provide true necessities, such as food or shelter, it is important to hear a child's feelings of lack, fear or unworthiness and emphasize that while things are unfair and unfortunate they (and all people) truly deserve better. We can reassure them that we will provide for them and put our every possible effort toward their well-being. With such a clear and noble motivation we will often find some way to make things better—even if the nourishment we end up providing is simply a model of love and courage.

The same holds true if we cannot provide optimal education, a non-racist or nonsexist world in which to live or if we cannot provide the same opportunities that they see other children receive. If we cannot spend as much time with them as they would like, or must miss their games or school performances because we must work or are ill, etc. they need to know that this is not because we don't care about them, love them or see them as deserving all the best life has to offer.

4) <u>Loss</u>

Loss is a variation on deprivation where something a child once had is now gone. When our child is sad we can wonder if there has been a loss we have not fully addressed with them (i.e. a divorce). There could have been a loss we are not privy to such as a friend excluding them at school.

Talking and connecting bridges isolation and helps us come to terms with losses.

5) <u>Trauma</u>

Scary or overwhelming situations, such as witnessing, or being the victim of, a crime, family violence, bullying or sexual or emotional abuse, can cause depression. Sometimes a child is ashamed of what has happened or is frightened to tell us. When depression strikes and we cannot figure out why, it is important to determine if anything might have hurt or upset our child. If trauma does occur, we take appropriate steps to protect them so that they will not be re-traumatized. By doing this we can ameliorate feelings of hopelessness or helplessness that fuel depression, and can reduce lasting effects of trauma. It is essential that a child know that trauma is not their fault.

Traumas such as a car accident or other injury are also likely to have emotional repercussions. If a child falls into depression, after something like this, we can encourage them to talk about what happened to process their experience and store it as true memory. Until trauma is stored as memory it is like a pop-up screen on a computer. It can intrude at random moments. If a trauma is particularly horrific, professional help may be in order and is most effective if it comes as soon as possible following the disturbing event.

6) <u>An Unhappy Family</u>

If a child lives with depressed parents, this is obviously a depressing situation. Before we diagnose our child as depressed, we want to take a look in the mirror and be sure that we are not the one who is depressed. A young child learns about who they are (and even *that* they are) from our interest and reactions to them—if we are depressed, they may come to believe that they are depressing. If we are suffering, it will help our children if we take ourselves to therapy.

7) <u>Lack of Hope</u>

Hope is an antidote to depression; it is the glimmer that something good will be coming. As parents we want to instill hope in our sad child, and this will be more effective if we actually believe things will get better. If our child lacks hope we need to consider what might help change that. We can encourage our child to dream, and support them to believe that they can make their dreams come true.

8) <u>Social Isolation</u>

Friends can be lifesavers. They are a huge part of what makes life wonderful. Being a good friend is at the heart of making friends. A child need not be popular, they just need one or two good friends and that can make all the difference. A shy kid will be miserable if they believe they have to be everybody's best friend. As parents we would want to help them pick the kids that they relate to, who have common interests and, most importantly, who they believe are the nice kids.

We can model being a good friend in how we behave toward our own friends, and we can support our children to make friends. When our kids are young this means going out of our way to set up repeated play-dates. This is what it takes to get bonds to form. As children grow older we can be there to listen and help them stay on the path of being a good sport and a kind and interested friend. Good self-esteem helps allow them to go out of their way to talk to new kids (i.e. when they start a new school) and run the risk of rejection it takes to bridge to new people.

9) <u>Realizing They Are Different</u>

When a child's brain develops to the point where they can think deeply, if they happen to be a little "different," they suddenly *realize* that they are. Good self-esteem will mitigate this, but the capacity for suffering intensifies along with the ability to think abstractly and infer things (i.e. algebra: $3x=9$; no friends=loser). The irony of the pain of feeling different is that we all secretly feel a bit different and have pockets within us that no one will ever fully understand. This is part of our human situation. We all struggle with the contradictory desire to fit in, be part of a community, and to be our own unique, distinct self.

If a darkening of mood comes on around ages ten or twelve, consider whether their advancing ability to think, and thus recognize limitations, may be contributing to it. The good news is that they are more able to talk about it; the bad news is that they may not want to talk to us. We still have to be there to listen just in case they decide to talk; they might be telling us they feel excluded by unconsciously freezing us out and making us feel what they feel at school.

10) <u>Hormones</u>

Hormones affect mood and so we want to keep the obvious fact in mind that puberty wreaks havoc on mood. If nothing else, a conscious perspective on how adolescence has been called developmental insanity may keep us parents from losing our grip on reality even when it seems our child has temporarily lost theirs.

11) <u>Genes and Brain Chemistry</u>

Sometimes brain chemistry is problematic and all the practical and loving attention in the world will not improve things. Outbursts that are frighteningly violent, complaints of hearing things or consistently odd behavior could indicate that a child has a genetic vulnerability to a more serious sort of depression. This is heartbreaking for any parent, but scientific understanding of such conditions continues to improve and increasingly effective treatments are likely to emerge. A head in the sand approach can allow conditions to worsen when help might be possible; as self-esteem spirals down a child becomes harder to reach and harder to help. When in doubt, we can educate ourselves, talk to our pediatrician and to mental health professionals and work with them to differentiate between what needs love and limits, and what needs therapy or medication.

What's In Our Way?

As parents we need to continually monitor our influence and impact on our child's well being. When our child struggles with sadness beyond what we would expect, given their situation, we can consider if any of the following are in our own way:

1) Our Bowl Is Leaky

If we lack a solid self we dodge or drown in the emotional overflow that our child needs us to contain. When we wish to be containing but are impaired by a leaky bowl, we can become angry with those who ask us to hold their feelings because their request makes us feel inadequate. Our bowl of self is our key parenting tool, and a lack of self can drag us into the closed loop of self-involvement. When we consciously strive to hold our children's feelings, even if it pains and strains us, our own bowl grows stronger. In this way being our best Self as a parent can bring us the self we had not yet managed to achieve. This will allow us to more fully enjoy our lives now, and long after the kids have grown.

2) We Are Depressed

The same factors we consider regarding whether our children are depressed or only experiencing normal sadness also apply to ourselves. If we find ourselves deeply sad (or angry, or irritable) for most of the day, every day, for more than a week or two, or if we are mildly sad for months on end, we should probably have a physical exam to be sure we're not ill, and then consult a therapist. Other warning signs include poor sleep, weight changes, lack of pleasure in things and thoughts about wanting to hurt ourselves. If we are depressed we need to seek help not only for our own good, but for the well-being of our children. It is very burdensome to a child to have a depressed parent. Depression sometimes brings feelings of guilt or worthlessness, but being there for our child to the extent we are able (some depressions can be utterly debilitating) is a way to snap out of depression and self-focus. What truly helps our child, ultimately, helps us as their parent.

3) <u>Our Own Childhood</u>

Whatever age our child is at any given moment, it's good practice to be conscious of what our life was like when we were that age. If we had a hard time of it in middle school or had a loss at the start of high school we are likely to be triggered into reliving these feelings as our child reaches these ages. If we are not conscious of this, we are at risk of becoming distraught but not knowing why, and our child is at risk of becoming the receiver of our unwanted feelings. We might mistakenly see the sad kid we once were instead of the actual child we have now. Over time a child may come to act in accordance with how they are seen and even fall into a depression that is rightfully our own.

4) <u>Denial</u>

Here we do not consciously see our child's pain and are truly surprised when we find out they are suicidal, or have been using drugs, etc. Denial can be subtle. Our child can feel that we pay a lot of attention to them and yet not really understand them, or love them for who they really are. Tolerating our child's feelings and not turning away is an act of love that helps them build their self. Denial is a way that we protect ourselves from painful truths. It is almost impossible to recognize on our own. If our children are suffering it is a bold act of love to ask a therapist if we could possibly be in denial about some things.

5) We Might Need an Unhappy Child

If we do happen to be in denial, an underlying thing we could be in denial about is our need for an unhappy kid. We can sometimes unconsciously use our child as a container for our own unwanted feelings; then our child becomes a portrait of our secret self. We want to try and be aware of our own insecurities, and sorrows, because when we are aware of them we become dramatically less likely to unconsciously script our child to carry or enact our own problems.

6) Guilt

Guilt acknowledges our failings but leaves us unavailable to our child because we are too busy beating ourselves up to actually take responsibility and improve. Apologize, repair where possible, don't repeat the same mistake, move on—this is the cure for guilt.

Broadening Our Perspective

"Your mom doesn't love you!"

Rob, a ten-year-old boy whose parents were divorcing, was having trouble dealing with feelings of confusion, rejection, hurt and loss. Rob was a nice looking kid and generally well-liked, but he liked to put other kids down in a ten-year-old version of a tough demeanor. In the turmoil of his family situation he was gaining weight and had become persistently insulting and aggressive with the other kids in his class. Rob insulted one of his good friends by saying, "Your mother doesn't love you!" For several days Rob repeated this insult as well as the comment: "You need to lose weight!" despite the fact that the target of his insult was a virtual beanpole. After several days of this, Rob's friend said, "My mom does love me and if your mom doesn't love you she's stupid!" I really like that comeback because it is self-affirming and affirming of Rob's lovability without being too uncool for an elementary school boy to say. This moment seemed to mark a turning point in the boys' relationship and the chronic "disses" subsided. Having a friend who Rob could respect, rather than bully, helped him learn how to be a better friend. This was good for Rob's self-esteem. As parents we can strive to live by the ethic that it is cool to be kind.

Kids who feel self-conscious, insecure and excluded but cannot express their feelings may in turn make other children feel these same feelings. This overall dynamic pretty much sums up late elementary and middle school unless skilled teachers and parents model and artfully cultivate pro-social behavior. It also helps for us parents to realize that it is not just our child who may be in pain.

Pain Is Information

Research shows that depressed people sometimes see "reality" more accurately than non-depressed people.[2] While reality can be painful, if we heed the wisdom of our sorrows and frustrations we will have a better chance at authentic happiness.

Bad feelings can be a way to learn that we are on the wrong path. Depression can tell us that we have been off track for some time and have gotten stuck in the pain of the past. Anti-depressant medications can be helpful when pain is too much to bear, but they help us cope by making us less sensitive. If we medicate but do not change our attitude, thoughts or behaviors, we miss the deeper message of our pain and our misguided path remains the same.

Just as physical pain serves a protective function (if we sprain an ankle but feel no pain we'll cause more damage), emotional pain tends to quiet down when we heed its message. If we're off our path our soul's pain alerts us to this. Pain can be jarring—like guardrails on a highway—but can keep us from going off the cliff altogether. If our children do not get love and connection when upset, we teach them to run the other way from their feelings. If we ignore our child's sorrow (or our own) that sorrow may resort to extreme actions to get our attention, and force a change of direction.

Manically avoiding pain (i.e. with substances or endless work) is not living fully and tends to mask feelings of emptiness and futility. If we slow down and allow feeling, we might learn what we are afraid of. Our child's emotional pain contains clues about what's really the matter as well as what might help. For example, if our child is feeling dumb or inadequate in school, we might take this distress as a cue to set up a conference with their teacher to seek ways to support them to have more success. This might mean we become more involved in supervising homework, or it could mean we need to become *less* involved in micro-managing them. Conversely, if our child has excellent grades but lacks friends and is unhappy, we might encourage them to realize that achievement alone does not bring happiness and that a B or C is not the end of the world. If modifications lead to improvement in their weaker areas this can boost self-esteem as well as set a standard of compassionate understanding and teamwork for our child to follow when they find themselves struggling with other challenges during the course of their lives.

The Black Hole: Major Depression and Bipolar Disorder

Balance is highly important in all things. While normal sadness is part of happiness, there are times when depression can be so deep that professional help is called for. In trying to assess when to seek professional help (whether for ourselves or our children) there are checklists of symptoms we can find in books or on-line, but we must also use our instinct as parents. In common sense terms, it would probably be best to seek a professional opinion if we find ourselves consistently wondering if our child is depressed or not. In this way we can rule out a serious problem quickly, or obtain help early on. The same is true in the case of our own depression.

Depression is bad enough to get help if it is a) not *that* bad, but is lasts for weeks rather than hours or days, b) if it is *really* bad (i.e. no pleasure in anything, thoughts of suicide, profound lack of energy, etc.) and lasts for days or a week rather than minutes or hours or c) if mood fluctuates very severely or there are sustained and frightening (hyper-energetic or violently destructive) episodes which then give way to black despair. Obviously, if a child is hearing or seeing things or is convinced others are trying to hurt them when this has no factual basis, professional help is called for on an urgent basis. With Bipolar disorder each manic episode is followed by increasingly dark episodes of depression so preventing manic episodes before they occur becomes an ideal component of treatment. While Bipolar and other psychotic disorders are relatively rare, they often first appear in adolescence, or even in childhood. The main point is if our child or teenager seems out of balance, it's better to get an expert opinion than to just wait and see what happens. If trouble is brewing, from mild depression to something more serious, it is better to put a team in place while things are still manageable rather than trying to scramble to do this when a child, and in turn a family, is in crisis.

Trust your own concerns and instincts and talk to your primary care doctor as a first step. It is important to rule out medical conditions that can cause emotional symptoms. If our child seems depressed, this could be a good time for a checkup. Sometimes parents miss the clues that something is wrong because it is painful to see our child suffer and not know how to help. We unconsciously turn away. The risk of missing warning signs of depression increases as kids move through adolescence, when we see and talk to them less than in early childhood. Deteriorating school performance, social withdrawal or even frequent "colds" (i.e. drugs can also make eyes red and noses run) could be red flags that something is amiss.

Drug and alcohol use can be a child's attempt to self-medicate if their mood, family life or brain chemistry is off. Drinking and drugs complicate the picture since it becomes unclear what the main problem is (i.e. drug or alcohol abuse vs. depression) and treating depression is complicated by the use of substances; for example marijuana and alcohol are depressants which can *bring about* depression with steady use. Conversely, stimulant use such as crystal meth or cocaine can be attempts to block underlying depression, but the rebound effect of the high is lower lows until a terrified kid finds themselves at the bottom of a well with no apparent way out.

As science moves along, we will gain increasing sophistication on diagnosing and treating all types of disorders. What had once appeared as a single disorder may prove to have many sub-categories reflecting different underlying genetics, brain chemistry and interactions between individuals and their environment.

It is frightening and depressing to think our child might be burdened by serious problems. Even where there are psychoses, rages or destructive impulses, beyond therapy and medications, a calm and supportive family environment is a key ingredient in helping restore mental health and decrease the likelihood and severity of future episodes.

If we have a child with Bipolar disorder it is important not to blame ourselves, as even outright poor parenting or a dysfunctional family will not *cause* it (although it can worsen the effects). It is important to seek help for our child but also to educate ourselves and work to learn how to effectively deal with very difficult moods and behaviors.

A friend who has a daughter with Bipolar disorder was eventually able to send her daughter off to an excellent college on full scholarship. She urged me to share some suggestions/opinions with potential readers of this book who might have a Bipolar child:

1) Don't put them in a group home if it is at all avoidable. Your own love is more beneficial. It is very scary to be Bipolar and our kids need *us*.

2) If mood or behavioral changes occur, drug test your child consistently and be sure someone is in the room with them and literally watching them pee in the cup (as many kids know how to tamper with the urine

to trick the test). Once their judgment is impaired by the disorder, you really don't know what drugs your child might take that they would never consider when they were stable.

3) Don't judge other people; their "bad" kid may be suffering from an illness, not just reacting to parents' divorce, problems in the home, etc.

4) Avoid shame and secrets, seek community support, educate yourself and help others.

Finally, it is worth noting that often people with Bipolar disorder have some extraordinary gifts in addition to their illness. Studies have found that first-degree relatives of people with Bipolar disorder (i.e. you their parents, siblings or their future children) are the most likely to possess genius levels of ability in art or science. Some Native American tribes viewed those who were different as having a special connection to spirit, and today's Bipolar may have been yesterday's shaman—respected and consulted rather than pathologized and medicated. For all we know these children see more of "reality" than we do. We should honor and support them in their efforts to handle the burden of their gift.

Collective Sorrow: We All Love All Our Kids

It can be a challenge sometimes to stay connected with our child when they are in pain because we care so much that their distress threatens to swamp us. In this sense it is important to consider our child's pain in the context of all the children who may be in sorrow or despair at the present moment, and to consider our relationship to these nameless and faceless souls even if that relationship is mostly out of our conscious awareness.

We may not realize it, but somewhere within us we love all the world's children and sincerely want the best for them. All children begin as innocents deserving love and a chance at a happy life. Whether we are conscious of it or not, we all carry the collective sorrow of those children who suffer. It serves us to not judge other parents who may, on the surface, appear to be causing children to suffer. We have to look into the eyes of a psychotic mother who is trying to do her best for her child, but simply cannot manage it, to understand the tragic dimensions of such situations. It's easier for us to vilify such parents in our minds (or to pity them as somehow less than ourselves) than to see that they are us and we are them. It is unspeakably painful to confront the needs of children whose sad situations we cannot personally transform. Collectively we turn away and those lost souls become invisible within our culture. We stop seeing them (or fail to notice them in the first place), and it is our collective disconnect from them, not their wounds or limitations alone, that threatens to extinguish their life spirit.

Often the most sensitive and artistic souls feel most acutely the collective sorrow of our world. In the spirit of collective concern I relate Laurence's story.

Laurence

Outside it was a brilliant Thursday in January. Inside, it was dark and smelly as Laurence, a fourteen-year-old boy, writhed next to me on the floor. He was in pain of the most excruciating sort—Laurence was mentally coming apart at the seams. He might have been just having a moment or he might have been losing it altogether—I wasn't sure which. That's why I had been paged to the padded cells of the "quiet area"—to decide which, and to decide what to do about it. He didn't respond to my voice and seemed far away in some unreachable hell, mumbling incoherently, eyes rolling back in his head, skin glistening with sweat.

The day before we had found Laurence in a closet having sex with a twelve-year old girl while beating her. Even more disturbing was that she had asked him to have sex with her in the closet and had insisted that he beat her, something that he had been less than enthusiastic about, at least to begin with. I tried to understand their behavior as some sort of shared re-enactment of past traumas that were turbo-charged by racing hormones, wobbly brain chemistry, emotional pain and free-floating panic. Since Laurence was bigger, older and male, his welcome to remain in the group home had fallen into question.

The next stop for our dropouts (if they didn't slip the system and end up on the streets) was generally either a locked psychiatric hospital or an out of state facility so remote that escape was pointless—where kids who misbehaved were locked in freezing concrete rooms without food or blankets until they broke, tough-love style. Some kids actually died in those sorts of places while others learned to behave but typically fell apart again once they returned and no longer had the rigid structure. Other kids ended up in the correctional system, which would certainly give you mental and emotional problems if you didn't have them when you went in. "Youth Authority" is a Dickensian horror, which, as one former inmate told me, sat directly adjacent to prison. The kids looked out onto their expected future every day until one day they turned eighteen and walked through a fenced corridor to begin adult life amongst hardened criminals.

It was hard for me to see how any of these alternatives would actually help the poor tortured souls in my care and so I tended to fight tooth and nail to keep the kids in the group home; even if we couldn't help them all that much we might at least prevent their situation from getting worse. There was an informal system of checks and balances amongst us therapists and supervisors that weighed the needs and misdeeds of a child against potential harm to the group. Was Laurence's behavior bringing the other kids down? Did the psychiatrist have the meds right? Was he too disturbed to function with the amount of freedom a group home affords? How much danger did he pose to himself or others including the staff? One of the most difficult things about my job was having even partial responsibility over the fate of people's lives. My supervisor was beginning to trust me, and I was going to have to weigh in on keeping Laurence, or giving him up for the greater good. Rough sex with a twelve-year-old was pretty hard to stomach, but if we got rid of Laurence there were plenty of other boys who would be happy to oblige the poor girl the moment her staff lost sight of her, as she had previously coaxed an even younger boy into a janitor closet.

Despite several months of therapy, Laurence had thus far told me virtually nothing. He refused to come to my office. When I tried to interact with him at the group home he would never meet my gaze and acted as if I were not there. I wasn't entirely sure he knew who I was or even my name— there was something ghostly about him. Yet resistance to therapy was to be expected; in the first weeks of treatment none of the kids told me anything about themselves or their feelings. The only attention I got from them, other than joking around or shooting baskets, was when they were trying to get something from me (i.e. a "level" increase which brought more allowance, a later bedtime or a weekend pass with their psychotic or alcoholic mother or father, if they were lucky enough to have a parent in their lives). And so it surprised me when Laurence started to talk, or at least mumble. "What?" I asked. He mumbled on, but it was incomprehensible. The room stank of burnt plastic thanks to a kid who had taken a lighter to the fire-resistant carpet; Laurence himself needed a shower and a clean pair of pants. Just outside the little cell a two hundred and sixty pound man with an earring and a goatee sat on a metal folding chair with line-backer arms folded in front of him as his walkie-talkie crackled about situations and take-downs.

Laurence's unintelligible words flowed like a polluted stream in a ruined forest; what was he trying to say? I leaned closer; Laurence's mouth and my ear were almost touching. I began to make out his words: "Ashtray, stick, rock, cord… Ashtray, stick, rock." It was like brutal, simple poetry. He whispered, "Beat me." And again, "ashtray, rock, stick…" Was he confessing, processing, or hallucinating?

"Rock, stick, cord," Laurence repeated like a litany, like a to do list. "Electric cord?" I asked him. He looked at me and nodded—we were in contact. "Beat me," he gasped. "Someone beat *you*?" I clarified. His eyes let me in and I entered his world of precarious psychological existence and unspeakable pain. There was nothing to say, but I was not experienced enough to say nothing. "Who beat you?" I asked. "Everyone. Mom, step-dad, brothers." He was whispering, but to me! I had been working for weeks to build trust and open the possibility for actually talking instead of constant acting out. Laurence was violent and out of control—but he knew why!

Once we can begin talking through what has hurt us we don't have to keep repeating past traumas. I found myself wishing that he hadn't broken so many rules... and wishing that he wasn't psychotic. Why did glimmers of hope with these kids so often come as the doors of possibility were closing, and the guys with the straitjackets or handcuffs were pulling up?

When the bowl of self disintegrates we fear disappearing into a yawning black hole of terrifying chaos; Laurence was looking out at me as he was being sucked inexorably into his insanity. This moment of human contact and lucidity was heartbreaking because we both knew that Laurence had to go—and seeing that he had finally pushed things past the limit, he could show me a glimpse of the real him that I was going to miss out on ever knowing or helping. He knew he was too crazy for our level of care, and when he momentarily unmasked himself and showed me his abject sorrow and piercing humanity it made me love him and want to shelter, keep him and help him. I was watching a boy drown who for a moment took my hand and let me feel the impossibility of holding on against a current bigger than both of us.

Laurence went to a local psychiatric hospital and I visited him there until it was determined by his Department of Mental Health caseworker that he needed to go to a state mental hospital. The last time I saw Laurence he spontaneously hugged me. He knew it was good-bye. His scent, bitter and forlorn lingers in my memory along with the texture of his rough and filthy jacket; I cried like a baby in my car at the human tragedy and at my complete inability to do anything to change it.

Two years later, I was having dinner at the group home when the phone rang and it was Laurence saying he was doing better now and wanted out of the state hospital, wanted another chance at our group home. For various reasons this was not to be, but the fact that he was "doing better," even if only in his own estimation, and the fact that he remembered me, and the home we had provided for a brief period of his life, warmed my heart as much as it hurt it and left me with a small torn thread of hope for him and for all of us.

Envision What We Want

It was doubly strange to come home from situations like Laurence's to greet my own children, who were thriving in the warmth of a reasonably sane and loving household. The group home deepened my gratitude for my blessings and at the same time evoked feelings of alienation stemming from the stark contrast between worlds that I now passed regularly between—and which are really much closer together than most of us realize.

While our child may suddenly appear to be just fine in contrast to Laurence, we want to go in a more positive direction and think about what they would look like if he or she were truly happy. As we architect a virtual happiness for our child to inhabit (even if only in our minds at first) on the way out of their depression, some things we might have forgotten to imagine could include:

1) They feel safe and generally relaxed.
2) They are productive (i.e. creative, do their school work, read for pleasure).
3) They are generous, fun and fun-loving.
4) They are interested in the world.
5) They feel talented at some things.

6) They are a good sport about others being better than them at things.

7) They know how they feel and are able and willing to express themselves.

8) They like themselves and they like their life (or at least hold hope for a better life if, for example, war, disaster, disease or poverty has hurt them).

9) They know that they are loved.

10) They feel understood, accepted and appreciated for who they are.

11) They have age-appropriate gratitude for the blessings that they do have and carry a sense of abundance and trust that there will be enough for them.

12) They have hope and confidence that their future will be bright.

While these are *ideals* (and not embodying them all does not mean a child is depressed or even unhappy), we parents could envision a world where these were every child's right. Working for a better world for all children could be part of our vision of our own happy life. If we can be happy we lead the way for our child and the world.

Strategies For Helping

Good Feelings That Last

In talking about sadness and depression we want to keep a positive direction in mind. Whatever else is going on, the goal for our child and our family is good feelings that last. The question of whether any given course of action, from limit-setting to losing our temper, will lead toward, or away from, good feelings that *last* is a good way to guide our behavior and decision making.

From mild passing sadness to hugely difficult depressions we must always remember that our children are unique and sacred human spirits, not diagnoses. Depression is a serious condition, but it is not a defining characteristic of a person. Diagnoses such as schizophrenia or obsessive-compulsive disorder can come along with depression or can be a contributing factor in becoming depressed. Whatever is going on for our child, big or small, we can strive for basics such as having and expressing empathy for what it feels like to be them, helping our child keep up their sense of hope and providing a low-stress and loving environment.

Target Self-Esteem

We want to think about what our child would probably do if they felt really good about themselves and make those behaviors the goal. For example, applying to college. An acceptance, even to the worst college on the planet, is better for self-esteem than a failure to try at all. Small goals, like remembering to brush teeth or feed pets, that are set, met and acknowledged can help both parent and child feel that progress is being made, which can be overlooked if we focus only on what is *not* happening. Depression can take a while to heal; focusing on self-esteem can engender and sustain hope, which is essential in climbing out of depression.

Advocate And Support Friendships

Friendship at different ages calls for different skills. Young children need to learn how to enter imaginative play. This requires listening to the game being played (i.e. house, fire station, monsters) and finding a way to enter the situation in character and keep with the imagined world. If a child has trouble reading social cues, role-playing a playground situation with them might help more than a technical explanation. It can be especially effective if they play at being the other kids and we, as the parent, have a chance to play our child and model socially adaptive behaviors.

When boys and girls are very young we can facilitate play-dates and build bonds out of school that carry into the classroom. If they do not click with their particular class they might find that good friend they need in activities such as sports, art or music. As kids develop, boys will almost always benefit in elementary school if they can play sports. Teaching a kid some basic skills when young, even if you are not into sports, will often do them a great service. Girls can be trickier and if we encourage kindness, inclusion and a long-view they will make and keep the right friends for them. Still, no child is spared their share of awful moments. Our task is to empathize with our child's pain and encourage them to trust that mean behavior comes from others feeling threatened, insecure and inadequate.

Hope

Whether we are trying to help our child not get depressed or get through being depressed, hope is a critical factor to instill, and keep alive in, our child. In therapy, depression tends to get worse when we start to work on it. Although this hurts more rather than less to begin with, long-term well-being and improved mood tend to follow. As I have grown more experienced as a therapist and have seen sorrow spike up and then subside numerous times, I am increasingly able to engender my clients' trust that the pain will pass and good feelings will come.

There are many things in life we cannot control, but one thing we can do is choose to love our kids no matter what else is happening around us. If this is a guiding principle we can receive even our child's difficulties as a gift; then our kid might also find meaning and purpose in their pain, which helps transform suffering. For example, our child might discover that they are stronger than they had realized as a result of personal struggle. Our confidence that things will get better, and our conviction to stick with our children no matter what it takes gives them every reason to maintain the hope that will get them through hard times. Hope springs eternal. As parents our love for our children, and for everyone else's children too, is a wellspring of hope.

Empathy

To help our children out of a stuck place we must start by truly understanding that place. When someone has a bad day it does not help when we say, "It's not so bad," or "cheer up." Advice doesn't help much either: "You need to put that ice cream away and go to the gym." In our dark moments, we need to be understood—that it hurts, maybe feels hopeless; even if this is not "reality," it may be how our kid feels at that moment. When our child is irritated or miserable it can be comforting to them if we are able to articulate the nuances and intensity of their feelings. It is better to say, "I hear how you felt tortured by that experience" (rather than "so-and-so didn't mean anything by it"). It does not help to minimize feelings ("that's no big deal"), put things in a context of the less fortunate ("kids in Darfur...") or to share our own tales of woe ("when I was your age...").

It is also important to remember that when our child is upset, they really do not care about what we feel. Just because our child lapses into moments of total self-involvement does not justify our doing the same. Empathy means not making it all about our selves. It is possible that our parents asked us to hear and hold their feelings and we felt burdened by that, but if so we can also ask if our parents presented a model of happiness we wish to emulate.

There is a Chinese parable in which a man has slipped on ice and cannot get up. Everyone who tries to pull him up ends up falling down on the ice. A master comes along and lies down on the ice next to the man who is suddenly able to get up. Sometimes quietly joining someone in their difficulty is more helpful than overt assistance. The next time our child tells us about something that hurt or is bothering them, we can try to metaphorically "lie down on the ice beside them." If we just try to *feel* their world from their shoes and not fix anything we might notice a difference in how they respond. They might not feel better right away, but they are more likely to let us in and connect with us—and that helps them up. If we turn away from our child when they are in pain it shames them and leads them to believe that since their pain is too much for us it must be too much for them too. This creates loneliness that can accidentally turn normal sorrow into entrenched depression.

Provide A Calm Environment

No matter what else is going on for a child, from homework to hallucinations, a tranquil and low-stress environment is a big plus. Bickering parents, shouting in the house, alcohol abuse, etc. will impair a healthy child's sense of well-being and are serious additional burdens for a child with inner struggles of their own.

We are wise to avoid being rude, sarcastic or cruel, not just toward our child, but especially within range of our child hearing or sensing it. Besides *not* making things stressful, we can actively strive for calm by getting more tranquil within ourselves (such as with yoga or meditation), and by choosing calm music, filling the house with good smells such as soups or fresh flowers. If we consciously put love into our home, our cooking, even our laundry, somehow it all helps bring about a subtle difference that can help the people who live in our home feel safer, more loved and happier. I once saw a T-shirt that said, "If momma's not happy—nobody's happy." Having a depressed parent is very hard on children. Loving our child means taking care of ourselves as well as our child—and finding a way to enjoy being alive and being a parent. Happiness on a day-to-day basis comes from doing the small things we enjoy. Gardening, cooking, sports, going for a walk or seeing a movie brings simple moments of happiness if we are present to them. Building Legos, throwing a ball or stringing beads are ways we can join our child in doing what they like and bring moments of tangible happiness.

Exercises To Consider

1. Draw your child out: We can make a point of listening to our child in a way that gets them to talk. We might express interest in how they're

doing or in what they are doing and then NOT offer commentary, criticism or helpful advice. Work to just pay attention and take interest in whatever they want to say, in whatever manner they choose to express it. The safer they feel to just be themselves, the more they will open up.

2.   Do something your child enjoys: Pick an activity your child has shown pleasure in, but keep it simple—like kicking a soccer ball around, drawing or going to the pet shop just to say hello to the animals. Sometimes kids will open up in the process of doing something other than overtly talking about feelings. Since small things bring happiness, if we consistently do small fun things good feelings that last might sneak up on our children.

3. Play a family game: Even if the whole "family" is only you and your child, let your child choose a game and then be fully present to them while you play. Games offer your child a way to connect and engage with you that is less dramatic and intense than "working on helping them." Games help teach them (and ourselves if we need to learn it) the fine art of just hanging out. For kids three to six let your kid create the rules of fantasy play (or offer suggestions: i.e. the floor is lava and a path of pillows and chairs are safe areas; a trip to the market is actually a trip to another planet and your car is a space ship); For kids six to ten a card game called Rat-A-Tat-Cat offers simple math and strategy; for nine or ten and older

games like Apples to Apples and Who Knew? engage children in thinking about other people's likes and dislikes which is a fun way to facilitate empathy and allow children to reveal new aspects of themselves. For kids older than eleven or twelve Settlers of Catan and Seafarers of Catan are interesting games of strategy and social relatedness in the context of goods, services and a race to develop pretend lands and seas. Kids also tend to enjoy Uno, Connect Four, checkers, chess (as they get older), Life (which helps them think about choices and their differing outcomes). Finally, playing any game our child has come to like (even video games that bore us and make us dizzy) helps meta-communicate interest in our child and builds relationship.

4. Envision many bowls: Imagine a bowl that you select to catch and hold your child's overflow feelings. Label it with their name in your mind's eye and put a baby spoon in the bowl so that when your child comes back for their feelings you can remember to give them manageable bites and not overwhelm them. If you have a leaky boss, friend or family member in addition to your child, or you are working to get a solid bowl of your own, it might help to envision an imaginary cabinet with bowls to store whatever those in our lives cannot. This way we provide a psychological bowl and not a sponge, and we do not have to be toxically burdened (and then get angry, resentful or rejecting and defensive) just because someone gives us their unwanted

feelings. Mentally keep your kid's bowl on the counter and take it with you until you no longer need to think about it (i.e. when you feel naturally strong and containing).

5. Do a bit of what you love: Being happy as a parent helps your child. Consider things you might like to do if anything and everything were open to you. If you already had all the health, money, power, and time you desire, then what would you like to do that comes from your heart? Music, sports, study, service, adventure... find your passion and then find a way to do it at least some of the time. If you can't tour the world in a rock band, get a guitar and take a lesson anyway; if you can't afford a classic truck you wish to fix up, buy a few parts anyway and see how it makes you feel. Be a little bit Don Quixote—it will nourish your soul and that's good for your child.

6. Use music: Pick music to create the mood you wish to have as a parent. Maybe classical to calm down or rock to pep up. Perhaps blues for consolation or a much-needed cry to let things go. Sharing music with your children can also be a lot of fun if they get into it or if you can be open to what they like and want to share with you.

7. Yoga: If you do yoga and you find yourself down, go to yoga class. If your child will consider it, take them along. If you have never done yoga but are out of ideas to improve sadness or stuckness in yourself, your child or your household,

take a beginner class and *then* evaluate if it helps. Initially yoga can seem awkward, difficult and intimidating, but the benefit is often clear only at the end of class with feelings of enhanced well-being, tranquility, clarity and improved mood. If you already are a yogi and feel glum, or are trying to help a gloomy child you can always do a few poses at home and see if they have a positive effect. Consciously dedicate the yoga to something (such as your child's well being, or to following the wisdom of your deeper Self). Consider inversions (hand stand, shoulder stand, head stand) to bring increased energy; try Supta Baddha Konassana (reclining bound angle pose with the soles of the feet brought together and drawn up close to the body), which is very restorative. Be sure to breathe slow and deep and fully exhale, as the breath is more important than anything else in yoga.

Finally, Savasana, or corpse pose, is excellent when we need to surrender and let everything go so we can open ourselves to whatever we feel, and drink in the nourishment of the yoga we did to prepare for this final relaxation pose. Savasana allows guidance and renewal to find a way into our consciousness through quiet meditation.

Chapter 6

Calm Ideas For Anxious Kids

If we hope to allay our child's anxieties and coax them into the safe harbor of the present moment we need to find ways to be present to the moment ourselves. When in doubt, slow down, breathe and invite calm into yourself; then invite your child into your calm.

Take a breath (don't just read about it, actually take a deep breath), breathe in love for your child and breathe out fear. Take a moment. Look around you and take in your current surroundings—whatever you can see, feel, hear and smell right now; note the year, season, day and time as you happen across these words. Observe your emotions. Take another breath and stay present to where you are and what you feel. Even when things are difficult, the present moment is a powerful antidote to anxiety.

Kidnappers, Robbers, Witches and the Anxious Child

Imagine you had planned to drop your eight-year-old at soccer practice and run a few errands but he or she gets weepy and frightened and doesn't want you to leave the park. They don't really want to talk about their fear but you press them and they reveal that they are afraid of being kidnapped. This fear is not new, but you thought it was over. They are fine at school, at friends' houses and with family but they get upset at any mention of an unfamiliar baby-sitter or a situation like the park even if it is with their coach. Maybe *your* child specifically fears robbers, ghosts, witches or monsters; maybe they feel ashamed because they know they are getting too old for their fear, but they cannot seem to stop their mind from thinking something bad is going to happen to them.

Maybe you have patiently explained to your child that they are always safe and protected. Maybe you joked that kidnappers would not be able to handle the whining and would give them back or that kidnappers usually want rich children and your family is not that rich. They may say that they know that monsters and witches are not real but the anxiety remains all the same. You want to help them feel safe but you don't really understand where this fear is coming from and nothing you have tried has changed the way your child feels. You feel sad for your child but also constricted in things like getting to the market as you both become prisoner of their fear.

What Are We Afraid Of?

If the big bad wolf is about to get us and we feel no fear we are, basically, dinner. But if we *feel* as if the wolf is at the door when there is no actual danger we are talking about anxiety. Anxiety is like fear on steroids—it is ultimately maladaptive, narrowing our horizons and exhausting us. When we feel fear, our bodies create adrenaline to provide extra energy to run away or fight, but when we feel fear in situations where our fight or flight responses are blocked (i.e. a traffic jam, sitting at a desk or sitting in circle at preschool) those same chemicals just float around in our bodies and make us agitated and exhausted—and then become artery-clogging plaque.

As parents our truest and deepest fears are about our child becoming severely ill, hurt or worse; this would be a body blow to our soul, and underscores how our love for our child transcends issues of our own comfort or even survival. Our top fears for ourselves tend to cluster around disability, illness and poverty, the essence of which distills down to our dread of isolation, abandonment and agonizing dependency. Children's fears boil down to pretty much the same things. Our worst nightmares of being abandoned in some sinister "old-folks" home or ending up homeless altogether are emotional equivalents to our children's worst fears of being orphaned, abducted or victimized.

The more a child feels secure that they are safe, the less prone to anxiety they will be. Sometimes we do everything "right," and we still have an anxious child. Where genes play a role we can help our child manage their heightened vulnerability to anxiety by providing a calm and understanding environment. Anxiety can come from circumstances beyond our control (i.e. hurricanes, war, accidents, etc.) and then we must work to set things right again—not with the world (that can come later), but with our child's world-view. We will generally have little luck talking an anxious child out of their anxiety with logic or reassurance. Relationship is our best parenting tool. Our chief goal, after being calm ourselves, is to accurately understand what our child is afraid of and empathically connect with them in their worry.

As our culture becomes increasingly materialistic, more of us *feel* poor and grow frightened that we too could lose our grip and get sucked down into poverty, desolation or decrepit dependency. We think we need more "things" but get little sense of security out of having them; all this trickles down to our children who feel increasingly worried about everything from gang violence, to getting into the right middle school to not being harmed, Columbine or Virginia Tech style, by emotionally disturbed classmates. We need to find tranquility in the good fortune that we do have and re-direct our anxiety into concern for those in genuine need. If we treat the world more compassionately we will be less afraid that it will leave us hanging if we fall on hard times; then our trust and security might set a calm example for our children to follow.

Separation Anxiety

I stand in an unfamiliar backyard, smiling stiffly as I try to encourage my three-year-old to join a swarm of frolicking, laughing children, but he is super-glued to me like a barnacle, arms and legs coiled around my leg. I try to carry on a conversation with another parent and appear un-phased to be wearing my child like a boot. I have my own shyness with these unfamiliar parents and I am extra self-conscious about being the psychologist-parent of the seemingly messed-up kid. I want to play it cool and keep in mind that it's all normal behavior (which it is), yet I feel irrationally sad about a future of tragic loneliness that I can't help but picture for my child, based on how things are going at a preschooler's birthday party.

It is a decade later as I write about it and smile with affection for that sweet clingy kid who has grown infinitely more trusting and confident and has wonderful friends—and feel compassion for the nervous awkward parent that I was.

If our child has fear of separation they don't feel safe without us and do not yet feel confident on their own. When kids dread separation it is because it evokes anxiety about us parents leaving them vulnerable or about us not coming back at all. This feeling can hit them when they first have to sleep in their own bed alone all night, when they have to go on an overnight trip in elementary or middle school or when they feel overwhelmed when away at college. By letting our children cling as much as they need to in the early and exhausting years, when dependency is so desperately intense, we can bolster their secure attachment in the future. When we have our own separation issues every drop-off at pre-school can feel like a tragic opera. There are also times when we pass our threshold of patience and empathy and our child suddenly just seems like an overgrown crybaby. There are moments when our child simply must go to school or cope with a baby-sitter, but when they panic we need to stay connected to their feelings. It's when we check-out emotionally that our children tend to freak out and get dramatic until we understand things from their point of view and at their level of intensity.

In the multi-thousand year sweep of human history it is relatively recent for things like professional day-care, and pre-school to exist. In cave-dwelling times a baby presumably was in the familiar arms of his or her mother, and of aunts, grandmothers and whatever sensitive men might have been around until he or she could begin to crawl away and explore the environment. A baby has no fear of strangers until about seven months—the time they are first able to crawl away. Evolution would seem to imply that there was not much need to fear strangers *until* we had the capacity to encounter them by our own actions. A child is probably meant to experience separation driven by curiosity about the world, rather than by being left with strangers because mommy or daddy has to work, shop or go to therapy. A naturally secure child organically learns to venture farther and farther from the safe base of mother until eventually they are discovering new worlds.

With the rise of civilization and the specialization of labor we eventually end up with professional child-care givers servicing kids who really just want *their* mommy. What is the message to a child when, instead of it being a sacred honor to parent them, someone has to be *paid* to take care of them? We working parents often feel that we have little choice but to pay someone and keep working to pay for the child's private education, etc. The child may not understand our feelings, only the fact that we are largely not there. While working sets a good example to slightly older children, very young ones really benefit from having us there and loving them in that deep way that transcends salaries and wages. As a society we do not make child-care and education true priorities, so even if we find a way to make things work for our child, they eventually tumble out into a world of largely unparented children. As a child develops into precocious social awareness, they see that caregivers are low-paid and hold low social status. The net effect is the devaluing of caregiving and the lowering of a child's sense of worth; parents are important and do important things—which does not include staying home to take care of that child. As a result we get more and more anxiously attached people who do not trust the world or their place in it. With increasing distrust and coldness things become increasingly materialistic (after all, our car and plasma TV won't leave us, and neither will a bottle of gin). Poverty and war grow out of our wounded ways of treating the world, and each other, like things instead of as containers of the sacred. Raising secure and loving human beings contributes to making it a better world by restoring the sacredness of relationships.

While "terrible two's" has a nice alliteration, three is really the killer year for separation, tantrums and hair-pulling moments with one's child. Just keeping this in mind can help us weather the storm of normal developmental tumult. Three is a particularly scary time for children because they are more capable of fantasizing about super-hero/princess sorts of powers as well as of scaring themselves about witches, monsters and villains. Their developing minds are able to terrify themselves but not yet able to protect or soothe themselves, and their dependency on us can take on a nightmarish dimension. It may also be inherently wise for a child to have a lot of fear at this point when they can easily get themselves into trouble, but not out of it.

If the first mantra of parenting is "We can't win," (and so we just have to love our child no matter what), the second mantra is "transition is hard." Routines lower anxiety, so explaining what is coming up and establishing consistent patterns helps kids calm down.

Kindness and sensitivity to transition will typically help children be less anxious. Even newborns will appreciate it if we don't just scoop them up and shock them but rather gently clue them in on what we're about to do (i.e. "I'm going to pick you up now"); they may not understand the words, but they will learn the music of our tone. When a child is fussy after a nap, or anxious about separating, we can directly say to them that "transition is hard" (or our version of this idea); over time this cues them that they are not inadequate and that this painful feeling has a name, is normal and will not last forever.

Trauma And Anxiety

Trauma can come as the result of something big like injuries that send us to the ER. It can also come from things that are less obvious to us grown-ups but still emotionally overwhelming to our child (i.e. having a consistently cruel sibling). Even big traumas do not necessarily lead to debilitating anxiety if we have a chance to talk them through. This helps the brain transform flashback-like feelings of living terror into properly stored, and less intrusive, memories. "Working things through" is especially difficult if we are very young and not yet able to fully understand what has hurt us, much less be able to talk about it. In such cases a skilled play therapist can help a child express their trauma through art or play. Kids are resilient but the chance to "tell their story" as soon after a trauma as possible is ideal.

Trauma can fuel widening anxiety because we may learn to associate fear, danger or bad feelings with the sights, sounds, smells, etc. that were present when we got hurt. If a flower pot falls on our head while walking down a cobblestone street we may forever feel dread when we see cobblestone—or when we smell whatever was cooking at that moment, or when we see geraniums. Our fear can generalize to the point where more and more innocuous things feel like cues alerting us to potential danger. In the extreme we become afraid to leave our house.

Everything our child thinks and feels makes sense to them. It is better to respect their fear and try and understand what they are afraid of and why rather than tell them there is nothing to be afraid of—that just makes us sound like we completely don't get it.

While it is important to be sensitive and responsive to our child's anxiety, we also want to avoid inadvertently reinforcing fearful behaviors by only giving love and attention when a child is scared while neglecting them when they are not in crisis. If we proactively pay lots of loving attention when our kids are calm and happy we teach them that there is no particular *need* to be worried in order to get love and attention.

Research shows that the single best predictor of a child becoming seriously overwhelmed or disorganized in their attachment relationships (which has long-term implications for their functioning) is *unresolved loss or trauma in the parent*. It turns out that we very subtly, and non-consciously, frighten our children if we haven't worked through our serious wounds. This pattern is particularly destabilizing to infants younger than two, because if we exhibit "bizarre" behavior (i.e. trancing out due to our own demons) our kid gets crossed wires in the face of danger with no escape—leaving them with a pocket of disintegration into which they subsequently fall when faced with stressful situations. This underscores the tremendous value for our children in us healing ourselves.

School Avoidance

If a child is having a hard time in general, school can become a dreaded place. If our child doesn't want to go to school, we want to strive for a clearer understanding of why. Beyond separation anxiety, if a child does not feel up to the social or academic challenges of school it may be that they do not trust in themselves and their ability to learn, grow, make friends or fit in. If school makes a child feel overwhelmed, frightened or bad about themselves they may naturally want to dodge those bad feelings by avoiding school altogether. It is important for parents not to simply tell our children that they have to go to school and that's that. We need to really listen to what they say about it. If we can figure out what they are afraid of we can support them to find coping strategies and build skills to better manage their situation.

Somatic Expression

Sometimes fears originate with thoughts but end up getting expressed in the body (body is "soma" in Latin, hence the term "psycho-somatic" illness). A kid who gets sick on Monday mornings (unless there is no school that day), or who gets headaches before music lessons or gets a stomachache when the baby-sitter is coming may be unconsciously trying to protect themselves from things they fear (i.e. separation or failure). It is important to keep in mind that people who tend to have somatic problems are not faking illness. Their complaints and symptoms are real and beyond their conscious control.

Anxiety feels awful, and sometimes we unconsciously prefer a stomachache or headache to our dread. The better we understand what our child's "somatic expressions" could be telling us the more we can help them deal with the challenges they face. When avoidance is no longer necessary (i.e. because a child feels good about going to school), symptoms that once helped a child avoid things tend to drop away.

Older Kids' Fears Are More Secret

As children grow older they may be more conscious of their fears and at the same time more ashamed to talk about them. Adolescents who feel lonely or angry may become confused by sexual or destructive thoughts that they dare not express, and become increasingly isolated and anxious. Throughout adolescence children have intermittent fears (mixed with big dreams) about how they will manage to get on in the world when childhood ends. Fears about rejection or acceptance from peers, colleges, jobs, etc. render the typical adolescent at least a little bit anxious a good deal of the time. It is important that as parents we continue to listen in ways that get our kids to talk; not judging what they say, but empathizing with how they feel. Teens may be mouthy, standoffish and embarrassed by us parents as part of their natural rebellion and search for identity but their secret is that they never want us to give up on loving them (which includes setting limits)—and even on giving affection. The graceful thing to do, as parents of adolescents, is to know that our kids still desperately need us but not force them to admit that this is true.

Shame is a key reason why a child or teenager would want to hide feelings or fears. Shame comes when we do something "wrong" that we know we were not supposed to do (i.e. using drugs, having unprotected sex) or when we somehow just feel "wrong" in being the way we are. Our children need to feel that they can come to us for help when they worry about the way they are, or when they "mess up," and trust that we will help them figure out how to learn from mistakes and make better choices. They must also know that they are lovable and acceptable and that bad behavior does not mean that they are "bad" kids. Limits and consequences are important but we do not want to be so severe that our child's primary concern becomes not getting caught or making us angry. Then they miss the point of behaving well for their own well-being. If kids get into troubling behavior they are very likely feeling neglected, unloved or overwhelmed and are trying to manage sadness and anxiety with behaviors that only get them into more trouble. This is especially true with sex, drugs and alcohol. We want our kids to feel comfortable sharing feelings and asking us questions so they have good information on what is safe and good for them.

Obsessions And Compulsions

Obsessions are recurring thoughts that are intrusive, consuming and generally unrealistic or grossly exaggerated. Examples would be constantly worrying that we left the iron on, fearing that we will shout out something inappropriate, thinking that we will get sick from shaking hands, touching doorknobs or going to a public toilet. Compulsions are actions that we feel driven to repeat in order to release anxiety or ward bad things off. Examples of compulsions include repeatedly checking (i.e. if a door is locked), counting, saying particular words over and over in our head (and fearing something bad could occur if we don't) or continual handwashing—often until the skin is raw. Compulsive actions can be mental or physical but tend to be excessive or illogical. The obsessive compulsive tends to feel that their obsessions and compulsions are not a choice, are not socially sanctioned, cause personal distress and that they would be better off without them if they could trust that they could stop and nothing bad would actually happen.

Obsessive-Compulsive Disorder (OCD) is an anxiety disorder that can come on in childhood and which sometimes carries shame when we feel that our thoughts or behaviors are wrong, or at least illogical, but we cannot stop them. Obsessions and compulsions can serve as a defense; they release stress and give an illusion of control (i.e. we *can* wash our hands, but cannot control most of what happens in the world). Since they momentarily provide relief, obsessions and compulsions are powerfully self-reinforcing.

If our child needs to touch the other side of things if they touch one side, or go through every door twice, we want to pay attention to when and where their behaviors occur with an eye on discovering anything that might spike their anxiety. If we suspect our child might have OCD we would want to consult with an expert to get an accurate diagnosis and provide compassionate and effective treatment. Many kids (and adults) without OCD have milder tendencies to be a little obsessive and here we parents need to be sensitive and understanding to help our child reduce and deal better with their stress. If a child repeatedly asks for reassurance but cannot be reassured, we can try to keep in mind that obsessions do not respond to logic—they are like hamsters that run on wheels to nowhere.

If our child is anxious and obsessive, we must be sensitive about helping them stop their compulsive behaviors. Obsessions and compulsions can serve to protect a person from feeling out of control. When we take away this sort of defense it can, at least temporarily, worsen anxiety. A child may then go deeper underground in hiding their behaviors from us, worsening feelings of shame and isolation and lessening the likelihood they will get effective help. We want to emphasize non-judgmental understanding to learn what our child is thinking and feeling.

Cutting

Sometimes a person can be so out of sorts that cutting or scratching their own skin actually feels calming and brings a grounding sense of realness at moments when they are emotionally or psychologically coming apart. Cutting can be thought of as a defense against feeling unreal. While cutting is a serious symptom of emotional disturbance, it is not the same as direct attempts at suicide (although the pain that leads to cutting can also lead to more lethal attempts to end suffering). If our child is cutting they need professional help immediately.

I worked with a fifteen-year-old girl who was a cutter. Her skin was an echo of the baby she had once been who had never felt safe and loved, the forgotten self that was forever coming apart and flooding her with unmanageable despondency. One time when she was having a particularly rough patch and needed to be hospitalized, we were waiting for the ambulance together when she started gouging her nails into her thighs. The staff was on stand-by to restrain her, but that would have also just added to her trauma. I told her that her skin was like her baby and that she needed to calm it. She was able to follow this directive, gently massage her skin and self-soothe. While it was going to take a lot more than that to heal her, I was struck by how telling her what she *could* do to help was more effective than telling her what not to do.

The younger our child is at the present moment, the more we need to soothe and massage them and help them know that they are real, sacred and loved. Through paying consistent attention to our children, and emotionally holding what they spill over, we help them feel real and contained. This helps remove the need to cut, scratch, pierce, tattoo or drug themselves in order to cope with underlying feelings of disintegration.

Free-Floating Anxiety

Sometimes we are tense and nervous but we don't necessarily know why; the Italians call it "agida," in Yiddish it's "the spilkes." When we can't put our finger on what we are nervous about that only adds to an out-of-control feeling. If we are afraid of flying we can stay off airplanes. If we are afraid of open spaces we can stay inside, but if we don't know what we are afraid of—only *that* we are anxious—we are haunted by free-floating anxiety that can plague us wherever we go and whatever we do.

Before we take away a defense (be it a teddy-bear or an obsession) we want to strengthen our child's underlying sense of security so we don't, inadvertently, make things worse. To stop being afraid of the dark only to fall into free floating anxiety is to go out of the frying-pan and into the fire. In this sense most specific fears could be understood as defenses against underlying and undifferentiated free-floating anxiety. As parents we strive to be a container for our children's fears as they work their way toward security and trust in themselves and learn how to manage their feelings. By using *our* feelings—even negative feelings—to more deeply sense and hold our child's feelings we soothe them and help solidify their emerging bowl of self. Facilitating our child's sense of self arms them with their best defense against free-floating or specific anxiety.

Annihilation Anxiety

In a newborn baby all anxiety is free-floating; as we begin to map our world we become slowly capable of fearing specific things. We emerge from infantile chaos into a dimly sensed fear that we could be swept back into the psychological soup we came from. If free-floating anxiety feels like hanging by a thread over an unknown abyss, annihilation is the feeling that the thread has snapped, and we have fallen into non-being.

In emotional terms, annihilation is about as bad as it gets. In the brain the black hole of annihilation has its correlate in the primitive fight-flight area; this is where we begin mental life, and it has no sense of time—all is the eternal now. That's great if you're the Buddha, but when it comes to dread, it is exacerbated by *feeling* as if unspeakable angst is eternally undoing us.

If we have a solid self we can (even if just barely) contain feelings of chaos, but if we have no bowl, the wordless, shapeless panic that roils in the minds of pre-verbal infants can evoke that very feeling in us, their parents. When a very young child is in distress, as parents, we may feel swamped, helpless, angry and frightened as they psychologically spill those emotions over into us. If our self is fragile we may emotionally cut off from our distressed child and mistakenly teach them that their feelings are too much for others and themselves. As parents we must grow strong and solid to be able to contain our children's primordial dread and not be destabilized by it; their emotional tempests must be held within our psychological teapot.

Children emerge from feelings of annihilation when they are new in the world, and then dip into them again at developmental transitions. Adolescence and the intensifying quest for identity leaves some children vulnerable to vast plunges into anguish and terror. When nameless dread grips us as teenagers (or adults) it is the darkest sort of despair that can provoke desperate measures from drug abuse to thoughts of self-harm—anything to bring relief from excruciating isolation, confusion and hopelessness. It is important to neither fuel the fireworks nor dismiss our overwrought teens as being fake or dramatic. They are always expressing some sort of emotional truth. If we receive their authentic "perform-ance" and let it move us to understand their tears, angst or fear, we acknowledge that their agony is genuine. This helps them stay connected with us when they are overwhelmed and regain their center. While "annihilation" is just a label, help-ing our child talk about and name their extreme feelings can help reduce fears of coming apart. We all parent together in the service of our shared world. Knowing this helps us face chaos with love and courage, and not lose sight of the inde-structible sacred spirit that lives in all our children.

Why Aren't We Calmer?
What's In Our Child's Way?

If our child is anxious or suffering from fears our inten-tion, as parents, is to help them feel calm and confident. In the service of tranquility and confidence it makes sense to consider what obstacles a kid might face that blocks them from feeling safe and empowered.

1) Inherited Predisposition to Anxiety

If one or both of a child's parents happen to be a little obsessive or anxious, that child may inherit a similar mind/ body package. Understanding that a person cannot help the wiring they inherit allows us, as parents, to validate our child's feelings and communicate to them that we believe that they are doing the best they can. Recognizing that genetics play a role in anxiety helps us seek timely treatment for our child, when appropriate, and avoid criticizing our child for what they cannot help, which would only make them more anx-ious and lower their self-esteem. An anxious child may be more like one of their grandparents than their parents, but wherever they got their predisposition from, our message to them is that we unconditionally love them and want to help them feel safe.

2) <u>Sensitivity</u>

Some children have high levels of sensitivity to sights, smells and sounds and experience strong emotional reactions to the world. These are kids who hate loud noises, tend to have allergies or asthma (which is the body's over-reaction to irritants) and can be hard to soothe as infants. Sensitivity amplifies hurts and minor annoyances and makes them feel bigger and more overwhelming. This increases a child's fear of the world—which is a recipe for anxiety.

To help a child manage a high level of sensitivity it helps to understand what it's like to be like them. Telling them that things are no big deal, or shaming them as weak or inadequate can make them hate themselves for being sensitive when we want them to understand and love themselves for who they are. If we minimize things that bother our child or shame them for their big reactions to small things we exacerbate emotionally painful experiences. Things that to a less sensitive person are little more than an annoyance (i.e. a scratchy shirt, a squeaky door, a stinky restroom) are an assault on the sensitive child's equilibrium. Their nails-on-a-chalkboard feeling is only compounded by shame or judgment coming from us not-so-highly-sensitive parents.

Validating our child's reactions (i.e. "that was startling for you") can help a child realize and handle the fact that they feel things more intensely than the typical person while simultaneously learning that no lasting harm comes from most of the things that startle or annoy them. We strive to help them manage sensitivity gracefully and even recognize it as a gift (i.e. a great sense of smell is an asset for a chef or a perfume-maker).

3) <u>Trauma</u>

If our child shows signs of anxiety but we can't figure out where it's coming from maybe something that we were unaware of has traumatized them or something we knew about has had a bigger impact on them than we realized (i.e. a violent video game or scary movie; or even our own unresolved traumas).

When something scares us so much that we are overwhelmed by it (i.e. a car accident), we may temporarily check out of our body to get away from the terrible feelings we *would* have had if we had stayed present to the trauma. Checking out is involuntary. It brings surreal, ghostly feelings and lingering effects; sudden flashbacks may be triggered by things that remind us of the original trauma (i.e. the smell of smoke if we were in a fire). If a child has been traumatized they may develop a persistent fear that the same thing will happen again even if that is highly unlikely. The younger and less verbal a child is, the harder it may be for them to process trauma. A skilled child therapist may work with sand trays, toys or puppets to help a child "tell" what hurt them by play-acting it out. Telling, drawing, explaining, etc. takes living terror and turns it into memory that can be properly stored so that it no longer intrudes unexpectedly as if it were happening in the present. Hearing about painful things, especially that have happened to our child (and possibly to ourselves at the same time) can obviously be distressing. Our natural tendency to avoid revisiting painful experiences inadvertently blocks healing and can worsen or prolong anxiety.

For very young children separation from caregivers can be traumatic and separation anxiety can result. Sometimes separation is unavoidable (i.e. when we must work), but as parents we can at least validate that being brought to preschool before they were ready or being left with a nanny had an impact on their basic trust. Acknowledging past hurts as real promotes our child's ability to trust that the future will not necessarily be a repeat of the past. Then successful separations (i.e. sleepovers or class trips) can finally put the past to bed.

4) <u>Lack of Basic Trust</u>

Too much separation, deprivation or hurt, early on, can teach a young child that the world is dangerous and bound to hurt them. This world-view is the opposite of basic trust, where we first get to experience the world as kind, nurturing, consistent and safe (based on our newborn experiences with our caregivers). If we carry a sense of basic trust we are free to explore the park, the preschool, new friendships, etc. and know that we will always find safe harbor with our family. The more good experiences we have with our family the more we internalize the trust and safety that allows openness, creativity and confidence throughout our lives. If our child lacks basic trust we must work to provide safety and understanding now, while validating and helping them work through whatever has been harmful in the past. Trust is hard to build and easy to break, so as parents we must find ways to manage our anger, curb our sarcasm and make our child's basic trust a top priority.

5) <u>Lack of a Self</u>

A solid sense of self is necessary in order to hold intense or contradictory emotions. If a child lacks a psychological bowl to hold fear, hurt and uncertainty they need to rely on someone else's psyche (i.e. their parents) to manage their emotional overflow. Child development is, in many ways, self-development. Understanding that it is natural for young children to lack a solid self (and to be easily overwhelmed by fear), helps us parents remember to be patient and compassionate. If an older child or teenager has not received enough attention and understanding early on, their self may not have fully developed and their ability to hold fear or deal with ambiguity may remain more like that of a much younger child. If we lack a self and cannot tolerate even mild anxiety we cannot take appropriate social, academic or emotional risks and our world stays narrow as we primarily focus on avoiding feeling anxious. Lack of a self is typically the real problem underlying poor self-esteem, which correlates with anxiety as well as depression. Accurate empathy and precise, non-critical understanding facilitates our child's self to grow stronger and their anxiety then tends to go down—especially if measured over a span of months and years rather than minutes and hours.

6) A Stressful Environment

A highly sensitive or anxiety-prone child may feel overwhelmed by what to most people would be a moderate level of loudness in our voice, or by typical levels of relational conflict around them. But even a hardy and resilient child can develop anxiety as the level of yelling and discord in their environment goes up, just as battle-toughened soldiers can still develop post-traumatic stress disorder if things get horrific enough. No matter what level of anxiety our child has, it helps to provide a stable, safe and tranquil home environment.

What's In Our Way?

To help our children feel calm and confident it can only help if we, as their parents, are calm and confident. To the extent that we are not, it serves us to wonder what may be blocking us.

1) Past Hurts

We re-experience childhood through our children as they remind us of our own experiences at each particular age. If we are transported back to awful times and feelings, we may emotionally checkout and stop being present to our child, which can spike their anxiety. Our child's anxiety may then grow out of our own hurt and mistrustful worldview.

Sometimes having an anxious child echoes our anxious parents and pain they may have caused us in childhood. Our past hurts can make us over-protective, which teaches children that the world is scary and dangerous. We need to stay clear that our child, anxious or not, is not responsible for our own childhood. Our kids love us and try to please us. They may even unconsciously take on our fears and sorrows in sad attempts to relieve us of pain by carrying it for us. Our conscious willingness to deal with our own pain, and to carry and experience our *child's* pain, helps us avoid inflicting our wounds or dumping our unwanted feelings onto our children.

2) Denial of Fear

If we engage in high-risk or self-destructive behaviors we may be trying to block or deny fear in ourselves. The immature parent, who lives an impulsive and irresponsible life, tends to have anxious children. Lack of parental limit-setting, boundaries and attention, combined with a child's unconscious fear that the parent will self-destruct and the child will be orphaned, creates a propensity for fear and insecurity in a child. Being kind and patient shows real strength and will breed calm confidence in our kids.

3) <u>We Feel Threatened</u>

Some of us get angry for similar reasons that others get anxious—because it feels like we, or our loved ones, are in danger. The threat can be to pride, as well as body, but once we are in fight/flight mode, if escape is blocked (even by our own ego), we tend to become aggressive. If we deal with fear by becoming aggressive or threatening, our loudness and scariness can naturally make our children afraid. We may think we are teaching them the way of the world, or keeping them in line, but if we were actually powerful and in charge there would be no need for shouting or cruelty. If our child is terrified, we can check-in with ourselves just to be certain that it isn't us who scared them.

Another threat to parents is the dreaded feeling that we are inadequate, unlovable or useless. If we think badly of ourselves, any perceived slight from partners or children can cause us to explode or retreat. This creates fear in those who must anxiously depend on us for their protection, food, love, etc. This dynamic of feeling hurt and causing hurt creates shame in ourselves (and later in our children), which makes us further withdraw and isolate—and in turn makes our kids more needy and anxious (or mouthy and rebellious).

The more we work on healthy self-esteem and compassion in the service of our children, the less we misread cues, overreact to small slights and cause anxiety in the people we love most in the world.

4) <u>Our Lack of Sensitivity</u>

The vast majority of people are not highly sensitive, so if our child *is* highly sensitive and we are not, our relative lack of sensitivity can cause their anxiety to escalate. The highly sensitive child does not understand that they feel things more intensely than others. If we treat them as if there is something wrong with them when a loud noise, or a strong smell, rocks their world we make them nervous about being who they are. If we have a sensitive child we can try to imagine the world with the volume turned up—imagine freezing showers, blasting radios, hot peppers and scratchy clothes to deepen empathy for the princess and the pea feeling of being highly sensitive. It also offers a possible explanation for certain children tending to shut down, or avoid things. This is not to say that sensitive kids are "special" and need to be indulged all the time, only that if we sincerely wish to help them feel less anxious it will be useful if we can be a little more sensitive to them.

5) Making Things All About Ourselves

We make a cardinal error in parenting when we make things about us. One problem with our self-focus is that it can teach our child to anxiously focus on pleasing us while disregarding what they feel. Later in life this leaves them vulnerable to pleasing others at their own expense. If our child is always trying to make us happy we are probably pretty unhappy, and nothing that they can do will make us feel good about ourselves. A child's inevitable lack of success in making us happy reinforces the idea that they are powerless, which only increases anxiety.

Obsessive preoccupation with being a good parent or chronic worry that things are all our fault is still making things about us. This may not seem selfish, but our guilt does not make our children feel loved and understood. If we always need to make things about ourselves, therapy could be a great plan where for one hour a week it *can* be all about us but in the service of it not being that way the rest of the week. Parents who really know their children and accurately understand, and respond, to them are most effective at cultivating security.

6) <u>Denial of Our Shadow</u>

If we are all about love and harmony but cannot be the "bad guy," set limits or allow our child to be unhappy with us we may be cut off from the Shadow part of our personality. Children naturally have aggression and inner monsters and they project their Shadow onto us when it's too much for them. Our ability to tolerate our child hating us because we said it was time for their bath, and maintaining that we love them even when they hate us, goes a long way toward taming inner dragons. Understanding and coming into a respectful relationship with our own Shadow helps us be a calming influence on our child. The Shadow is potentially destructive but also carries our power; when we acknowledge and respect our Shadow as part of us it becomes more like an inner bodyguard. A good relationship with our Shadow empowers us to give love *and* set limits.

7) <u>Obsession With Money</u>

Joseph Heller, the author of "Catch 22," was at a party where someone pointed to a Wall Street tycoon and said that he made more money that year than all of Heller's books would ever make. Heller replied, "Yes, but I have one thing that guy doesn't have and will never have: Enough."

As a culture we are obsessed with money. We project our free-floating anxiety onto money and gain pseudo-clarity about our problems (i.e. that they are because of a lack of money) and then fantasize that more money is the solution. If we model for our children that money is the be-all and end-all they may emulate our world-view and behavior and end up like too many of us, affluent yet isolated, empty and restless. If we try to help distressed children feel calm by buying things we fuel their anxiety with our lack of faith that love might help them feel better than another meaningless purchase. We are poor so long as we believe that we don't have enough—and that belief, rational or not, will make our child anxious.

If we labor under the delusion that we do not have enough, when we are actually affluent, we are in no position to truly help our children see that their irrational fears and beliefs are in fact unfounded. Money is a culturally sanctioned obsession that masks collective fear and loneliness. It has become a stand-in for real problems, such as widespread isolation and collective dread, and serves as a carrot-on-a-stick answer. Happy people are not always the ones with all the toys. We need to realize that we already have enough in order to perceive the hamster-wheel of chronic getting and spending and not model an anxious poverty mentality for our children. When in doubt of our abundance, we need to give more to others; the amount is not important, but the love that we put into it is everything.

8) Illness

When we are ill we are less present to thinking about our child. When we are less mentally and physically available our child may regress, grow anxious, over-eat, act-out, etc. While we cannot avoid getting sick sometimes and must work to heal ourselves as best as we can, we can at least validate the impact it may have on our child. We can also make our love for our child a key motivation in our healing. Giving love is as curative as getting love.

Broadening Our Perspective

Anxiety Is The Unremembered Past Projected Into The Future

If we experience shame as a child we may fear that our disappointed and disapproving parents will withdraw love, protection and nourishment, and thus we learn to associate disappointing others with loss and abandonment. We may then grow up into an anxious people-pleaser out of unconscious fear of abandonment if we disappoint others—not realizing that the future we dread is an emotional snapshot of our past.

The actual traumas of our past may have little resemblance to the scenarios our anxiety causes us to fear, but the underlying feelings are the same. For example, being yelled at or neglected in very early childhood may have made us feel out of control, ashamed or annihilated, but we may have never really understood those feelings or put them into words. Although we cannot remember being hurt in this way, we may dread feeling out of control or annihilated. We might then develop a fear of flying that is, deep down, a trace memory of some emotional catastrophe dating from our pre-verbal, pre-memory past. Our strategy to avoid feeling out of control may include staying off planes, but anxiety can generalize into other fears (i.e. open spaces, crowds, etc.)—haunting us with a desolation that we cannot seem to prevent... because it already occurred.

If we won't consider the possibility that our anxious child really has at least *felt as if* they were annihilated, shamed, orphaned or abandoned we fail to validate their emotional reality. Attempts to soothe our children with logic about the future (i.e., "you have nothing to worry about") inadvertently block them from accepting and working through past hurts—the very thing that would liberate and calm them. Even if our actions have hurt our child, we need to transcend guilt and shame to empathize with their experiences. Validating that a child's fear makes sense in terms of the past supports them to face the discomfort of *not* repeating avoidant, compulsive or obsessive thoughts and behaviors they may rely on for relief from anxiety.

Sometimes past trauma can even date back to the uterus. A psychoanalyst presented a case about a client who had repeated nightmares of the ceiling being ripped open and something like a big arm or machine entering her home and trying to get her. The analyst came to suspect that this was a symbolic representation of an abortion. He encouraged his client to talk to her mother about it and the daughter learned that there had in fact been an abortion attempt; when the client's mother became pregnant their country was at war and the husband was called to the front lines, so they didn't think they could bring a baby into the world. The abortion attempt failed, and the very next week the war ended. The husband returned and they happily kept the pregnancy. They loved their daughter and raised her well, but a terrible feeling of impending destruction always plagued her. Once the abortion story was affirmed and she understood the validity of her dream—but as memory not premonition—both her nightmares and waking dread evaporated. In the end she was not angry with her mother and in fact felt freer in their relationship and in her own life overall.

Fear Is Intelligent

Appropriate or realistic fear is adaptive in that it helps keep us safe and alive. Fear is gut intelligence while anxiety is the domain of an over-active head. An anxious brain is like a car alarm that goes off every time a car passes. An anxious brain is not always our best friend; sometimes it is more like the domineering mean kid at school— and so we don't want to blindly do whatever our brain tells us to do. Our heart and our gut are better friends—less pretentious and generally wiser than our brain.

If we somehow manage to comprehend the intelligence in the underlying or original fear, back before it became anxiety, we might be more effective in getting kids to feel safe and calm. When our child is anxious we must respect that anyone who had the same mind, body and past experiences as our child would be affected the same way. It's often best to acknowledge the way they *feel,* soothe jangled nerves with hugs rather than words and help our child discover that, while they may have been rattled by the past, they may no longer be in danger. The more we support our child to trust their gut, the more they will learn to operate from a place of heart as true intelligence and the less anxious, needy, clingy and dependent they will become.

Nightmares As Wishes

Our child's dreams are a window into their psyche. Most children have bad dreams on occasion and some are troubled by recurring nightmares. Our dreams are architected by our deep Self and we create everything that happens in them. One aspect of dream interpretation is finding the wish hidden in the dream. All the people, places and figures in a dream could be seen as representing different parts of our own psyche. In this light the monster that chases our child in their dream may represent their own angry, devouring Shadow aspect.

If our child's unconscious brings them a nightmare then at some level they *want* to be chased by the monster. As to why anyone would *wish* to be chased by a monster, a possible interpretation is that when we feel alone or abandoned, being chased and "desired" (even as potential dinner) can feel better than believing that we are completely unwanted.

Children sometimes dream about their parents dying. If our child is, in a sense, writing and directing their dreams, one reason they might unconsciously kill us off could be that they are hurt, mad at us and, cartoon style, want to exact revenge. They may also wish for us to understand how bad it feels to be hurt and give us a taste of our own cruel medicine. They may just be fed up with being small and bossed around. But dream violence is like cartoon violence where shadowy figures die and come back again.

Sometimes dreams show us our inner situation, and offer us opportunity to make changes. For example, we might dream of being back in school and having test anxiety; a possible interpretation is that we are confronting something in our life (such as parenting) that requires new learning. A child may learn to confront or talk to their inner monster over a series of recurring dreams; the child may realize that they cannot get away, but when they face the monster it will generally teach them something and transform into a more benign form (i.e. the "friendly monster"). Orphan situations in dreams may relate to unconscious wishes our child has to reassure themselves that they *could* make it on their own, much like Oliver Twist or Harry Potter, if they absolutely had to.

When a child has bad dreams and doesn't want to talk about them a possible guess is that we, the parents, have come to harm in our child's unconscious. Gently intuiting this and making it safe to talk can dispel anxiety by allowing children to release their "secret." To children, a bad dream about their parents being hurt is a secret because they dimly intuit the power hidden in the dream and fear that they could somehow make it come true by speaking it aloud. If our kid has bad dreams they "can't remember" or don't want to talk about we can, just to be kind, find a way to cue them that we are sorry if we have hurt their feelings, and that even if they are angry at us, we still love them as much as ever. If we happen to get it right their bad dreams may fade away, and even if fear persists it won't hurt for us to validate that we sometimes hurt their feelings and that we are committed to doing better.

Shadow Holds Our Power

The "message" of the Shadow is generally related to power. If we are not comfortable with our own power we tend to project it onto others. The child who is not ready to accept the beast within will see the monster in every shadow on the wall, and in every "mean" word from mommy or daddy. Children are small and vulnerable and naturally have fears; they also delight in playing at having super-powers, but know that they cannot yet trust themselves to use power in a good way (hence the endless kid shows that depict evil child-geniuses). When the Shadow remains untamed, power and authority cannot be trusted and a child remains more likely to mistake those trying to help empower them (coaches, teachers, parents) as trying to hurt or mock them.

If our child can learn to become gradually more powerful and autonomous (i.e. in charge of whatever they can manage about themselves from picking out their own clothes, to ordering at the restaurant, to telling the barber what kind of haircut they want, etc.), their overall level of anxiety may go down.

Secrets Can Be Scary

Sometimes a child has anxiety because they are carrying a secret. Secrets have a lot of power, whether it is the secret of our own bad behavior or someone else's that we have been told not to talk about. The concept of "don't tell" implies an "or else" (i.e., we will be punished or will lose someone's love). If something is totally fine it generally doesn't need to be a secret.

Kids *hold* secrets for fear that telling them will make things worse. In such cases the secret itself creates anxiety and the fact that they can't talk about it ramps it all up. For example, a child who secretly watched a scary or violent film or saw something on the internet that they know they should not have viewed finds themselves burdened with double anxiety—the impact of the images they saw *and* the fact that they can't tell their parents for fear they will get in trouble. Maybe that child then tells a friend every graphic detail and scares them too, but swears them to secrecy; this recreates the emotional experience of secret fear in their friend who may become anxious and act out on another friend or sibling.

Kids *create* secrets for various reasons (i.e. to bond with friends or gain belonging to a group by excluding others). Children who have been wounded, neglected or had their trust broken are more vulnerable to being pulled into harmful activities about which they then find themselves bound to secrecy. In extreme examples lonely children are induced into drugs, sexual behavior or gang involvement by being coerced into doing things that must remain secret. This allows others to further manipulate and control them and widens the gap between the child and their caregivers, teachers and others who genuinely care about them.

I worked with a child who had been in a gunfight when he was eleven or twelve and didn't even know if he hit anyone, only that the firing across the street stopped. Getting to a safe place and being able to confess and not get in more trouble helped allay his anxiety. I hoped this would also lower the risk that he would continue his violent behavior or induce others into it.

When our child is holding a heavy secret, we need to intuit this and make it safe for our child to confess. Parenting is not the Spanish Inquisition and we do not need to know our child's every "secret," rather we need to spot the times that they are so anxious that whatever they are holding has become too much for them. At times like this they will want to tell us, and a gentle and comforting interest in their plight will often prompt them to spill it all out. We must not fly off the handle when they tell us, but help them grasp the lessons inherent in the natural consequences that stem from their mistakes. This deepens trust and sends the message that when they are in a real quandary or out of their depth, parents are the best people to go to for help.

Tikkun

There is a Jewish mystical creation story where God makes a vessel to hold the world, but the cosmos turns out to be so vast that when God pours it into the vessel it shatters.[1] The world we then come to live in is really just the remnants of a torn and broken former totality. The purpose of life is for each soul to gather up and tend the particular shards of the shattered universe that are meant for them and thus participate in Tikkun—the collective repair of the world.

As parents we provide a psychic and spiritual vessel for our child's self to form within. The world asks so much of children, from disadvantaged to privileged, that sometimes they cannot hold it all and go to pieces. Rather than seeing them as broken Humpty-Dumptys and rushing them to the psychologist for repair, we might consider our children as the most sacred of our shards and lovingly gather them up in the spirit of Tikkun.

Envision What We Want

Take a moment to imagine yourself in a fantasy of tranquility. It may be a spa, a forest, a beach, a mountain—whatever you find calming and transporting. Make it as real as possible; note the sights, smells and sounds. Envision your child feeling safe and confident in your paradise, and then imagine them going back to their "real" life, but in a calm and happy manner; see them feeling good about themselves, being a good friend, trying their best and being proud of their efforts. Having a vision of our child living in joy and harmony empowers us to work toward our child's well-being, rather than against their anxiety.

When I feel anxious I may try to recall the smells of the countryside and the sound of birds and bleating sheep as I walk past ancient ruins with rain falling lightly on my face—and soon I feel just a little better. I may imagine walking along with my happy family or, from this place of recaptured calm I may try to share the spirit of my gratitude and feelings of good fortune with my children, my clients and with you, the reader who may hopefully find encouragement toward your own tranquility in these words.

Strategies For Helping

Given that over-talking does not help anxiety, we strive to make our strategies for helping anxious children simple and concise.

Get Calm

I cannot over-emphasize this. Children respond to our energy as much as to our words and actions. If we want to help our children be calm and secure we must find ways to be calm.

Don't Make It About Ourselves

Question: "How many Jewish Mothers does it take to change a light bulb?" Answer: None ("I'll just sit here in the dark").

Not making our child's anxiety about our own worth or validity is an important strategy for parenting. Not making things all about ourselves is generally a good approach to life—it makes us calmer and more effective and leads to greater freedom and happiness.

Co-dependence and people-pleasing involve manipulation and control, which are Shadow aspects of over-giving. The people-pleaser unconsciously tries to get their needs met vicariously, by making other people happy—and they avoid dealing with their issues by having others hold their problems for them. On the surface they may appear noble and self-sacrificing, but it is not truly selfless giving, it is neurotic giving owing to the lack of a solid self. This is the parent who gives to us but somehow always makes us feel guilty about it. The parent who gives and gives but seems forever depleted, unsatisfied and unhappy over-gives as an unconscious strategy for getting love, or ensuring closeness through making their children remain dependent well into adulthood (i.e. through giving money in ways that block the motivating influence of reality and mute the need to work and grow strong and independent). Manipulation and control in the guise of helping and protecting are likely to worsen anxiety and depression in children.

It can be quite hard to stop making things about us. The wish and intention of this book is to offer love, support and understanding for you, the parent, and hope that the combined effort of my writing and your reading will help us both be less self-conscious and find more calm, love and confidence to share with our children. By being as conscious as we can about our own insecurities and letting them go when we parent we can see our children for who they are and attend to *their* needs and not our secretly projected needs that we might unconsciously place on our child.

Find Some Way To Make Sense Of Things, Even If It Seems Like Non-Sense

A good way to calm an over-excited child, for example as we help them get ready for sleep, is to go over the day and all the things that happened. Even on a good day this helps them find structure for all the stimulation that may still be buzzing around in their heads. On days where painful things happened, big or small, it is even more important and calming to do a sort of post-game wrap up and review of the day's events.

Making sense of nightmares, even in a fantastical or absurd way, can help quiet a child's anxiety. One of my sons had recurring nightmares about being kidnapped by a witch and no amount of reassurance that he was not going to be abducted by an old woman in a babushka could stop the fear until I offered the unconventional idea that maybe he *was* kidnapped, but in a past life. He found this idea comforting and validating and while I have no idea if it could possibly be true, it proved emotionally true and the dreams stopped. It could be that his "past life" was merely the early childhood experiences that he could not recall. The past life idea got me thinking about his early childhood, and we later went on to discuss an alternate, more rational explanation as well. His baby-sitter had taken him to distant parts of the city on a bus when he was very little and had not told us about it, but as my child became able to speak he told us how he had been given treats and told not to tell about the whole thing—which he only dimly remembered. Going to an unfamiliar neighborhood while his babysitter took care of personal business may have felt like being kidnapped by a "witch." Beyond protecting our children from baby-sitters who betray our trust (or simply miscommunicate), once our child is carrying anxiety that we don't understand, we need to find creative ways to make some sort of sense out of fear (even if it means making up stories that may only reflect feelings and not facts) so we can help put fears to bed.

Listen In A Way That Makes Talking Feel Safe For Your Child

Obviously, we don't want to start irresponsibly blaming others for our child's anxiety or making up stories about child-abuse or neglect that never happened, but neither do we want to dismiss our child's fears or shut down their expression of feelings. Helping with fears of witches does not mean going on witch-hunts and vilifying people without evidence; projecting the Shadow is all too easy. Helping a child make sense about what they feel is primarily about helping that child feel validated and taken seriously in their fears—and protected where legitimately necessary. If we listen in ways that make our child feel safe to talk, they will be more able to tell us if, and when, something terrible really does happen to them and trust that we will take steps to protect them and not just tell them they are making it up or that we don't want to hear about it. A number of people I have worked with were abused as children and tried to tell a parent but were met with denial by a fearful grown-up who didn't want to risk their own relationship or whose guilt blocked them from helping their child. This is the sort of scenario that leads to entrenched anxiety as the victimized child must make sense of trauma on their own and may feel unclear about what actually happened, and if it was somehow their own fault—a sure-fire formula for shame, low self-esteem and anxiety.

The more we receive and take a "customer is always right" approach to their complaints and perceptions, the more they will tell us. Keeping the flow of information coming helps our child process their fears and not get bottled up in secrets, shame or isolation. Once our child feels heard and understood they may grow less anxious and then be more open to feedback or suggestions.

Explain The Plan

"What time is it?" "Are we there yet?" "What are we doing today?" "What are we having for dinner?" "What are we doing tomorrow?" Kids like structure and they like to know what the plan is. Very young kids will watch the same DVD over and over and delight in knowing everything that is going to happen. Particularly in times of trouble or transition, spelling out the basic road map (i.e. we will pack up in boxes, then a big truck will come and we will unpack in the new place and eat dinner and have stories and sleep in our new beds) can be very helpful to young (or regressed under stress) kids who cannot necessarily anticipate what we hold to be self-evident.

Exercise

Physical activity is a great way to help manage anxiety. Taking a walk, shooting baskets, hitting golf balls, swimming, bike riding—anything that takes us out of our heads, gets us breathing more deeply and breaks up feeling anxious and stuck is a good plan. When we get our hearts pumping, endorphins bring a natural boost to our mood while we flush the toxins that stagnate when we feel fight/flight adrenaline but neither run nor fight. Burning off those chemicals helps us feel calmer in the short-run and helps us avoid clogged arteries in the long-run. So if our kid is anxious and we run, bike or play ping-pong with them we will help them calm down and feel more connected with us, and we will improve our own mental and physical health as well.

Yoga

Like parenting, yoga has to be experienced to be understood. It is a superlative path to mind-body calm. Some people are uncomfortable with the religious icons in many yoga studios, but yoga is a path we can walk down with Jesus,

Moses, Abraham or Buddha—it's the *walking* that helps us calm down and open ourselves to the universal spirit that transcends us all... transcends all words and images. *That* spirit can easily empower us to be better parents.

Many yoga studios offer pre-natal or mommy and me classes. There are classes geared for young children and, beyond nine or ten years old, we can bring our children to class with us if they are willing. Kids may initially resist yoga as weird and unfamiliar, but it can be just the ticket for an anxious child or adolescent who struggles to quiet their racing mind; if yoga brings them a good feeling by the end of class they may then be interested in doing it again. It is best to make it available but not push and to emphasize the non-competitive and spiritual nature of yoga.

Panic Is All About Breath

Panic attacks feel like a wave of out of control and overwhelming anxiety. Panic attacks come on when our nervousness gets us breathing very fast but shallow, resulting in decreased oxygen to the brain. We become lightheaded and this odd feeling gets misread as something being really wrong and so we get more nervous, breathe even faster and feel even more lightheaded until we are on the verge of losing consciousness. Panic attacks can be so intense that they feel dangerous, but the worst that happens is we do pass out... and return naturally to normal breathing.

If we purposely breath fast and shallow we can actually bring on a panic attack; once we realize we can bring one on, we also realize we can stop a panic attack—by breathing slow and deep when anxious. If our child is prone to panic, we want to emphasize slow deep breathing over talking about the irrational nature of their anxiety as they swoon.

Read Fairy Tales

For children old enough to understand a story like *Hansel and Gretel,* reading fairy tales can be an interesting hedge against anxiety. Fairy tales have a way of taking the forbidden (and mostly unconscious) fears and desires of children and giving them life, but in an arena safely removed from their own day-to-day world. The original Grimm tales are often graphic and gruesome and it may seem counter-intuitive to read such provocative fare to impressionable and wide-eyed innocents, but fairy-tales can serve as a safe vessel into which a child can pour their anxiety. The characters and situations in *Little Red Riding Hood* or *The Three Little Pigs* offer ready-made monsters and witches onto which children can project their own inner turmoil. Unlike movies where a child can be overwhelmed by the filmmaker's imagery, in hearing a story read a child uses their imagination to modulate how graphically they visualize things.

When I read fairy-tales to young children I like to make it clear that the story is "just pretend" and that no matter how scary it might get, it is going to end happily ever after. (Note that some Grimm tales are just plain horrifying, but the classic favorites tend to end reasonably well). If anxiety is the issue, make it a point to read through a story before you just lay it on your child, and use your own judgment about whether it seems okay. When we read fairy-tales to our child we are with them as they imagine scary situations where kids, ne're-do-wells and naive but kind animals triumph over wolves and witches—in other words, the grown-ups.

In *The Uses Of Enchantment,*[2] Bruno Bettleheim psychologically deconstructs a number of classic fairy-tales. With enhanced understanding of underlying meaning, we can select tales to match our child's emotional issues. For example, if a child fears separation or abandonment *Hansel and Gretel* or *Rapunzel* may be helpful, while if monsters loom large in their nightmares, *Little Red Riding Hood* or *The Seven Goats* might be more on target. Bettleheim also suggests *telling* rather than reading fairy-tales to children.

Beyond fairy-tales, books such as *The Miraculous Journey of Edward Tulane* and *Because of Win-Dixie* by Kate DiCamello[3], or *Dear Mr. Henshaw* by Beverly Cleary[4] can be good choices for kids in the nine to twelve range to vicariously deal with the dread of losing a parent and fantasies about being able to survive on their own. Books on tape are an option, not just for holiday travel, but also for trips to and from school, etc. When children have a chance to identify with, and hear about, other children who face adversity, fear, loss and sorrow and nevertheless manage to learn, grow and prevail, it teaches that they too can somehow prevail no matter what happens to them.

Exposure Therapy (A.K.A. Dealing With It)

If we have an irrational fear, however it got started, one of the best ways to get over it is to face that fear and learn that nothing lastingly terrible happens when we do. This is called "exposure" (i.e. to the feared object or situation) with "response prevention" (i.e. not hand-washing). If someone has a phobia about snakes, for example, a therapist who specializes in anxiety disorders may help them make a hierarchy of fears ranging from thinking about snakes to holding a snake. The therapist guides the client to make their way up the hierarchy, first in imagination and later in actuality looking at, and then touching, a snake. By touching a snake and not perishing, the formerly phobic client convincingly learns that they can handle their fear. Now we might think, "Who cares about touching snakes?" But fears tend to generalize, and spread, until yesterday's fear of snakes can become tomorrow's fear of open spaces, crowds or public restrooms.

In severe cases an expert on anxiety disorders is called for, but when it comes to the basic concept of exposure therapy we *can* try this at home. For example, one of my sons became terrified of public restrooms when he was about two years old. It took some time to zero in on the real problem, which turned out to be an abject dread of electric hand-dryers—specifically the loud roar they made.

The cure came progressively. Firstly, with the gentle but firm insistence that we were going to keep trying to get over this fear, even though my child was scared and prepared to never go to the bathroom or wash his hands in public again. We built trust by deliberately going into an empty restroom and simply looking at the dryers from across the way—and then going back out. Next we worked on moving closer to the dryers so he could see the machines better and learn about how they worked without turning them on. Later we worked up to having him stand far away while I turned it on, and finally to my son, held in my arms, triumphantly pressing the button himself and us celebrating and laughing. We may have looked ridiculous but today I am the proud parent of an adolescent who is able to use an electric hand-dryer.

Creative Expression

Sometimes it helps children to put their fears into a tangible form, such as drawing, writing and collage or by playing with dolls or puppets (depending on their age and their expressive style). Perhaps we encourage our kids to draw a picture of the dragon that has been haunting them in their dreams and then make it into a paper airplane that can fly back to its own world. Maybe we help our child make the witch into a paper boat and sail it to witch island (which just so happens to be in the center of that fountain at the mall). Trust the power of symbol and ritual—and make it fun.

By helping a child make up a story about dealing with their fears they engage their own creativity to bring about change. One way to co-create a story is to have our child say the first sentence and then we say the next one, taking turns as the story develops; another option is where they give us characters and settings and we weave them into a story. If we help a child make up a story where the dragon becomes their friend we encourage a spirit of empowerment and integration of their fuller Self. To the extent that we guide and shape the stories, it is better to suggest transformation and integration of the "bad" than aggressive story-lines where monsters, bad-guys or dragons are killed; kids tend to love their dragons even as they fear them and do not want to see their misunderstood, unconscious and primitive aspect killed off. Taming is much better than killing when it comes to our Shadow, as it is not killable anyway and will come back with greater and greater force if we try to kill it off in ourselves.

Humor

Humor is a healthy coping strategy for life's pain, especially if we can gently and affectionately laugh at ourselves. Comedy is also laced with anxiety. As a character in a Woody Allen film says, "Comedy is tragedy plus time."[5] Most comedy is based on watching other people in painful or humiliating situations; we laugh partly out of relief that it is not us and partly in anxious identification with the character in pain, having felt those feelings ourselves. With laughter we release anxiety and tension. Laughing releases good chemicals in the brain and helps lift mood and enhance healing. Laughter can be spiritual—even the Dalai Lama is prone to childlike bursts of it.

To really know our child, and enjoy them, is to know their humor and be able to laugh together with them. Kids love to tell jokes and our best Self is a good audience. If a young child fears monsters we might be able to get them laughing by inviting them to imagine the stinky brute in his underwear tripping and making a big mess. Little kids are easy to crack-up and a good laugh can release a lot of anxiety and help shift the bad character into a vulnerable, funny and even friendly character. If we have an anxious child we might watch comedy with them (*Mr. Bean*, Buster Keaton, *School Of Rock* depending on their age)[6] and notice whether some good laughs ameliorate their anxiety or not.

Laughing is cathartic—when we laugh we are in the present moment. When we find ourselves laughing hard from our gut at the same time as our child we drink in the sweetness of parenting in the here and now.

Exercises To Consider

1. Do things that make you a little anxious: Consider some situations or things that scare or disturb you; going to a restaurant alone with a book, or going to a party where you don't know anyone and talking to one new person. It could be capturing

227

a spider and letting it out of the house if you are afraid of spiders. By confronting our own fears we deepen our empathy for our child's fears. And whether or not our child sees or knows about our attempts to overcome our limitations we become calmer and more confident in the service of our child. If our self-directed "exposure therapy" works, we can gently encourage and support our child to do things that makes them a little anxious—maybe join a sports team, ask someone over for a play-date or work up to petting a dog if they have a fear of dogs. By doing the things that scare them (but which are not really all that dangerous), our child can increase their sense of self and their positive self-esteem through success experiences.

2. Read to your child's anxiety: When we read stories that thematically relate to our child's anxiety we speak to their inner situation without raising their level of discomfort by making things too directly about their issues. Think about an issue that gives your child fear or anxiety. Try to distill the issue down to its essence: for example, is it more about the wish to get love, to be powerful or about a wish to feel safe? If a child seems to feel unloved (maybe due to sibling rivalries, parental conflict or a sense that their own differences have made friendships difficult or scarce), consider tales where love comes, but after much trial and tribulation such as "Sleeping Beauty," "Rapunzel" or "The Frog Prince." If our child struggles with feeling inadequate, dumb or ugly, stories like "The

228

Ugly Duckling," "The Three Languages" or "The White Snake" might be good. If a child is terrified of witches, boogey men or monsters, stories like "The Three Little Pigs," "Little Red Riding Hood" or "Jack And The Beanstalk" could bring relief by allowing a child to vicariously experience fear and resolution. Often a child will really respond to a particular tale and want to hear it multiple times—this is a sign that you are on the right track and they are drinking in what you are providing.

3. Fear into art: If our child is struggling with a specific fear we can shift gears from logical explanation, into a fun art activity. We don't need to spell out the purpose (which might make them resistant), instead we want to make things light and if they are wondering what to draw, we might casually suggest they draw that monster, bully or problem they were worried about. If a child feels overwhelmed by anxiety, they can gather objects or cut out pictures related to their fears and put them in a special box. This may help them "put away" obsessive thoughts and emotions so they can have times of respite from worry. Here a shoebox becomes a transitional "bowl" in the service of developing a more containing self.

4. Shadow work through active imagination: In active imagination we recall a dream and vividly imagine that we are back in it, but with our waking consciousness. Active Imagination can turn enemies into allies and mentors. We can dialogue with our inner monster, villain or

wicked stepparent and say something to the effect, "I know that you are a part of me. What message, complaint, gift or guidance might you have for me?" We might get coaching on how to get what we consciously want (i.e. a better relationship with our child), or wisdom about what is wanted for us by our deep Self (i.e. to relinquish fear and rise to our potential through loving and being of service to our children and the world). If our child has bad dreams we can coach them in active imagination and help them dialogue with their Shadow to creatively transform terror into playfulness, confidence and personal power.

5. Unlock anger: Anxiety draws us into our shell where we may stew in isolation, resentment and anger, but if we can find a way to let anger and resentment be expressed and released this moves us out of ourselves and back to the world. We can sometimes free up our anxious (and secretly angry) children by inviting them to (in a safe context) throw rocks, break, smash, splash, shout, tear, cut, etc. By making it a cathartic sort of game and being together with them as they get their stuck energy moving, our child learns to let things out and also learns that their anger and aggression do not have to be a secret that separates them from us.

6. Yoga for fear and anxiety: Yoga is a very good remedy for anxiety. Remember to dedicate your yoga to something—for example, to your child's well-being. Then your yoga can harmonize

parenting goals and spiritual growth. If your child will consider it, a beginning level yoga class or a DVD at home can be a great thing to do together and a way to build confidence, balance, strength, tranquility and introduce the concept of non-competitive success. Particular poses that decrease anxiety include hip openers (fire-log, pigeon) to help release the stress, sorrow and anxiety we hold there; child's pose and down-dog are grounding; forward bends (seated or standing) are cooling; mountain pose (standing still and straight) and tree pose are balancing; supported bridge, shoulder-stand or legs up the wall pose (Viparita Karani) are very calming and restorative; and Savasana (or corpse pose) really cuts to the heart of letting go of everything including anxiety.

Chapter 7

Understanding and Dealing
With Oppositionality

"Out beyond ideas of right and wrong there is a field. I'll meet you there." Rumi

The Impossible Child

Sophie is four. She is adorable, smart—and a nightmare. Friends come over and Sophie declares that other people's things belong to her. She lies, fabricating elaborate and highly creative stories to manipulate and control every situation. Whatever anyone says to Sophie, or about her, she says the opposite.

She has hit babysitters, repeatedly hurt her generally loving eight-year-old brother and provokes her parents into atypical moments of shouting that seem utterly out of character with their calm and kind personalities—moments which are becoming sadly more typical.

Sophie demands and receives attention like a diva and flies into rages when challenged or confronted with any limit. When she blows, everyone is in for forty-plus minutes of ear-splitting and unstoppable screaming. The entire family has become structured around doing everything possible to not set Sophie off. Her exhausted and broken-hearted parents love her and want her to be happy and since they have another

child who is not a nightmare it can't be *entirely* their fault...
still, they guiltily look forward to times of respite when they
are not with her.

So what's really bothering Sophie, and what could be done
to help her and her parents? Is it chemical? Developmental?
Emotional? Could it be an enactment of hidden depression in
the parents or unspoken conflict between them? How do we
tell "normal," albeit frustrating, oppositional or limit-testing
behavior from more serious underlying problems of which
oppositional behavior is just a symptom?

This chapter is about deepening our understanding of,
and compassion for, the child who is driven to act out and
be oppositional; mouthy, rude, disrespectful, defiant, deceit-
ful and even violent or destructive. It's also about helping
you, the parent, deal gracefully and effectively with this
behavior. Although your child may only occasionally exhibit
rude, disrespectful or defiant behaviors, the techniques in this
chapter will prove all the more relevant to, and effective for,
minor-league or relatively fleeting problems— and help prevent them from escalating into more daunting challenges. So,
while situations like Sophie's could be the result of a number
of different factors, there are some general approaches and
attitudes, which we will explore and encourage, that tend
to facilitate calm and reduce chronic conflict. As with other
parenting challenges, it is easier to know, theoretically, what
to do (i.e. balance love and limits, be consistent, not make
things all about ourselves) than it is to actually be able to *do*
them, especially to do them consistently. Therefore this chapter is, at heart, about encouraging you, through deeper understanding of your child and your dynamics with them, to find
more patience, non-judgment and tenderness for your child

and for yourself. In the context of better relationships with us, our children's relationships with themselves can naturally improve and their negative behaviors spontaneously transform. Just try to remain open to the possibility of healing.

Is My Kid Out of Control?

"Out of control" is a relative term. Much depends on our past experiences as a parent. Our first baby's first tantrum has a different impact on us than our second child's umpteenth one. When my two-year-old pitched his first true fit at a restaurant, we were utterly unprepared for its sheer ferocity as he howled, kicked and literally climbed the walls. Public displays of oppositionality feel all the more intense as we parents may feel scrutinized and judged by others.

Out of control behavior generally suggests a child's need for more containing limits. If a small child throws their toys on the ground that is par for the course, but if an older child or teenager breaks things in anger, if fights result in stitches or other significant injuries or if we ourselves break things, use physical aggression or abuse substances or alcohol then things, sadly, are already out of control and the purpose of these words is to sincerely encourage you to seek treatment for yourself and your family.

Who? What? Where? When? And Why?

As we strive to understand and help diminish our child's "bad" behaviors it can be useful to try and be as objective and non-judgmental as possible. We can take another look at our child's situation through the lens of the journalist, asking, "Who? What? Where? When? And Why?"

"Who": We must consider a child's age, their developmental level, their physical and neurological wellness, their temperament, past experiences, and other unique qualities. Tantrums are never fun, but two or three-year-old children are virtually expected to tantrum; whereas chronic out-of-control tantrums in a ten-year-old are more of a concern.

Claire was eight when she suddenly started to have extreme rages. Her parents wondered what they were doing wrong. The pediatrician was concerned and after a series of tests they discovered that a brain tumor was causing the behavior. Although the vast majority of time a child's negative behavior does not mean they have a tumor, it's important to rule out physical problems before concluding that a problem is emotional. Once Claire had proper medicine the rages were brought more under control. As scary as the situation was, it was essential to discover the real problem and treat her tumor. After that, it was still important to help her cope with the moods and outbursts, which were as terrifying to Claire as they were to her family. Knowing that she truly could not control her behavior helped her parents be compassionate and containing rather than seeing her, or themselves, as "bad."

It is important to distinguish a child who refuses to do things from a child who can't stay focused and fails to comply with directives despite actually trying his best. A kid who is truly oppositional is often acting out emotional issues while a kid who has Attention Deficit Disorder (ADD) and is *unable* to focus can easily end up feeling stupid, ashamed and unlikeable *because* of their differences. Undiagnosed and untreated ADD can then, over time, lead to feelings of anger, low self-esteem and school avoidance, which can be misread as oppositional defiant behavior. An oppositional teen could be struggling with ADD as both an underlying issue that needs attention *and* a contributing factor to their oppositionality born of anger and lowered self-esteem. Oppositionality and acting out may be a child's cry for help that has grown loud, messy and disagreeable after meeker cries for help fell on deaf ears.

"What": What does our child actually *do* when they are acting out or opposing us? Is it mostly yelling, refusing, crying, insulting, physical aggression, lying, stealing, etc.? Do they break things? If so, what do they break? Do they oppose everything we ask or just some things? If so, which things? Knowing the particular "what" of their problematic behavior is part of cracking the code of learning what's wrong and helping them.

"Where" and "When:" Do problems happen mostly in the morning when everyone is rushed and stressed? Or is weekend time with less structure when it all breaks down? Is bed or bath time the witching hour, or does their blood sugar drop in mid-afternoon when they get fussy or worse? Do they act out primarily at home or at school? During certain subjects or sports; on the bus, in crowds, or at the store? If we can read the clues about where and when they feel threatened or overwhelmed we can better help them feel safe and good about themselves and there will be diminished need for chronic bad behavior.

"Why:" When our kids defy or insult are they *trying* to make us feel terrible or just discharging tension they can't hold? It's possible that our suffering child unconsciously makes us feel powerless or dejected as a way of getting us to feel the way they feel.

The more we place ourselves in our child's shoes and ask ourselves, "Why would *I* yell, lie, throw things, etc.?" the closer we get to breaking through the angry isolation of their pain. We yell when we don't feel heard. We refuse to do things when we can't see the point of doing them—when we think we will only fail, or be just as bad off as we were if we didn't bother at all. Maybe we get more attention when we are difficult and contrary than when we are easy.

Josh Is Just Like His Father (Who's in Prison)

Josh was a skinny nine-year-old with big expressive eyes who came to the community mental health clinic with his mom—who had been sent by the court. The boy sat meekly as his mother practically pleaded with me to protect her from this alleged monster-child who had repeatedly hit her, threatened her with broken glass and caused her to barricade herself in her room and call the police.

Josh's mom was a sturdy woman twice the size of her son, but she reported that he had dominated and hurt her ever since he was an infant. When I enquired into the boy's early life and the whereabouts of his father I was horrified to learn that the man had not only been violent and brutish, but had actually beaten the mother *with* the infant Josh—using the boy as a weapon to hurt her. Poor Josh had been scripted right down to his cells to attack is mother, and she had been scripted to play the victim. The father had left when Josh was still in his crib, but they were continuing to play out the initial drama/trauma nine years later.

Whatever it was that drew Josh's mom to be attracted to a violent abuser in the first place may have also driven her to unconsciously script her child to be a dysfunctional partner and container for her own unconscious rage and aggression. In attacking his mom, Josh was also unconsciously reenacting the trauma of his infancy, as the assault on the mother had also been a bashing of his own body as well; unaware of the real story, he was driven to re-live it... and each time he was "bad," Josh was reinforced to believe that he truly was bad to his core—just like his father. Kids are impressionable and Josh had been pervasively taught that he was bad, and had little choice but to "please" his mother by agreeing with her and playing the part of the villain. It was poignant how he seemed to try and do his best as the bad guy, but was unconvincing in his role. He showed no rage or irritability as he good-naturedly agreed with his mom that he attacked and terrified her. It was odd to see his playfulness and sense of humor in contrast to his mom's melodramatic pathos—chronically worried, not about her child, but about herself.

If our child has been traumatized, abused or rejected (directly, or by vicariously witnessing cruelty and abuse), we need to help them better understand what they've been through and liberate them from the need to continually act it out—and we need to free them from playing any sort of destructive roles that we might unconsciously need them to play. Time and again, chronic parent self-focus (i.e. on our own fears, needs, etc.) seems to show up in families where kids are acting out.

Rites of Initiation, Rites of Passage

Sometimes oppositionality in children is best understood as a normal side-effect of transitioning to a new level of development. Throughout history teenagers have had to find a way to become adults. Some cultures have structured rituals and ceremonies to help kids manage the process of initiation into power and responsibility. Such rites of passage create structure for transitioning into adulthood without necessarily needing to tear down the old society (and the poor grown-ups who represented that society). It makes sense that modern children and teenagers may feel overwhelmed and bewildered about how to become the next, more grown-up, version of themselves. Falling apart, regressing, tantruming and being oppositional may be ways that our kids express their inner confusion and need for us parents to help at least frame the questions that they face about who they are and what they are supposed to make of their lives in an ever-changing world.

The destructive aspects of teen rebellion are neither personal nor pointless, even if they make us parents feel confused, devalued and attacked. Without clearly defined rites of passage, each generation of teens must invent not only themselves as young men and women but their own unique *way* of becoming those selves; one generation does it hanging out on the corner, the next hangs out at the mall and the next does it on online, which will itself, soon enough, be old-school. Throw-away kids with bleak prospects may engage in violence as an initiation into adulthood while the privileged trek off to expensive colleges where their relatively tepid rebellion is often fully funded by mom and dad; frats may be joined, beer ingested, mid-terms and finals come and go, and in the end it's not uncommon for the young person to end up back in his parents' house with neither clue nor inclination for truly making his (or her) way in the world. Adolescence for the well-off tends to be very drawn out, with true adulthood beginning in earnest around twenty-seven, while many disadvantaged kids have told me that they didn't expect to live to see thirty.

With or without privilege, the messy process of self-transformation often calls for kids to define themselves in stark contrast to those of who came before them—and so a natural dynamic of "us" (the kids) and "them" (we the parents) gets set up in the service of identity consolidation. By holding limits (i.e. curfews) we provide a force for our kids to challenge, oppose and define themselves against. One key aspect of effectively parenting the transitioning rebel is to not personalize their temporary need to see us as lacking in order to see themselves as adequate.

Innocence, Angst and Sociopathy

Todd is a mischievous kindergartener with impulse control issues who threw something in class and hit another child in the head. He was sent to the principal, a moment most five-year-olds would presumably dread, but Todd pointed his finger at her and said, "You're dead meat!" The principal had to momentarily leave the room… in order to hide her laughter. Obviously Todd was out of control, but to really understand this situation it might help to know that the child's father happens to be a comedian who makes his living being outrageous. Out of context this kid might sound like the demon seed, but actually he's a sweet kid who needs a little coaching about limits and respect. Comedy and acting out behaviors are both based on pain and anxiety; when clowns and comics suffer we laugh, but when our kids suffer and act out we cry.

Since most of the time kids behave reasonably well, provided they feel safe and good about themselves, we can think of "bad" behavior as a barometer of underlying unhappiness. Mildly upset or fussy kids are difficult in the moment and get back to normal relatively quickly; *oppositional* kids have fallen into repetitive patterns of being difficult as their cry for help grows louder and louder (i.e. "what's it going to take to get my parents to realize that I feel truly hopeless and need limits and guidance?"). By the time a child has moved onto *conduct disordered* behavior (i.e. vandalism, theft, hurting others or animals for their own amusement) we have to ask ourselves if the cry for help has been taken to the streets, or to the heavens, in the hope someone beyond the family may notice and do something. It is when compassion and empathy die that sociopathy is born; it is a mystery as to how much of this is genetic versus environmental, but if our best efforts at love and discipline fail to help our child, our obligation as parents is to reach out to the wider world for wisdom, guidance and assistance. Secrets, shame and denial will only make the troubled son or daughter more defiant and rebellious; asking for help as a parent models trust and humility for our children.

Why Aren't We Getting Along Better with Our Kids?

What's In Our Child's Way?

If children who feel safe, loved and secure are generally pretty well behaved, and our child is relentlessly oppositional we want to ask ourselves what could be making them feel anxious, unlovable or inadequate?

1) Lack of Attention

Children thrive on attention. Feeling noticed, known and understood by us parents is a primary way that children are able to take in the love that we have for them. Listening to what our children think and feel is the sort of attention that nourishes the developing soul and makes kids feel centered, tranquil and like they matter—and reduces oppositionality.

2) Lack of Limits

Children feel calm and safe when there are clear limits, rules, boundaries and expectations about what behavior is okay and what is not. It is natural for kids to test what they can get away with, but when there are no limits it makes them anxious. Setting and holding limits is exhausting, but in the long run it saves work and does right by our kids.

3) <u>Lack of Consequences</u>

While limits are highly important, when kids cross the line on the clearly defined expectations of behavior (i.e. when they are disrespectful, aggressive, destructive, etc.) there should be consequences. Consequences should not be about us discharging our frustration ("That's it—no more TV for a week!"); nor should it be that the same infraction gets a consequence when we are in a bad mood but we let it slide when we are in a good mood. Be consistent, patient and emotionally neutral when you give consequences; this is effective teaching, which is what consequences are really about. Also, with discouraged, oppositional kids, you can take every "thing" (and privilege) away and they may not seem to care (or at least not improve their behavior). Depressed kids lack motivation and while we need unpleasant consequences at times, the vast majority of our effort should be on positive consequences—on noticing, praising, being interested.

4) <u>Too Much Stuff</u>

Besides making kids spoiled and obscuring any sense of what has value, giving kids too much places an over-emphasis on things rather than on people and relationships. The result of this is that kids may then start to treat others as dismissively as they treat their unappreciated over-abundance of toys, games, gadgets and clothes.

As a culture, we are terribly lonely. We strive to acquire things and achieve goals, yet often end up disillusioned by the emptiness we feel. Contemplating our own materialism and whether we give "things" rather than love and attention may inspire us to hang out more with our kids and include them more in our lives.

5) <u>Poor Role Models</u>

If we find ourselves with a rude, mouthy or obnoxious child we must ask ourselves, "Where did they learn that?" If our child is disrespectful to teachers or baby-sitters we need to consider whether we are rude and dismissive to the people our kids see us interact with (i.e. waiters, clerks, nannies, people on the street or on the road when we drive). If we don't like what we see in our child, we might need to take a look in the mirror and make some changes—not just in the way we parent, but in the way we interact with everyone in our lives.

6) <u>Inappropriate Shows and Games</u>

Perhaps allowing our children to watch shows where rudeness and aggression are modeled contributes to their negative behaviors (i.e. to the *way* they express their frustration or unhappiness). Another negative influence on kid behavior comes from violent, anti-social interactive games. When children role-play aggression, cruelty and problem-solving through violence they increase their likelihood of turning to those strategies in real life when they are frustrated or want to get their way. Games can be addictive, giving a false sense of mastery, power and accomplishment, (i.e. "I beat the level!") and depriving children of other activities where they might develop actual self-esteem, social relationships or skills. Games also hijack the brain and create the false experience of bodily activity while leaving the actual body sedentary, which can lead to chronic exhaustion. On top of everything else, spacey and over-tired kids are not likely to be at their best in terms of responsiveness, respectfulness or happiness.

7) <u>Depression and Underlying Low Self-Esteem</u>

The wellspring of defiant and oppositional behavior is unhappiness and not feeling good about oneself. Happy kids are generally well behaved, so if our kid is behaving badly we might need to see it as a symptom of inner suffering. This perspective can help us shift our thinking from blame and irritation toward compassion and helping.

Depression often shows up as anger and defiance, particularly in males. Understanding that our angry young man or woman may be depressed could be a good first step to improving both their mood and behavior. If life feels like it sucks for our kid, we will get nowhere lecturing them about how fortunate they are and ought to feel (i.e., how wrong they are to feel unhappy); if instead we finally get the message that they are hurting and we are willing to listen, perhaps they will feel less alone and it will help them heal—and behave better.

8) <u>Medical or Neurological Problems</u>

As mentioned earlier, sometimes a child's contrary, erratic or explosive behavior has its roots in underlying medical or neurological conditions. Children with ADD, for example, may appear oppositional owing to trouble staying focused—and so asking them to do things they cannot do only lowers self-esteem and may provoke them to "act out" their anger and frustration. Rages, intense mood fluctuations and oppositionality can also be part of the diagnostic picture with depression and Bipolar disorders, underscoring the need for a thorough evaluation when our child's behavior goes beyond what we instinctively feel is normal.

What's In Our Way?

If our child is angry and oppositional it's fair to at least ask ourselves if we might be failing them in some way. Some of the usual suspects include:

1) <u>Our Painful Past</u>

A good question to ask ourselves if our child is suddenly having problems is, "What was our life like when we were the age our child is now?" Our kids drag us through all the memories, conscious and unconscious, of our own childhood as they develop. Sometimes our child's "crisis" is really our own secret crisis and a message that it's time to get some help and put our own demons to rest.

2) <u>We Can't Stand to be Seen as the "Bad" Person</u>

We may be so invested in being the loving parent that we are uncomfortable being an authority figure. This may be particularly true if we had harsh, cruel or volatile parents, or if we grew up in the uncertainty and explosiveness of an alcoholic or drug-abusing household. Kids need limits in order to feel safe, and if we are "nice" to the point of being overly lenient then we fail them; our "niceness" eventually feels like weakness, which creates anxiety in children. Being firm is kinder than giving in; we can be compassionate about our children's frustration when we hold the line on things like safety, chores, school work, proper nutrition or hygiene, but we still have to hold the line. Also, if we play the role of indulgent push-over but expect our spouse to be the "bad guy" this leaves the parenting team wide-open to a divide and conquer strategy by the children. Kids need both parents to model successful limit-setting to help them learn how to say "no" to unhealthy or unsafe behaviors, substances and situations.

3) <u>Our Low Self-Esteem</u>

Our ability to pay attention to our child, and hold boundaries and limits, is impeded if we lack a positive sense of self. Symptoms of low self-esteem include rudeness to others, lack of positive relationships and self-destructive behaviors, all of which model a problematic example for our child. Without the bowl of self, we struggle to contain our own feelings much less hold the overflow emotions of our children. When we fail to help our children with the intensity of their feelings, they may come into conflict with us because they are frustrated and feel uncontained. If nothing else has done it, perhaps our child's pain-driven negativity can mark the tipping point that gets us into therapy (or 12-step recovery, meditation, yoga, etc.) to confront our own wounds and build healthy self-esteem.

4) <u>Finding Closeness In Conflict</u>

Some of us are uncomfortable with direct affection and kindness. Perhaps we have learned from our parents' example that shouting, slamming doors, leaving and coming back, fighting and making up, etc., is how people show each other that they care. If there is chronic conflict between us and our child we need to take note of our own patterns of behavior such as creating drama by being moody, inconsistent or volatile; maybe we tend to stir up jealousy, insecurity, feelings of exclusion or shame.

5) <u>We Might Have ADD or Another Diagnosis that Interferes with Parenting</u>

Given that our paying consistent attention is so important for our children, if as parents we might possibly have Attention Deficit Disorder (ADD) this might be something we want to identify and seek treatment for. If we had a lot of trouble staying focused in school, are always "on the go" and like to multi-task while finding it hard to stay with any one thing for long, we might talk to our doctor about ADD to see if it could be an issue for us. Obviously an ADD kid and an ADD parent could be either a recipe for understanding and empathy or for unfocused disaster. Getting appropriate help for ourselves is an act of love and good parenting for our children.

6) <u>We Have an Addiction</u>

If our child is oppositional, and acting out, they are certainly suffering from something. We parents need to be sure that it is not because we have a drinking or drug problem (or because we are enabling a spouse or partner with these addictions). A household in which caregivers are fighting over substance abuse, are emotionally unavailable, or passed-out or in which the parents must be lied about, covered for, or taken care of by their kids is going to leave children feeling angry and anxious. Their oppositionality and rebellion may be our last chance to wake up, heal and hold onto them before they take their needs to the outside world, where they are all too likely to follow in their parents' footsteps or else attach themselves to someone with the same sort of problems they are used to catering to. If this sounds even remotely like your situation, go to AA or Al-Anon, just in case, and let *them* tell you that you don't need to be there.

Broadening Our Perspective

Drama is Conflict

Leo Tolstoy, in the famous first line of *Anna Karenina*, says, "All happy families resemble one another, but each unhappy family is unhappy in its own way." When it comes to novels, plays and films, happy families are *boring*, but the key ingredient for happy family life is lack of conflict or minimal drama and respectfully handled conflict.

In The Age of the Child, the Parent is a Hero for Our Time

While doing for others is a defining characteristic of the hero, it is a quality expected of parents. The essence of leadership is service, but if our children are failing to follow, we must ask ourselves if we are failing to lead. Every era has its particular sort of hero, such as prophet, king or revolutionary—those who stand for what is prized, or needed, in a given epoch. It is my conviction that the biggest need we have, in our families and in our larger world, is for a more compassionate understanding of how we all share this planet and need to take better care of it and each other—starting with our children. The heroes who are fit to lead, inspire and encourage our world are those women and men who are ready, willing and able to take loving care of it—in short, to parent it.

Parents have always loved their children, but at no time in history have we had such a child-focused culture of specialists, books, activities and expectations of, and for, our kids— not to mention so many parenting books. The collective hunger for support in parenting reflects a zeitgeist of insecurity, perhaps born of the of the paternalistic "science" that rose to dominance in the middle of the last century, and which divided many a parent from her instincts (i.e. suggesting that formula from a bottle was superior to breast milk). While these ideas may now seem misguided and out of fashion, the insecurity they bred ripples to the present day; we may have traded in the *flavor* of our parenting gurus and experts, but not quite gotten back to actually trusting our own instincts. While I like, espouse and may embody many of these new ideas as a "parenting-expert" in my own right, my central point is that they are only guidelines; when they are blindly embraced by insecure parents as unbending doctrine, they are no longer natural nor holistic in practice. The call to the hero's journey as a parent is all about leaving the wide, and at times crunchy, trail and heading into the forest of our own true path with our own children—learning to trust ourselves *through* stepping up to do the unsung hard work of being there for our kids and by learning, via our own trials and errors, what works for us and our children. Passionately doing this is heroic. On the other hand, times, and cultures, do actually change and our massive collective wish to be our best Selves as parents also reflects an ascending ethic of healing, nurturing and appreciating our children and the world we will leave them—a newly emerging, care-giving-as-heroic, zeitgeist. While we must each find a way to make parenting our own, by doing this as our best Selves we meet again in the collective town square to discover that we have made a better world for ourselves and for our children.

Parenting is a role, but it is also an *attitude*. We bring the spirit of the parent as hero to life in the way we interact with our children. The parent-hero may be the actual parent of a child, but she may also be a teacher, a nanny, a grandparent—anyone who steps up to get involved in child-rearing, educating, guiding and nurturing. This quiet sort of hero *relates* to and tends the world rather than conquering, exploiting or controlling it. I see these caregiver heroes showing up all around us—on field trips, at baseball and soccer games, at yoga class. I hear her compassionate heroism in the loving way she talks about everyone's children at carpool, and in the way one man roots for the other man's daughter as well as his own. It serves us parents to rethink our beliefs about what constitutes the hero. This may help us deepen our respect for, and improve our relationships with, the nannies, coaches, teachers and therapists with whom our children interact.

Teaching Manners in a Culture of Entitlement

Manners are extremely important; they are a way of expressing kindness and genuine regard for others. Just as the original purpose of shaking hands was to show that our hand held no weapon, good manners help us find our place in the group in a positive and life-affirming way. Manners are more than the shared rules of an organized society; they are a culture's language of values, respect, inclusion, trust and cooperation. Manners help us connect with each other and find joy, meaning and community—when we feel those things we are much less likely to be oppositional, destructive or hurtful to others. When we model and teach manners we equip our children to positively adapt to the world and find their place in the group; the children who *we* fail to bring into the warmth of the group turn in opposition against us, the disappointing or rejecting parents, teachers and authority figures. Alfred Adler, who coined the term "inferiority complex," felt that if we could not find a socially positive way to be true to ourselves *and* contribute to the group our essential nature would express itself in opposition to the group, even in criminality; manners help us put our gifts and our authentic character to use in the service of society.

We must not yell, dominate or make any child feel small or stupid, as cruelty is the antithesis of manners. Our overbearing behavior may initially seem impressive to a child, but it is not impressive in the grand scheme things and tends to be copied by our child and look dreadfully boorish when it comes back at us. Our children may justify rude behavior by saying, "so and so does it," to which we must teach compassion for "so and so's" ignorance, unfortunate circumstances and/or low self-esteem. As the Tao Te Ching teaches, "What is a good man but a bad man's teacher; what is a bad man but a good man's charge?"

Good manners show self-respect and good self-esteem. If we yell at housekeepers or devalue waiters we are insecure and trying to toss off our bad feelings onto others. A pervasive sense of entitlement is a psychological symptom, not something to be proud of or aspire to; an approach to the world of getting what we want and others be damned is a compensation for underlying feelings of inadequacy and sends a perpetual message to our kids (and ourselves) that we cannot get what we want or need by being honest, caring and decent. This only deepens feelings of inadequacy and isolation and we end up perpetuating the very same ill-mannered world that we use to justify our shabby behavior.

Many of the parents with whom I work want concrete suggestions for improving their child's manners; the following are some ideas to consider:

- Make dinner a teachable moment where all wait to eat until everyone has been served and/or has sat down. Hold to the expectation that children stay at the table until everyone has finished. This communicates that they are wanted at the table and are an important part of the family group.
- Teach and model being genuinely attentive: this means looking people in the eye when you speak to

them, inquiring how others are doing, and paying attention to their responses.

- Do not use expletives or other words that you do not want your children to use; consider that even if you personally do not mind profanity, it may be inconsiderate for you, or your children, to use these words in front of others.

- Driving aggressively and angrily models rude behavior, and it may frighten and even endanger your child. Similarly, cutting in lines at the store or speaking loudly on the phone in public spaces teaches entitlement and a general disregard for others.

- Shouting at your child, or other children, during their sporting events/games is bad form (and ineffective coaching to boot).

- Beyond saying thank-you when we are given something, thanking others for coming over (i.e. for play-dates) helps create good-will and communicates a feeling of being liked and valued to the other; this teaches our children how to be gracious and put others at ease—which cuts past social convention and gets to the heart of good manners by treating others with true kindness and consideration.

Materialism

Often it seems that wealth and privilege breed just as much rudeness and oppositional discontent as do poverty and deprivation. While it is fairly easy to understand why children living in a group home or suffering from neglect or emotional pain might be prone to rage, tantrum and disrespect people and property, it is harder to comprehend why highly fortunate (at least materially) children might behave with absolute contempt for parents, teachers, peers, nannies and virtually everyone with whom they come in contact.

We may think we lack enough money, but what we really probably lack enough of is time. When our kids get a lot of "things" instead of time and attention from us, they feel empty and this pushes them toward negative behaviors—both to express anger and frustration and to try and get our attention by any means they can come up with.

It makes sense to think of materialism more broadly than being only about "things" like cars and clothes; the "things" our family prizes may be about status or power such as degrees, titles, trophies, report-card grades or admissions to Ivy-League colleges. Sometimes we do too much for our kids and are then dismayed when they seem unable to do anything for themselves and have zero frustration tolerance for things like sports or homework. Sometimes our well-intentioned but over-anxious wish to facilitate excellence can end up squelching it. Perhaps it is our own anxiety and narcissistic need to appear successful through our child (or get a re-do of our childhood) that makes us push our child aside and reach for their kindergarten, fourth or eighth grade project and pretend we're helping when we are really doing it for them. The diorama, poster or video arrives at class looking amazing, but the teacher and our child both know that we, the parent, did it. This too is materialism in that it tells our kid that the product must be excellent, even if this means cheating, while the all-important *process* of learning and growing is devalued and denied to them. Over time, our child becomes more intimidated to take chances and try things and their anxious avoidance starts to look more and more like oppositionality.

When a family's ethic is too focused on achievement or acquiring things, children themselves may start to feel like "things" that exist in order to generate pride and glory for their parents. If our kids cannot meet our misguided or inflated expectations they may give up, and to us relentlessly achieving parents this looks like oppositionality. Even when they do achieve, these children may end up feeling alienated and disillusioned in the midst of their lonely accomplishments; they eventually *must* rebel because to conform is to follow a path that they intuitively sense leads to the restless unhappiness of their parents. Many a rebel is born out of families that look good on the outside but are privately disconnected and depressed. Yet, sadly, rebelling is really just conforming in the opposite direction; and it is just as unlikely to lead to authentic happiness. Happiness is not about *anti*-materialism. We can have a lot of things and be great parents, provided we are truly happy and thankful for our blessings—we just can't be miserable and expect our children to be happy and well-behaved, much less to be enthusiastic about chasing after the same sorts of things that have failed to bring us peace, happiness or the true "success" of being a loving, generous and secure human being.

Hate and Love

A mom came into my office one day clutching a letter that her thirteen-year-old daughter had written and left conspicuously for her to find. It was a poison pen rant against this mother, who was criticized for everything from her hair to having no friends to being totally ugly to the opposite sex. The crass language would have made a rapper blush, and hate dripped off the page. My client sat on the therapy

255

couch stunned, her face streaked with tears, her hands literally shaking with hurt. None of the insults in the letter fit either the bright, charming and attractive mother nor her equally bright, charming (usually) and attractive kid; the vehemence of the attack, however, did indicate that the child was stressed, insecure about herself and spilling her pain over into her mother.

It took some convincing to help this mother see that the letter was really a twisted sort of love letter. The opposite of love is not hate but indifference, and her daughter was far from indifferent. Once the mother accepted that the letter was about her daughter's need for containment and not about the mother's allegedly unruly hair, she resolved to try and help her daughter by not crumbling, personalizing or retaliating—by being the grown-up and loving her daughter even in the face of insult and attack.

The proof of this approach was in the pudding; by the next session the mother and daughter were closer than ever, the daughter was behaving much better and feeling better about herself. Her hateful outpouring turned out to be a momentary convergence of hormones, transitions and stress about her parents' troubled relationship. By being loving and gracious my client was able to contain her daughter's painful feelings and at the same time feel better about herself and her parenting by seeing that it was effective.

When our kids actively hate us it hurts, but there is strong emotional contact with them and great possibility for positive change if we are able to love in the face of hate. Conflict is unpleasant, but it is an opportunity to taste the essence of what plagues our child when they bring their pain directly to our hearts with their vitriol and savagery. While we want harmony with happy kids, their in-our-face anger is full of hope, love, need and possibility… if we realize that it's not all about us.

Splitting

Splitting is the oldest play in the kid playbook: if mom says no, try dad, if you like dad's answer go with it, if you get busted by mom say, "Dad said it was okay." That's called splitting: if you're a kid you divide in order to conquer (and while you have to try, you secretly hope that you will fail). The parents' task is to remain a unified team and hash conflict out later, politely and behind closed doors. The more we present a unified front the better contained our child will feel and the better we will feel in our marriage, or even in our divorce.

We aid and abet splitting when we share secrets with our child and exclude the other parent; it can burden children with guilt and place the other parent in the unfortunate roles of third wheel, ogre or irrelevant fool. "Don't tell your father" and "Don't tell your mother" are tantamount to giving our child slow-acting poison. Our kids need parents to respect and support each other and resist competing for the child's favor.

Splitting is like "Red Rover": parents set limits and kids respond to them as a challenge and try to break through; if we hold the line we get them on our side, if we let them through they take a little bit of us back with them onto their side of fear and anxiety. The more we lose our grip on appropriate power as parents, the more frightened our children become. In turn, they "act out" their anxiety by further testing limits—begging us over and again to set and hold them. To feel safe and calm, kids must fail to create instability by playing one parent against the other.

The Sadness Below the Badness

Ernie had been in the group home over a year and was "working his program" when Martin had shown up and Ernie had taken him under his wing. Ernie mentored and encouraged Martin and repeatedly admonished him to quit smoking pot because he would get kicked out. Martin did not listen to his would-be big brother and, after repeated warnings, got busted and kicked out of the group home. It was my job one afternoon to tell Ernie that this had happened and I knew that he wouldn't take it well. I did not anticipate that he would threaten to have me killed.

Ernie had been in the system for years. His mom died when he was eight or nine and he failed to find acceptance with a successful aunt who wanted him to give up his baggy pants and *cholo* ways. He repeatedly ran away, bouncing from the street to various placements until he made a good bond with a prior group-home, where he started to work hard and follow the rules. He was proud of the fact that he had earned the chance to be at our group home where he could earn independent walks and increased allowance money with his continued good behavior. But he also remained proud of the fact that his cousins were powerful members of a notorious street gang who "had his back" if anyone ever threatened or disrespected him. Ernie had a good heart, but he also had a wicked temper and had been in his share of serious fights including a gun-fight, so when he looked me in the eye and said, "I'm going to call my cousin and tell him to kill you" I could not completely dismiss it as empty talk.

By the time the threat fully sank in, Ernie had already slammed the door and dented the wall of my dingy trailer office and was halfway across the blacktop on his way to god-knew-where (to the group home, to run away and go AWOL, to find a phone to call his cousin?). With adrenaline surging, I had competing thoughts about dying in the line of fire as a group home therapist, my kids growing up without a father and anger at the clinic administration who made the decision (against my vote) to get rid of Martin for having a drug problem. Something quickened inside my gut, feelings of compassion mingled with fear and sorrow. I ran out of my office, caught up with Ernie on the deserted yard and challenged him:

"Even if you have me killed, what good will it do?"

As my own human fear, rage sorrow and powerlessness collided with his, there was a flashing second where we each recognized our Self in the other—and the fact that while I couldn't change his or Martin's situation, I was *for* them and not against them. He broke my gaze and walked away, but I knew that he no longer wanted to hurt me. This was a turning point for me as a therapist as it transcended analysis and interpretation and made raw use of my soul. It marked the affirmation in my core that I *did* care and that actual caring makes a huge difference; it doesn't necessarily cure or solve much of anything, but it helps bridge shame and isolation which only fuel the dark impulses toward hurt and destruction that we all carry.

Later that afternoon I looked in on Ernie who was alone in his room in a somber mood. He asked me if I wanted to talk and indicated that I should close the door. I had worked with him for well over a year, but that moment on the blacktop marked a shift in our relationship. He opened up to me and told me about how after his mom died of cancer his aunt told him it was his fault—that his wanting toys as a four-year-old had caused her to work too hard and get cancer from the stress. Ernie had been trying to make up for it ever since, mentoring Martin and failing had tapped into his feeling that he was a selfish, bad person who could not help hurting those who cared about him (and this was also unconsciously re-played when he threatened to hurt me). Ernie and I realized together that we can feel horribly angry *and* care about someone at the same time; this was a big developmental step that he never fully got to experience when he was a child. After he confessed his secret agony that he was responsible for his mother's death, he lay face down on his bed and cried as hard as I've ever seen someone cry. Eventually the tears passed and he was drained, but also cleansed and renewed. We never really talked so intimately again, this was not his style, but he continued to do well in the program.

Ernie's mom's love for him was still his rock even after she had died. Children carry our abiding love with them forever, long after we are gone; they soak in our love and attention even as they fight with us. Wherever we see angry and oppositional behavior in our child it is worth considering what hurt and sorrow might be driving negativity or cruelty; if our kids make us scared (i.e. for ourselves or for their safety), sad or angry, perhaps this is how they feel. Understanding their sadness can make all the difference in reaching and helping them.

Sex, Identity, Rebellion and Danger, or Why We Probably Shouldn't Drop Little Red Riding Hood Off at the Mall

While oppositional boys typically act out by rebelling against authority figures, angry girls may be more prone to act out sexually. Boys and girls both tend to act out more in circumstances where parents are absent or emotionally una-vailable (i.e. alcoholism, depression), but even if everything is fine at home, sexual development is fraught with anxiety and potential drama. *Little Red Riding Hood* is an archetypal story that offers centuries old insight into the dangers that come with emerging sexuality. The title character could be under-stood as a girl-woman whose body may be ready for sex (i.e. tempting to the wolf) but whose heart and mind are not. She doesn't listen to her mother and "stay on the path" and ends up in a compromising situation. In the original Grimms' tale, called *Little Red Cap,* the girl is not rescued in the nick of time, she's swallowed up just like grandma—consumed if not consummated. The rescue comes when a passing hunter, who calls the wolf "old sinner," cuts them both back out of the belly of the beast.

If good little girls merely wander off the path, angry rebellious teenagers run wild into the woods, blindfolded, holding scissors and texting wolves to check out their online profiles. We can't just *tell* our kids to stay safe, we have to protect them from their own curiosity and under-developed judgment. The wolf seduces by cloaking his desire in *attention*, which is as irresistible to Little Red as it is to most teens. The better to see you with, hear you with, etc. underscores how attracted Little Red is to *being* seen and heard.

The moral of *Little Red Riding Hood* for parents may be that if we want to minimize our kids' (boys as well as girls) vulnerability to seductive wolves we need to pay close and loving attention to them—and not just drop them at the mall, the unsupervised party or the deep dark woods. When our kids demand freedoms that we sense will only get them into trouble, we need to stay firm and involved even if this means that we suffer the slings and arrows of their outrageous hormones. Kids are at risk when they need love and attention so badly that they will have sex (or take drugs) that they don't truly want in a pathetic bid for what they mistakenly think will be love.

Both boys and girls, but especially girls, tend to form cliques in middle and high school and this means a lot of drama around acceptance and rejection—and vulnerability to risky behaviors as a way to try and fit in or make so-called friends. Our guidance or protection may sometimes come out all wrong (i.e. "you can't go out wearing that!"). We need to supervise, but in the end we really can't stop or control our children so much as we can proactively encourage them to make choices that truly feel right to them. The more non-judgmental we can be, the more they will talk to us and the less likely they will be to make poor choices out of hurt, anger and loneliness. Open communication with our kids can help them feel safe to wait until they are ready for sex, and also allow us to reinforce the reality of sex's possible consequences.

Sexual development is difficult for boys as well as girls. A twelve-year-old boy dreamed that he answered the door to find a girl from his class standing there just as he realized that he was in his underwear with a stick of dynamite hanging on his belt. The boy had no idea that he even had a crush on the girl and not the faintest glimmer of understanding about what the dynamite could possibly symbolize. This was particularly apparent in the fact that he shared the dream with several classmates—including the girl who was in the dream—merely thinking that it was weird and funny. The dream illustrates the emotional experience of sexual development coming on all at once and in the way the dynamite mysteriously appeared on his belt—attached to, yet not actually part of, his body. Dreams come from a place of deep wisdom; this boy's unconscious was showing him that he was coming into his desire and his sexual power, and that this was potentially dangerous as well as exciting and a bit embarrassing— and not something to be rushed into or trifled with. The more we understand our children, and their ambivalence, the less we need to police or control them and instead we can honor *their* need to take things slow.

When our kids have questions, they can sense whether we're embarrassed or open to discussing things. We generally need to talk with our kids *before* they pick up a lot of misinformation from precocious but confused peers; this typically means talking with them when they are younger than we might have thought, perhaps around nine, ten or eleven (rather than middle school or high-school by which time they've been deeply schooled in whatever their peers have to say about the subject). We must be comfortable to frankly talk about details: for example, "sex" to some kids means intercourse, and so if they're having oral sex they may honestly believe that they are not having sex. This sort of confusion can get them in trouble at both the emotional and the viral level. Although we may be asked about ourselves, it is good to keep in mind that our kids mostly want us to understand how *they* feel and to respect their feelings and support them in their power to make choices. It's best to listen in a way so they will talk and have a chance to express their anxiety, their fears and their ambivalence. Love, support and understanding will tend to lead to better choices than control, shame or neglect. If we give them a chance to talk about the pros and cons of their potential decisions they are more likely to make good decisions and stick by them.

Why the Adolescent Brain Is Maddeningly Difficult to Parent

From birth through elementary school we really can't count on our children to consistently and reliably keep themselves safe or make mature and wise decisions, and we parent accordingly. Then comes middle adolescence and it seems that our child is growing up; the level of discussion becomes more sophisticated and our kids are increasingly convincing when they tell us that they can take care of themselves, at least in limited situations (i.e. so long as we keep feeding them and paying for everything). One of the most frustrating things about parenting teens through young adults is that because there are moments when they "get it" and seem reasonable and responsible we, in turn, let them take the car, loosen their curfew or let them be unsupervised for a night... and it's a disaster! They break our hearts, our trust (or, most horribly, injure themselves or others) and we are left feeling like they lied to us. Rather than conclude that they are devious little sociopaths never to be trusted again, we could chalk this dynamic up to normal brain development.

As we mature, the cells of our brain develop a coating that helps it work dramatically faster. In vastly simplified terms, as our brains develop we progress from not knowing where or who we are to being able to think abstractly, use symbols (as in algebra) and make increasingly sophisticated predictions about life, giving us more of a fighting chance of handling ourselves in a complex and often unpredictable world. If we are fortunate, the center of our consciousness moves from the impulsive, fight-flight, pleasure seeking, discomfort-avoiding lower brain toward the higher brain where we do things like appreciate, connect, intuit and empathize. Some of this depends on how we were parented, some depends on the sort of brain we inherit (i.e. more obsessive vs. more easy-going) but a big portion depends on the brain naturally developing over time. The tricky thing about the adolescent brain is that the process of getting up to speed is patchy, so in some spots it seems like the cake is done and in other spots it's still batter. A mature brain is better equipped to *consistently* temper impulses and anticipate what might happen if we were to drink too much, have unprotected sex or spend money that we don't have. In terms of reliable good judgment, the teen years are like a field full of holes that the teen brain crosses blindfolded. Parenting the teen brain requires a lot of hand-holding and limit setting for which we often get excoriated instead of thanked.

Given that the process of brain maturation is not complete until we are in our early to mid twenties, communicating with teens and young adults can be like talking to them on a cell phone where one minute they have reception and another they don't. Since our teenager's judgment is spotty at best, their ability to choose *not* to be surly and oppositional may also fade in and out. This may, at least some of the time, account for why they seem to defy or appear to lie to us when we thought we had a clear understanding about what was and was not okay; faulty communication due to half-finished brain wiring may also help explain why our teens often feel like we don't trust or believe in them when all we're trying to do is protect them so they can mature into having a happy, purposeful and rewarding life.

Intermittently awful judgment can give rise to dark moments where a child who is depressed may impulsively cut or hurt themselves—and underscores the extreme importance of compassionate supervision whenever a child doesn't feel safe from others or within themselves. In general, good counsel for destructive impulses is that if it is really a good idea it will still be a good idea tomorrow morning. With my clients, as well as with children, it has been effective to help a person in the grip of painful emotions understand that it is unwise to make life decisions when in distress; we can validate *feelings* while suggesting that it makes sense to put off big actions, or life-altering shifts in direction, until the current mood has passed. Since intelligent decision making about whether to have that next drink, try that drug or get into that car can be wildly unpredictable, we need to maintain a consistent and compassionate emphasis on safety above all else, offering our children the trust and freedom to call and ask us for help or a ride home without fear of negative consequences. Sadly, until our children's judgment is solid, we parents must think in terms of worse case scenarios and deal with our kids accordingly.

Envision What We Want

Envisioning our most cheerful Self handling our kids' limit-testing, defiance and negativity, helps us to feel tranquil and confident in our love and its power to create the right conditions for our child to heal and grow. Our paradigm of success becomes based on *our* thoughts, feelings and behaviors and not necessarily on the result or reactions of our child. The essence of right action is that we do it with nobility and sincerity, but do not control the outcome of our action. Of course we hope for the best, but we are only in charge of what *we* do. When we let go of the results of our action, we create space for our child to suffer, rage or oppose and still feel connected and understood. Ironically, this liberates us to stay loving despite our child's acting out and empowers us to break through and effect real change in the family.

It may be useful to use post-it notes, daily voice or emails to self, or other reminders to take time and visualize ourselves as centered, positive and happy parents. If our mindfulness can become second nature we can go to the next level and as vividly as possible picture our child at her best—happy, feeling respected, understood and proud of herself in her positive role in the family and in the community. In a sense, our loving visualization of our child becomes a *mental right action*. We enshroud our child in our positive wishes and stay open to the subtle changes that may occur in them and us.

Strategies for Helping

Mindfulness

We don't have to parent so much as we *get* to parent. Our hearts naturally want to do a good job. When we feel safe we are generally patient and kind and the beauty and natural nobility of our child is easy to see. For this reason, mindfulness (or centering, meditating or whatever else we call being aware of, and present to, the eternally living moment) truly is our most powerful strategy for being our best Self as a parent.

When our child is challenging, frustrating, worrying or infuriating us, a good first step is to pause. By simply *not* reacting right away, we eliminate a great deal of the potential errors we could make as a parent. Pausing is a key factor in anger management (i.e. counting, disengaging, recognizing the signs that we are on the verge of losing our temper). Pausing gives us an opportunity to stop and breathe *before* we respond.

Our pause can be a working silence where we breathe in love, wisdom or patience—whatever we need at that moment. In our pause we can breathe out fear (i.e. that we are a bad parent) and desire (i.e. that our child should be different). When we see our child's suffering or anger with an open and non-judging heart, they unfold like a flower before our eyes and natural compassion awakens without effort.

In difficult moments we need help, not to change things but to be present to suffering and to beauty. When we pause and bear unflinching witness, everything that wants or needs to change becomes free to do so on its own. We are guided from within to be a force of loving kindness; we find peace and happiness, even in the midst of great challenge—and cultivate the ability to softly enshroud our children in calm and loving energy.

Yoga

While mindfulness is a tried and true way to handle all sorts of things well, it takes discipline to practice consistently. If the path of peace and calm has eluded us, perhaps a yoga class might nudge us in the right direction—especially if we dedicate our yoga to having a better relationship with our child, or to their healing and well-being. Yoga can help take our mind off our worries and help release toxins, stress and sorrow; at the end of yoga class we spend some minutes in "Savasana," or corpse pose, which looks a lot like lying down with eyes closed and doing nothing—and it is here that the benefits of the poses and the intentions we had set get absorbed into our bodies, hearts and minds. Yoga for the parent may not seem like a strategy for dealing with an oppositional child, but if it helps us be calm and peaceful we help our child.

Mindful Eating

Our food is truly a wonder—it allows us to live. We often eat without giving much thought, much less thanks, to the cosmos contained in a piece of bread or grain of rice. In folk wisdom they say we are what we eat, and sometimes we end up eating a lot of processed, "fast," chemical-laden food. Besides being obviously bad for our body, food lacking in soul is probably bad for our soul.

In an intriguing case study on nutrition and wellness, troubled teens who had been previously unsuccessful and disruptive in a mainstream school setting, and who had subsequently been sent to Appleton Central Alternative Charter High School, found their vending machines proffering junk food and soda removed and replaced with a menu of health-focused and freshly prepared foods and water coolers placed throughout the school. The accepted norm of students eating chips and candy on couches, the floor or at computer stations was replaced with an expectation of eating real food along with teachers at round tables. Soothing music and even aroma-therapy helped to create a more homey milieu. Subsequent to these changes, teachers and social workers reported decreased levels of acting out, improved mood, enhanced concentration and decreased complaints of physical distress.

While the data is anecdotal, and therefore falls short of allowing definitive conclusions, this case study gained wide attention in venues from *The Today Show* to Michael Moore's

Sicko. As parents it makes common sense to give our children wholesome foods and a homey and respectful environment to support their well-being and to decrease their propensity for irritability and oppositionality. Poor nutrition alone certainly does have clinically significant negative effects on mental and physical functioning, and it follows that children skipping breakfast (as most of the Appleton kids reported doing) and eating mostly processed foods high in sugar, salt and fat are not going to feel especially good. Food can be a loaded issue, potentially fraught with struggles for control (i.e. children refusing to eat what we cook for them, insisting that all their friends get to eat all the junk they want, etc.), and especially in light of the obesity epidemic, we parents struggle to get food right. However, we are also busy, and it can be all too easy for drive-through dinners to become a staple of our children's diets.

Interestingly, the teachers in Appleton expected the kids to object to the removal of the vending machines, but when they explained the plan to offer better nutrition, the children readily accepted it. It seems clear enough that when we go out of our way to take good care of our kids, they feel it and respond positively to our authentic efforts to help them heal, grow and flourish. So while eating well is always a good idea, if your child is struggling with irritability, defiance, depression or apathy, it is well worth trying a course of enhanced nutrition. Also, be sure to sit at table together with your child to meta-communicate that whatever the issues may be at present, you are still a family and your love for your child remains unflagging.

When I was a group home therapist, I spent at least one night a week cooking and eating with the kids. One night we were making burgers and one of my staff, who'd grown up in the hood, said we were making "ghetto burgers." When I asked what made a ghetto burger different than any other burger he explained what his grandmother had taught him: "You have to put love into the meat." We did just that and they were the most delicious burgers we'd ever made in that dingy kitchen. I still try to remember to put love into everything I cook.

Non-Violence as a Guiding Ethic

When dealing with defiance it is key to strive for non-violence in our own hearts and actions. If we wish for our children to be non-violent, honest and respectful we must be this way. Non-violence in parenting can include respectful communication, kindness, manners and not taking opposition personally. With non-violence we set forth an expectation that there be no name-calling, blaming, labeling or defining others in the family (i.e. "you always do such and such," or "you're lazy, mean, rude," etc.) and, of course, no physical aggression. If we live and model this behavior, we set the tone for greater love and harmony in the home.

Giving in to our children's demands, or catering to them to avoid upsetting them, is not the same as non-violence. Non-violence calls for the balance of love and limits. Non-violence is compassionate, even as it is firm, and thus stronger than coercion, intimidation or brute force. As parents we strive for kindness, compassion and self-restraint as emblems of strength and power.

Non-violence is like water on stone—ever-flowing softness conquering obstinate hardness. Even at the personal level, non-violence is a political act. If we can tame fear, anger and cruelty in our families, we are also part of the solution to "world" problems that are also born of suffering, fear and greed such as poverty, war, racism and oppression.

Avoid Shame

Guilt is feeling bad about what we did while shame is feeling bad about who we are. Shame-prone people tend to get angry, show little remorse, not take responsibility— and thus repeat bad behavior. Shame prone kids are more likely to use drugs and have unsafe sex.[2] When kids misbehave we need to be sure to convey that it is their behavior that is "bad" and not their core character. We want to avoid labeling our kids as it negatively shapes their self-concept. Shame is typically based on the assumption that a person did something that they knew, or at least should have known (if they had bothered to listen or pay attention), was wrong. A more generous view is that people do the best they can and that bad behavior is our cue as parents that better understanding, teaching, limits or supervision is needed. By this approach we model taking responsibility for ourselves.

We Are the Best Parents, We Are the Worst Parents

As we mature we come to understand that the cruel and the terrible exists within each of us; we learn to manage our cruel impulses and cultivate kindness. Children split the world into good parts and bad parts (i.e., they want to go straight to the chocolate cake and stay miles away from the broccoli). The more vociferous our child is in hating us at any given moment, the more certain we can be that they desperately believe that we have what they need (i.e. love, understanding, validation) and are deliberately withholding.

This secret idealization of us, as giver of all good things, is as distorted as is their outward insistence that we are the worst parents ever. No one gets enraged at an earthworm for not giving—we devalue those who have the love, luck, power, ice-cream or television privileges that we think we need but don't have.

When our child shouts, "I hate you!" we can try to keep in mind how weak and out of control they probably feel in their immense dependency on us and how obviously important we are to them. Our task at such moments is to not take it personally. If we manage to remain calm and empathic we can communicate that we know they hate us but we love them anyway. In this way they internalize the image of a calm and loving parent who loves them even when they are hateful. Over time, they will come to be able to be angry with us without it becoming such an intense experience of hate. While we can communicate that we too have feelings, and we can be hurt by our child's behavior, it may be more effective to talk about this when our children are calm and we are able to engage them in a more productive conversation than those we generally have in the midst of high drama. When our child is enraged or highly distraught we are better off to remain focused on accurately recognizing what he or she feels at that moment, rather than on trying to evoke empathy in a child who is operating in fight/flight mode.

Devaluation comes from suffering. When our child devalues us it is not a job evaluation as a parent, it is a desperate cry of pain. Whenever we find ourselves devalued, bear in mind that our child is at the very same time unconsciously looking up to us and inadvertently revealing how much power we hold for them. If we see our child's fear and pain instead of our own inadequacy, we spontaneously regain compassion, wisdom and patience. If we can be kind in the face of their suffering-driven cruelty, we teach them how it is done, and we heal ourselves in the bargain. Then the worst of times, as a parent, truly do give way to the best of times.

Use Role Play and Story-Telling to Cultivate Empathy

Often children will come home from school and "act out" cruelty, disrespect or aggression they have experienced or witnessed. In a sense, they unconsciously try to make us, or their siblings, feel the smallness, fear or confusion that they felt. Sometimes we get the call from the teacher that it was our child who hurt another child. However cruelty gets started, our task as parents is to recognize hurt without blaming one child or the other and cultivate empathy and compassion. Yet with children between ages two and seven this is a dodgy proposition because their brains are still essentially "pre-empathy." If a five-year-old has hurt another child and we ask them, "How do you think *she* feels right now?" they sheepishly mumble, "bad," but they really don't get it.

Certain techniques can "speed the plow" on compassion, such as role-playing a situation that led to hurt bodies or feelings, but having our child "play" the other child while we play the role of our own child. We talk it back and forth, and if our child can get into their role of speaking and feeling from the *other* kid's point of view they may find themselves arguing the opposite of their own opinion and may grasp the frustration and pain that drove that other kid to behave in an unkind manner. This is the essence of empathy—leap-frogging their not yet developed brain to awaken understanding and organic compassion directly in their naturally wise hearts.

Another tactic is to make up stories about thinly veiled characters who represent the relevant children in our kid's life. We can create virtually identical scenarios to the social problems our three, six or nine-year-old is facing, but if they are said and done by squirrels, dinosaurs or wizards, our child is often enchanted and very eager to hear; they soak up advice and coping strategies as they listen to the story. When they notice that a character who is awfully similar to them has good results with kindness and courage, and ends up making friends, getting rewards and feeling good about themselves, our child may unconsciously have that story in mind the next time they interact with their nemesis of the moment.

Right Touch

Research shows that babies who receive a daily massage of their little bodies are easier to calm and get less colds than non-massaged babies. These differences hold up over time, long after the touch they got in infancy has passed. So whether it's our newborn baby or our twelve-year-old, loving touch is a good way to get beyond words and soothe them at the most fundamental level of self. The art of right touch often hinges on timing as children grow older; when kids are alone, and particularly when they are tired, they may be a little extra open to the sorts of cuddles they loved when they were little. Beyond the big cuddles that middle schoolers and teens are unlikely to favor, a gentle arm on the shoulder or a little hug when they come in the door (even if they merely accept it with seeming indifference) stimulates the nerve receptors deep in the lower layers of the skin that send messages of closeness and attachment to our kids' brains. If we are not hyper-sensitive to rejection, and so long as we are attuned to our children's self-consciousness in front of their peers, it may be good practice to continue to offer hugs, pats and arms around the shoulders despite apparent non-responsiveness. They may nonetheless be a salve to the unseen wounds of loneliness and feelings of isolation.

Some of the group home kids I worked with would tantrum to the point where staff members would have to physically hold them down, and I came to realize that the "take-down," rather than being merely a negative consequence to violent or unsafe behavior, was actually an enticement to act out. Certain kids were too big, lonely or angry to ask for a hug (not to mention not having anyone *to* ask), so they would get that physical human contact in the only way they knew how. They would get it literally kicking and screaming, spitting and swearing—and it was heartbreaking to know that it was all about getting a twisted version of a hug. True to the little children that they remained within their secret selves, invariably they would need to nap after being restrained. Over time, I found that I could sometimes explain this need for hugs to these wounded teenagers and they would actually see it and even agree with me. Sometimes this even resulted in them acting out less.

Dealing With Power Struggles

Don't Take The Bait

When it comes to power struggles there is one primary rule that takes precedence over, underscores, and supports all other techniques, rules and guidelines: DON'T ENGAGE IN POWER STRUGGLES! While this will not always be possible, as a parent, the moment we enter a power struggle we have already lost. As the parents, we have power and authority; when we stoop to threaten, count down to consequences, yell, use physical force or haggle and bargain with our child we unwittingly elevate them to our level, and thus they have a fighting *chance* and that's all the reason for them to keep fighting. If we parent like corrupt dictators, our kids become rebels, which leaves them anxious and disappointed in parents, and dooms them to keep testing limits until they find out where they actually are. We don't want to "win" power struggles with our children, we want not to have them.

End A Culture of Negotiation

If our child is three we cannot possibly live by the ethic "one family member, one vote" without lapsing into chaos. Despite intentions of fairness and democratic reasonableness (i.e. we'll have Mexican food tonight, but then tomorrow we will have burgers) we can end up with a family culture of constant haggling and deal-making. If we treat our family like a supply and demand driven free market, either the parents will come to be seen as oppressive hypocrites (because the kids had been given the impression that they were equally in charge only to find out that this is not true), or the kids will seize power and probably rule poorly. Even if the kids do a good job parenting their parents—which is a sad state of affairs—they end up robbed of childhood.

Negotiating as a family culture puts a yardstick on everything. When we foster a family culture of negotiation (be it in haggling over what kids should earn for doing extra chores, or bargaining for how many cookies they may have: mom says "one cookie," child says "three" knowing that mom, who is fair and reasonable—and wants to be well-liked at all times—will "settle" at two) it tends to monetize or quantify everything. Having some sort of metric for every interaction can leak into a child's sense of how much they are worth (i.e. especially as children have limited power in the family as well as limited earning power). Love is powerful, but it is not always directly lucrative and therefore becomes of questionable value when the benchmarks are all materialistic. Inadvertently turning our kids into deal-making pit-bulls can bleed over into devaluing house-keepers, tutors, teachers and anyone else who caters to our children. We must remain clear that the more money someone makes does not make a person that much more lovable, special or even happy. It's not just a matter of what we *say* in front of our kids, they are highly sensitive to our attitudes and subtle messages.

No matter how powerful we think we are in the world, our children will quickly remind us how little that counts for in the realm of parenting where we truly have to earn our kids' respect. If we have painted ourselves into a corner by over-negotiating everything from story-time to curfew it will help to gently shift our family paradigm from a failing democracy back toward a benevolent monarchy. Here the parents are like lionhearted kings and queens; they serve their heirs, and groom them for power, responsibility and service, by a firm and loving example. We are the parents not because we are better than our children, but simply because we are older and it's our time to play the parent role—but we must play it and not abdicate.

Be Consistent

It's better to say no kindly than to say yes and then get mad about it later. If we are consistent with things like TV/electronic games, junk food, bed-times, etc. our kids will start to know and trust the rules, they will take what we say more seriously and feel calmer. We can always decide that it's time for a rule to change—but we should ponder this when we are not under stress, and bear in mind that if a rule changes, the new rule applies whether we are in a good mood or not.

Be Like Water

Chinese wisdom holds that because water prefers low places, it is above all things. This is good power struggling wisdom. When confronted with our angry and obstinate child, our Zen ideal is to be egoless, like water. If water is a teacher, it shows us that when we are calm we reflect truth like a mirror—without judgment. Water acts powerfully, but without intention; when it comes to an obstacle it finds a way around it; when it finds stillness it stops. Kids love water and are drawn to it. Just as the ocean accepts all rivers, our deep Self accepts, with love and understanding, whatever emotions our child brings us.

Empower: Give Areas Of Control

We want to let our children have as much say-so, power, control and autonomy as they can responsibly handle. If we give too much freedom we frighten them, but if we give not enough freedom we also scare them into feeling that they cannot do much of anything for themselves; such timidity and low-self confidence leads to sour and contrary kids who make us feel as if we can't do anything right (because that is how they feel). With innocuous things like bath time, we can give our kid some choices: do you want to stay in a few more minutes and have less reading time or get out now and have extra reading time? Choice empowers kids and teaches them about the logical consequences of their own behavior (which will serve them much better in the real world than "Do it because I said so"). We all don't feel like doing things sometimes—the art of parenting is striking a good balance between pushing and nurturing.

Anticipate

When our child has to do something difficult, they themselves may become difficult. Bring along a snack and the mantra, "transition is hard." We avoid being blind-sided by anticipating trouble. Just as we parents must know our own limits, if our child is acting out we want to consider whether they can really manage all the activities we so lovingly chart for them (music, sports, art, religious school, tutors, etc., on top of homework); are we preparing them for joy and success or dispiriting and grinding them down?

When it comes to anticipating drama, homework is a prime suspect. If our kids feel maxed out they are not going to feel very happy about doing a lot of homework; and if they are feeling bad about themselves they will find confronting anything that makes them feel dumb very tempting to avoid—procrastinating, picking quarrels, teasing siblings—anything to put up a smoke-screen, and avoid the pain of what is hard.

Recognizing feelings without prematurely trying to change our child's attitude can help. If they are grumpy, low on blood sugar, or just feeling momentarily overwhelmed a potential conflict may be averted with a snack and a kind ear. We may need to help our kid find a structure for doing their homework—how much down time, whether to do the hard or the easy tasks first (they usually like the easy, but then they are out of energy when it's time to do the hard), etc.

Take it seriously if they claim they are trying but not feeling successful. Perhaps they need a tutor, perhaps they have a learning difference; as parents we need to communicate with teachers and school staff to support our child. We may need to encourage our kid to talk with their teachers, ask for help (and possibly find a different class, school, etc. if it turns out to be a poor fit for our child). This can be a lot of work, but not doing this work leads to problems that are even more work to deal with. If our child is already into the problematic zone of acting out and refusing to go to school, a more appropriate learning environment may make all the difference. We generally don't like to see our child "fail" out of their school, but very often the right social and/or academic environment makes it possible for a kid to feel like a success again.

In the realm of anticipating trouble, it can be effective to structure time for our child to de-compress and do nothing. The fine art of hanging out is one very few adults seem to have mastered. Kids benefit from a little time being "bored" (not hours of neglect, more like ten minutes of staring out the window without the distraction and constant stimulation of radio, TV, computer, and a steady stream of newly invented gadgets). Setting limits on mind-numbing, over-stimulating, interactive electronic games can reduce anxiety and diminish the exhaustion that comes when the brain is tricked into thinking that the body is doing all sorts of activity when, in reality, we are moving little more than our thumbs.

Catch Them Being Good

It makes obvious sense to pay a lot of attention to our child when they are doing the right things so that we reinforce pro-social behaviors and positive self-esteem. But the more our child is struggling, the harder it may be to "catch them being good." If our child has been very difficult lately, "being good" can be redefined to mean simply "not being bad" at any given moment.

A strategy for jump-starting renewed happiness and hope in our child is to suddenly give them extra love and attention for absolutely no reason—not contingent on their accomplishments or behavior, but simply because we love them and have decided to make giving positive attention our top priority. We can also engage our child when they are in a neutral mood and treat this as if it is positive behavior (as it is, at least relative to their problematic behaviors). Above praise or rewards, sheer interest is a powerful force when applied with sincerity and consistency. I worked with a child who ignored me and refused to leave his classroom for months until one day he was ready to take a walk with me. It took four months for him to trust the non-verbal message of sincere interest contained in my showing up time and again. So if your child shuts down your overtures of interest, treat this as a prelude to a better relationship, and be ready to offer a rather long prelude. If you don't resent your child for inelegantly, or even selfishly, expressing what ultimately amounts to his pain, and if you do not give up on him despite his rejecting behavior (which, again, may communicate how he feels rejected—perhaps by you, perhaps by his other parent, maybe by peers) he will eventually realize that your love is stronger than his down-heartedness.

Make Directives Positive

While a kind tone is helpful, what makes a directive "positive" is that it is something a child CAN do, rather than a warning telling them what NOT to do. The more we make our instructions clear and doable, the more we set our child up for success.

For example, if two kids are fighting, us shouting, "Cut it out!" or "Stop fighting" is hard for them to comply with. In heated situations it's better to calmly command, "Hands DOWN!" When kids are in the red zone of fear and rage it helps for us to be like Simon in a game of Simon Says, and keep it simple: "Come here," "Look at me," "Take a deep breath"—these commands redirect behavior and diffuse tension. Talking and reasoning will only be effective after our children are calm.

Negative directives reinforce a negative self-image. If we're coaching sports we might say, "Go out there and win" or preferably "Do your best," but we certainly ought not say, "Just don't lose." "Don't make a mess" is not as good as "Work neatly." "No TV" is not as useful as "It's reading time now." "Please set the table" is more motivating than, "You're a lazy brat—you never even set the table." And, "Please put a napkin, a knife, a fork and a spoon at every chair" may be even better because it's specific. Let them tell us, "Dad, I know how to set the table," before we assume they know where the silverware drawer is. Frustration with us thinking they are younger than they are is not nearly as damaging as their perception that we think they are lazy, rotten or deliberately bad.

Quantify

When I worked with troubled kids, progress was often measured in millimeters. For every child we would have one or two behavioral goals that were linked to their underlying diagnosis. An example of a treatment goal might be to reduce depression as evidenced by increased participation in group activities from zero times per week to three times per week. Another typical goal might be to increase self-esteem as evidenced by reduced instances of aggressive behavior from five times per week to two times per week. By sharing our treatment goals with the child, we could help make it clear that we did not think the *main* problem was aggressive behavior, so much as their behavior was more a symptom of their feeling sad, angry and dejected. Every week we would chart progress and quarterly we would revise goals. Because the steps toward healing were often so tiny, by keeping track we could see when we were getting somewhere—and so could the child.

It helps to identify our oppositional child's underlying issue (typically depression, anxiety and/or low-self-esteem) and then view problematic behavior (i.e. outbursts, work refusal, substance abuse, self-destructiveness, running away, etc.) as a place to target behavioral intervention. It doesn't need to be fancy; if our kid loses their temper daily, we hope to reduce angry outbursts from seven times per week to six or less. Making a goal and keeping notes can help us have a more accurate picture of the problem as it really is, and help us recognize overall progress. This helps avoid concluding that our kid is a total disaster just because they have a bad moment. Behavioral goals help us maintain clarity of focus and help our children better understand what we want them *to* do. An example of a positive behavioral goal might be: Raise self-esteem as evidenced by increased helping with household chores (such as making the bed or taking out the trash) from zero times per week to one or more times per week.

Give Your Child Strategies For Saying "No" To Bad Ideas

Once a child is in trouble, we have already missed our best opportunity, which would have been to proactively intervene. By the time our child is six or seven they will generally be most receptive to discussing issues that they will face in a year or two. By working a couple of years in their developmental future they are more likely to find the discussion pertinent (rather than old news) and feel valued as mature by us, which helps them take themselves more seriously.

By the time our kids are having sex, the last thing they want to do is talk about it with their parents; however, when it's still a little ways off and vaguely titillating and terrifying they are more likely to talk with us about hypothetical situations (albeit, with some coaxing on our part and a fair amount of resistance and attitude on their part). Kids don't typically think things all the way through—and so it's our job as parents to help them do that. When they are eleven or twelve we can teach them about birth control, abstinence or the importance of waiting until they are ready but if they are fifteen, sexually active and *now* we think it's time for "the talk," we've missed the boat.

Drugs are another issue that calls for detailed discussion *before* drinking and drugs become a common reality amongst our child's peers (and that, sadly, may be younger than we imagined). When they are not yet going to those sorts of parties we can ask them to use their imagination to picture being offered things they do not want and coming up with ways to say no with confidence and style. Having these sorts of discussions is meant to encourage our children to share *their* opinions, mentally practice situations with us and get to creatively try different strategies for saying no to things before they encounter them in the world.

Be A Nerd, A Geek And A Loser (At Least In Your Child's View)

As our children develop they need to differentiate from us and assert their difference and uniqueness. Their once-flattering desire to be like us evaporates into a need to be as unlike us as possible.

Even though our kids may find us a colossal embarrassment 'round about middle school, they don't really want us to get a hipster make-over. Being anything like our kids at these points in development can seem like an insult of the highest order. This is because it threatens their sense of self at a point when they don't exactly know who they are. If we happen to like their music, their slang or their style we might have to keep that on the down-low until the adolescent storm passes. The more secure our child becomes, the less insulting they will be. In the end, for child and parent alike, it is not being in style that is cool but rather being true to our authentic selves.

Give Logical Consequences

Kids are smart, and they are curious. They want to know why they need to do the things we ask them to do. If we bother to think through and explain to our child why they should do things like go to school, do homework, brush teeth or have good sportsmanship (and if the reasons make sense to them) they are more likely to trust our parenting and comply. "Because I told you so," is a lame reason for anyone to do anything. Since we don't want to teach our kids to be mindless drones, we must welcome their questions and treat them as teachable moments. We need to continually think through and adjust rules, limits and freedoms along with our child's evolving development.

In nature every action brings a reaction; if we drop a pebble in a pond, a ripple of waves follows as a natural consequence. The art of effective consequences in parenting lies in crafting "logical" repercussions for inappropriate or dangerous behaviors. For consequences to be logical they should bear some resemblance to what would actually happen in "real life" if our child were to indulge in problematic behavior out in the world. To organically arrive at logical consequences we have to think scenarios through. For example, we can imagine our child being a grown-up, living independently and doing negative behaviors. What would happen? Would they have any friends? Would they lose their job? Would they end up hungry, lonely or unhappy? Still, we modify consequences to give a taste of logical reality while protecting our kids from the harshness of the world. Criminal-style penalties and attitudes often do little to deter or remediate bad behavior and instead tend to deepen shame and entrench human beings in dead-end ways of being. For example, if our child keeps watching TV after we say turn it off, we don't take away desert (what do sweets and watching TV have to do with each other in the real world?), instead the next time they want to watch TV, we might kindly inform them, "Yesterday when you ignored the rule about turning off the TV you used up an extra fifteen minutes and so you get a fifteen-minute penalty." If they are upset, we can help them see that in life, when we spend time on things, we make choices and there will be less time left over for other things. We need to leave room for our child's emotional experience where they are free to disagree with our decisions and be upset, sad or angry. Only after they have calmed down will it make any sense to them if we lovingly and compassionately explain how the limit at hand is meant to keep them safe, or promote their growth and was not just because we said so—and certainly not because they are worthless or undeserving. The consequence is the teacher, not our mood or reaction. Consequences help us protect our kids from what lies on the other side of limits—we teach children that fire is dangerous *so* that they will not get burned.

We can tailor consequences to teach specific lessons. We don't want to pull out our "big gun" consequences and take away all our child's toys and privileges for every hint of insubordination. In the face of overkill punishment children quickly grow apathetic and no longer care about the things they used to treasure since they're only going to lose them. Even worse than overkill consequences is the chronic empty threat of overkill consequences. To shout, "No TV and no dessert!" for a minor infraction, and then let them watch TV and have dessert makes us into a windbag to be largely disregarded. Casting TV and junk food as rewards does the disservice of suggesting to children that mind-numbing toxins are objects of desire. In the actual world, if we mess up we don't typically lose TV—in fact we are probably more likely to watch a lot of TV if we fall into a dead-end life.

Consequences can also be positive; whatever happens after our child is kind or industrious teaches them whether or not this sort of behavior is a good idea. We don't have to buy them a bike for taking their plate to the counter, but simply *noticing* things is a form of reinforcement since kids thrive on attention. We can use rewards (i.e. do a good job, get a cookie), but as soon as possible we want to transition away from rewards so that positive behavior itself becomes self-reinforcing and thus self-sustaining. We support this by emphasizing our child's own feelings about themselves, saying things like, "I hope *you* are feeling proud of yourself" rather than, "I am proud of you." Rewards are good for establishing behaviors, but they lose their effectiveness quickly. Reward-trained behaviors tend to drop away again in the absence of reinforcements, so we must get good behavior going and then wean away rewards the way training wheels can come off as soon as they are no longer needed. What we are really hoping to teach is joy in a job well done, and in the process of doing that job; happiness and a sense of purpose are the natural consequences of working hard and contributing while the logical outcome of chasing fun is to feel bored and empty.

Factor In Rebellion

Since children are going to test boundaries and cross lines, we need to set limits a little tighter than our ultimate intent. For example, if our child asks if it is okay to drink alcohol, we might want to consider what we really think (and what behavior we model). Let's say we feel that a teen approaching adulthood could have *one* drink if they were moderate about it and did not drive and we say as much—and the next thing we know our child has had four or five too many. You are the best expert on your particular child, but if they are the daredevil sort you want to take that into account when you decide where to draw the line on issues like curfew, closed bedroom doors when boyfriend/girlfriends are over and access to drugs, alcohol and the internet.

With some kids, if we say okay to alcohol they'll try marijuana; if we say okay to pot they'll have to try coke. For the kids who will likely go past whatever we say is okay we must make the rules a little more strict than we ultimately intend so that they won't get into too much trouble when they rebel.

Be the Change

Teaching our children by example—by being mindful, compassionate, authentically happy and as healthy as possible—is *the* strategy for helping them when they suffer or struggle and, as a result, behave badly. If we want our child to have a good attitude then we must have one—even in the face of their bad attitude. If our child is rude, we can be ceaselessly polite; if our child is unmotivated, we can muster the energy to bear empathic witness to their dejection—this teaches that they too can stay with painful feelings and grow.

If we want our kids to have a good work ethic then we ought to have one; this means more than working hard, it means finding pleasure, and meaning, in our work and saying so to our kids. It means coming home tired, but not too tired to talk to our own kids. If we can find the courage and love to be our best Self, our kids will eventually follow suit. If we can show that being kind, loving and generous, as well as hardworking, makes us happy our kids will take more notice than if we complain that we're living a depressing or oppressive life all supposedly for them.

Exercises To Consider

1. Authority inventory: Bring to mind authority figures such as police, judges, bosses, teachers, clergy, politicians and parents—and notice what sort of feelings they evoke in you. For example, do you feel warmth to recall being mentored by a teacher, or angry about being harassed by police? Consider whether you tend to have a balanced view, or if you have had a lot of bad experiences and an understandable distrust or dislike of people in charge. Now think about the impact that your attitude toward authority figures might have on your parenting; maybe you are too soft on your kids because you want to avoid being the bully at all costs, or maybe you go too hard on your kids because that's the way you were treated. Greater self-awareness frees us to more consciously choose the sort of authority we would like to be; in this spirit, think about what you personally believe constitutes a positive authority figure and identify one positive authority trait that you would like to cultivate or strengthen in yourself. Write it down, carry it with you—keep it in mind and try to bring it to your parenting.

2. Love-hate meditation: If you can find the time, make a list of things you love about your children and another list of things you hate or devalue in them. Now try and come up with at least one positive thing about each negative trait (i.e. being less gifted at something can inspire us to become more hardworking; being short in basketball can

make us learn to shoot from outside or be a better dribbler); come up with one negative thing about each positive trait (i.e., being smart can make someone arrogant or lower frustration tolerance because they expect that things will always be easy for them). Now try and pair one negative and one positive trait and notice how they balance each other and create a sort of harmony (i.e. being talented at music compensates for being hopeless at sports; struggling with a learning difference might be part of why they are patient and kind with younger children). By creating our own yin-yang relationships between the light and the dark aspects in our child we deepen our understanding, patience and sensitivity to them—and feeling more accepted and understood tends to decrease our child's acting out and oppositionality.

Next, make a list of behaviors that your child does that makes you angry, hurt or just a little crazy. Try to come up with reasons why someone might behave in these hurtful ways or what they might hope to gain. For example, braggarts probably want to be admired, noticed and feel good about themselves, the greedy person feels deprived and wishes to have enough, the cruel person feels hurt and wants others to feel their pain, the cheater lacks trust in the world and themselves and feels that they need to manipulate and control to get what they want or need. Consider the uneasy likelihood that whatever bugs you in your kid might very well be something that you also do sometimes, but probably in a more covert or unconscious way. Hopefully this sort of thinking can bring more compassion and less judgment toward you and your child and lessen the conflicts between you.

3. Conflict analysis: Think about a major area of conflict with your child. Note *when* problems, arguments and dramatic scenes happen (i.e. after school, waking up) with an eye on which transitions are most destabilizing for your child; note what precedes conflicts (i.e., if your child loses at something, is teased, gets frustrated doing homework) to better understand triggers and the pain that drives bad behavior. If they get fussy when they are hungry, keeping extra snacks in the car may help head tantrums off at the pass. If conflicts serve the purpose of avoiding something (i.e. homework, chores, bedtime), supporting our child to feel more able to do their homework (i.e. by having a tutor) or feel safer to go to sleep (i.e. by talking about how they might understand and deal with nightmares) may eliminate the need for acting out. The more closely we study the cycle of build-up, overt conflict and aftermath, the more we may gain clues about how to have a more harmonious relationship with our child.

4. Brainstorm logical consequences: First, pick one key problem behavior your child repeatedly does such as showing disrespect or refusing to do what they are asked. Next, try to intuit underlying reasons for negative behavior such as your child is sad, anxious, guilty, or is suffering from

low self-esteem or feelings of neglect. Imagine "real world" consequences for their behavior; maybe they would lose relationships, money, opportunity, freedom or privileges. Pick a logical consequence tailored to the lesson you want to teach or reinforce. Possibilities include: repair damage (i.e. doing extra chores, cleaning up); lose privileges (i.e., going out, talking on the phone or texting); time outs/cool downs (i.e. a more instructional variation on being grounded); treatment (i.e. therapy, twelve step-recovery, family therapy, drug testing). Sometimes the natural consequence of our children feeling bad is enough, and no further intervention is needed. Finally, implement whatever consequences we devise with either compassion or emotional neutrality; reinforce success by helping our children feel noticed and appreciated when they are on the right track. Note: we don't have to think of, or give, consequences in the heat of the moment. Take time, craft consequences well, take the time to explain how and why the consequence is logical, but not until our child is relatively calm.

5. Play un-Monopoly: An antidote to a world that makes everything about money and competition is to play games, such as Monopoly, with our kids, but instead of everyone just trying to win we can try and make the game last as long as possible by sharing money and property and being kind and compassionate citizens. Agree that everyone gets good properties and revenue, and let each

other off the hook if someone can't pay. The goal is for everyone to be generous, compassionate and have no one lose. The real "game" is to turn individual self-interest into collective teamwork. This sets a new paradigm for family harmony and cooperation. We can still coach our kids to compete in the world when appropriate, but also how to differentiate when to compete from when to work together.

6. Background music: Music can affect mood, set a tone or help us relax. Taking an interest in our kid's playlists and hanging out with them to listen can be a good way to connect. Another way to bring calm into our home is to consistently play "easy listening" (mellow, not necessarily cheesy) music at a low-volume. It can be a radio in our room playing very quietly, but the calming effect may draw our kids unconsciously toward us and the soothing sound may be there to help fill awkward silences and relax tense muscles (like at the dentist's office).

7. Yoga: This chapter on oppositionality begins and ends with mindfulness. In a sense, there is no opposition so long as we are not against our child, only the perception of it in our hurting kid. Through mindfulness we can let go, see more clearly and find the wisdom, love, kindness and patience to be our best Self and find a naturally harmonious relationship with the best Self of our child. Yoga to help us deal with oppositionality, should be as soft and simple as possible. Down

Dog, Child's Pose and forward bends are cooling and quieting; balancing poses can teach us a lot about quietly staying to our center, but most of all we will make progress by sitting quietly and comfortably and emptying our mind if we can, or by simply gazing at anything handy (i.e. a flower, a rock, our child) and seeing it as completely as we possibly can. Paradoxically, when we empty our minds our hearts awaken and fill with guidance and compassion. When sitting in meditation, we can place our thumbs and forefingers in the gesture of "okay." This particular "mudra," or seal, is symbolic of the unity between the individual self and the universal SELF—a nice way to think about us and our child, our family and the world, etc. We can place our hands facing up to receive energy, or facing down to ground ourselves; we can place hands in prayer at our hearts, or make a bowl in our lap. It's all about setting an intention to be our best Self, to create favorable conditions for our child's growth and happiness and to have a better relationship with our child. While an oppositional child may be unlikely to join you at yoga, your first step is to take yourself; after that, you can invite your child if she is old enough, or if there is another, age-appropriate, class available. The younger you start a child, the more yoga can be a natural part of their lexicon if, or rather when, bumpy times arrive in their life—at which point yoga can return to calm them down.

Chapter 8

"I Knew That Was Going To Happen": Using Intuition To Parent Better

From Common Sense to Sixth Sense

It is easy to picture an exasperated parent saying to their frustrated four-year-old, or sulking fourteen-year-old, "I'm not a mind reader!" But what if we *could* read our children's minds? Imagine how much easier parenting would be! Or would it?

Maybe mind-reading our child would be like perpetually streaming our child's private diary—and maybe it would hurt to know every big and small criticism, to face how our outbursts really make them feel, or our not having time for them, or our drinking or other shameful things that we like to imagine they don't know about. Maybe just knowing their every thought would be exhausting and mentally overwhelming as most of us can barely keep up with the things they already do tell and ask us, not to mention our own thoughts and feelings. What if telepathy was a two-way street and our children actually knew and felt it when we had angry or critical thoughts about them? We would have to do even more than just saying and doing the right things to be our best Self as a parent—we'd even have to *think* the right things.

Or maybe, at an unconscious level, our families are an interconnected web of shared thoughts and emotions—and maybe this could help explain some of the inexplicable problems that we seem to have with our children (i.e., not even realizing we are flooded by their unexpressed feelings or that they are drowning in our unconscious fear or sorrow). A scenario of intimate wordless connectedness would be a potential paradise if everyone were safe and happy, as misspoken words would no longer jumble our messages of love and compassion for our children. Often, however, it seems that we unconsciously mind-read (and feel the effects of) waves of unspoken blame, criticism, contempt and resentment that fly around under the radar in our families. Perhaps if we tuned into our children's messages of suffering and sent them consistent telepathic messages of love, or even just managed to achieve tranquility and remain clear in our love we would, in turn, emanate some sort of "good energy" and our children, ourselves and our families might feel happier.

Many great sages throughout history suggest that our minds create our reality— and that if we master our minds we can create the reality we desire. Some of us hear this sort of idea and think it's nonsense (but don't necessarily have any better ideas about achieving happiness or the life we want); some of us hear these ideas in forms such as *The New Earth* by Eckhart Tolle or *The Secret* and think it sounds exciting and empowering. For a week or two feel as if we are "manifesting" things but within a short span of time most of us have forgotten about meditating or mentally architecting better experiences for ourselves and are on to the next quick fix. Whether or not it's possible to mentally conjure up wealth, fame or excellence, simply trying, by any and all means we can think of, to have better relationships with our children seems like a hugely important yet reachable goal worth pulling out all the stops for—even including the temporary suspension of disbelief and an over-reliance on logic and rationality.

This chapter is meant to be an organic and logical extension of the ideas of the previous eight chapters, emphasizing patience, attention and the attitude that we don't have to parent so much as we *get to* parent, but now framed in the context of the subtle and intuitive links that exist between parents and children. We will explore different ways of conceptualizing the intuitive, animal and possibly telepathic connections that we have with our children and look at ways we might use them to help our children and our families feel happier and more harmonious. Even if "mind-reading" proves impossible, the *attempt* to intuit, as an act of love, may translate into closer relationships with happier children.

An open mind is a good thing to have in parenting and in the world. Yet even the best ideas need to be applied consistently over time to have optimally positive and lasting effects. This chapter is not about doing magic as a parent, it is about opening the doors of perception just a little wider and then using whatever we gain to stay on message, which is that we love our children and truly want the best for them and for our collective world. Opening the "third eye" and stepping into the sphere of psychic parenting may seem an unconventional notion in a parenting self-help book, but I have found the concept extremely helpful in my clinical work with parents and children as well as in my own parenting.

Earth and Air

My perspective on the "mystic" realm is both trusting and skeptical. As is generally true for each of us, I am a combination of my parents. An image I carry emblazoned in my mind is walking into my parents' room to typically find my father in bed reading the Wall Street Journal and my mom lying beside him holding crystals and meditating. Over the years I have come to see that it is actually my father who sees the world through rose-colored glasses, and my mother is the pragmatist. After fifty years of marriage they make a pretty good team.

As parents, we need to roll up our sleeves and be sure that the basic needs of our children, from safety and nutrition to love and attention, are being met before we concern ourselves with esoteric aspects of care-giving. The psychic in parenting is like adding spin to the ball in tennis or golf—it is interesting and worth talking about, but it is not a substitute for mastering fundamentals, such as listening (not to thoughts, but to what our children actually *do* say), setting clear limits and expectations with our spoken words and providing logical and consistent consequences with our actions. And yet, if we *were* able to better tune in to what the world, and particularly our children, are "saying" when they are not actually speaking, we might be able to better attune with our kids at times such as when they are too young to talk, or when they are too wounded, angry or mistrustful to listen.

Over the years as a therapist, I have come to experience occasional connections with my clients that could be called "extra-sensory" or psychic; sometimes I might pick up an ache or pain, an emotion or an image that pops into my mind. I have learned to trust such "messages" and talk about them with my clients, understanding these instances as acts of trust where my client wants me to know more about how they hurt, or unconsciously feel, so that I can help them. Physical symptoms are sometimes a way that our bodies hold and experience emotional pain that has not been recognized, or which was initially overwhelming, and has gone into hiding in the body. I slowly learned that if I ignore the pain I am "offered" by my clients I feel ill and exhausted but if I comment on it, my own discomfort quickly releases (and often my client's pain either releases or at least decreases). By treating a sad or painful connection as helpful information, we serve the deep Self; then pain becomes a shared, and thus transforming, experience and source of inner guidance that can lead us to our right path and our happiness. While this sort of psychic connecting may sound mysterious, it feels more to me like I have learned, over years, to get my ego out of the way and trust that if I am present, open, honest and natural then what my clients need me to know I will somehow come to know, even if they can't always directly tell me with their words. When two people form an authentic connection, growth and increasing happiness tend to spontaneously occur and healing often takes care of itself. As parents, if we can create favorable conditions for our children to trust that we are listening, we will be better able to attune with them at all levels, from spoken to psychic, and they will be more able to heal and grow naturally from within.

The Child Who Was Upset For her Mother

I have occasionally encouraged adult clients to experiment with using their thoughts to finesse a delicate parenting juncture. For example, a mother whose child was having anxiety and repeated nightmares. While the young girl had no conscious awareness of it, the mother was highly upset about her aging father's upcoming marriage to a woman younger than herself. It turned out that her dad had left her mom when she was the same age as her child was now. As the child was too young to really understand this situation, and it would not necessarily have been appropriate or helpful to spell it all out even if she could, I suggested that at bedtime she gently rub her daughter's back as she was falling asleep and "explain" things, but only in her mind and actually say nothing. Something along the lines of mentally saying, "I know you are feeling scared and you don't really know why. Long ago when I was your age my dad left and it made me sad, angry and scared. And now grandpa is getting married again and it is reminding me of those bad feelings and somehow you picked them up. So you can give them back to me and I will feel bad about this myself and you can sleep peacefully as you have nothing to be afraid of."

I also explained to the mother that if it worked, she herself might feel more sad, scared and angry, but that her child would feel better. As is typical, the mother was more than willing to go ahead and feel a little awful if it would spare her child pain. Our work to make the unspoken and unrealized pain more conscious freed this mother to make the hard but loving choice to work through her own hurt and to release her child from it. She and I were both delighted to find that the child's anxiety level dropped within the week and the nightmares went away. Of course this doesn't "prove" anything about psychic transmission, and it is entirely plausible that the mother's simply *trying* to communicate with her child mind-to-mind turned out to be an effective way to clarify her own thinking, soothe herself and help contain her sadness and anxiety. Still, whatever helps mom or dad to be patient, calm and confident generally helps their children to feel happier and less anxious. So whether the message really found its way into the child's psyche, or the mother's different "vibe" of loving calm, in and of itself, made the difference, *something* about at least attempting to psychically soothe her daughter brought good results for this mom, and for other parents who were willing to give it a try.

The Silver Canoe

In my practice I am primarily interested in positive results. Due to the success that the quasi-psychic approach has found with a good number of parents, I have increasingly found myself suggesting that parents psychically tell their children certain things that are better left unsaid at the audible level.

I wrestled in my mind for a long time, not just on whether to talk about psychic parenting at all, but also about *how* to convey it in a way that was earthy and understandable, especially to skeptics and those who might be open to the possibility of the psychic realm being real enough, but who personally don't feel that they have a strong intuitive, much less psychic, capacity. These are the readers I wish most strongly to reach and to encourage to experiment with these ideas. If "psychically" telling our children that we love them somehow makes a difference when nothing else seems to be working, what's the harm? Even if it doesn't change things for our child, perhaps it helps us stay connected to what we truly feel—and be more effective in challenging times. Being an intuitive sort myself, I pay sincere attention to my own dreams as well as those of my clients. So I put my dilemma about whether, and how, to conceptualize, and talk about, "psychic parenting," to my dreams and soon had an interesting one: I was on the bank of a beautiful river in a dense forest where an Old Guide gave me a silver canoe. The Guide explained how I, as a parent, had to counter-balance my child, who was placed at the front of the canoe, and we paddled off, drifting with the current along a winding river.

Dreams can have many meanings, but I took the silver canoe to be a visual representation of psychic containing. A canoe is a vessel meant for going through water (i.e. navigating the unconscious). Silver is the moon's color, and is connected to the realm of the night, the feminine and the intuitive (signaling that the dream is addressing my questions about the psychic realm). Silver is also Mercury's color, the archetypal messenger who is able to cross into typically inaccessible realms, such as into the unconscious. The Old Guide is a classic "Wise Old Man" who gives me the canoe and counsels me on how to use it. In offering a way of picturing how the deep Self, or soul (the silver canoe), can serve as a psychological and spiritual container for the ego-self, and for the selves of our children, the dream seemed to affirm the concept of psychic parenting and, at least I hope, my endeavoring to write about it.

Why Aren't We Intuitively Attuned With Our Children?

It is possible that we are all born intuitive but are taught to heed the five senses and disregard the sixth. If we didn't learn to ignore it, intuition and attunement with others, especially our children, would be a natural complement to seeing, hearing, touch, etc. Perhaps all it would take to cultivate our natural intuitiveness would be to calm down and pay closer attention to our emotions, sensations and the seemingly random thoughts or images that come into our heads or show up in our dreams. Networks of neurons that are very much like brain cells also surround our intestines and hearts. We literally have a "heart mind," and a "gut mind"—the question is whether we have ignored these for so long that we no longer hear what they say, or by ignoring them have made *them* ill or depressed; maybe they have locked themselves in their room and shut down, just as our child does, maybe we're trying to listen but have forgotten how to understand the language of the heart and the gut.

Most adults generally experience the world in a "normal" and mundane way—and if they don't, they know enough to keep quiet about it. In speaking with many people, however, it seems that most of us can report at least a few unusual experiences that we can't really explain by rational means, like falling in love and suddenly just knowing that someone is "the one," or when we sense from afar that a loved one is ailing or in danger. A common telepathic occurrence is when we randomly think of someone with whom we rarely speak and moments later the phone rings and it's them.

If we take the position that being attuned with our children is the natural state of things yet find ourselves utterly in the dark about what our child is thinking or feeling, or are sadly unable to convey love and calm to them, it makes sense to ask ourselves what might have gotten in the way of their, or our own, instinct and intuition?

What's In Our Child's Way?

1) <u>We Parents Have Talked Them Out of Seeing the Magic All Around Us</u>

When kids are first born perhaps they see angels, elves and faeries but find it no more astounding than seeing faces and clouds. As they mature we confuse them by first reading them stories that confirm what they've always seen, and then telling them that such stories are just make-believe. Since they want our love and they want to succeed in the world where those who feed and love them live, they systematically learn to ignore their perceptions and conform to agreed upon reality. While I say this in the spirit in which *Peter Pan, Alice in Wonderland* and *Harry Potter* were probably written and while I no longer see elves, etc., I suspect that once upon a time I did.

Maybe it's worth truly listening to our children's tales of past lives or mystical perceptions without fearing that we'll teach them to be crazy.

2) Natural Development

The shades of darkness that obscure the magical or numinous world close naturally as our children grow and busy themselves with the "real" world. When it comes time to no longer believe in the tooth fairy and Santa, we would hurt our children if we infantilize them by insisting (or tricking them) that they keep believing. But just because they no longer believe in the commercially propagated myths doesn't mean they aren't increasingly interested in the witchy realms of power, magic and mysticism which validate their real-enough inner worlds. Perhaps the great success of *Harry Potter* is that it evokes the world as late elementary, middle and even early high school kids feel it to be. They may recognize it as fantasy, yet there must be some sort of truth in such successful stories that teach kids about dark and light energy and the wise use of power.

Maybe, as grown-ups and parents, we mature to the point where we are safe enough in our so-called sanity to peek behind the shade once again—and hopefully wise enough to use whatever powers we can conjure as power to love and help our children.

3) <u>Wounds</u>

If our children have been hurt by neglect, or by inappropriate intrusions, they may have had to wall themselves off and focus on survival and self-protection. With most energy going to watching for problems in the real world, energy for play and fantasy dies and with it their openness and sensitivity to intuition. Kids who have to grow up too fast, for whatever reasons, may become harsh and cynical, or they may start to live in a fantasy world of their own making to escape from an overwhelming and toxic world.

While such a child may not be in contact with their playful and imaginative side, they probably aren't in positive connection with real people either. Before such a child can come back to trusting their intuitions, they may need to heal their traumas.

4) <u>Psychotic Experiences and Disorders</u>

When children are ill with fever they may hallucinate. When kids are very badly hurt they may do more than lose touch with intuition, they may start to perceive things as real that truly are not there. This is a delicate issue because playful intuitiveness is good for most people, but extremely hurt or psychotic children need help with reality testing and not enhanced imagination. In these tragic situations it would be healthy and positive for the child to stay firmly rooted in agreed upon reality. Still, it is worth keeping in mind that certain other "primitive" (or perhaps "natural") cultures have viewed psychotic people as having special abilities to see a fuller view of things and so they were honored and valued in the group for the perspective they brought.

When children enter into psychotic states they may unconsciously share, or evoke powerfully destabilizing feelings in us at a seemingly psychic level. While in general most of us are probably too closed down to the intuitive or psychic realms, psychotics are too open. As parents in such cases we may have to use our intuitive abilities to help contain and bind our children's terror.

5) <u>Warding Off Our Negative Spill-Over</u>

Some children are not shut off from their intuition, but they are closed off from us parents. At times, and in moderation, this marks healthy development as children separate and strive to become more independent. But sometimes, especially if they are depressed and anxious, our children may intuit that they need to close an imagined door between us because our anger, bitterness, sorrow or anxiety is spilling over into them. Instead of feeling contained by us they may feel swamped. If they are blocking us at the intuitive level, it may be necessary that we at least work to recognize and contain our own issues and hopefully begin to send apologies, love and comfort along intuitive channels.

What's In Our Way?

1) <u>Not Believing</u>

A primary potential obstacle to psychically parenting our children is for us to simply not believe that it's possible. Or perhaps we just think of ourselves as not very gifted in this area and so keep ignoring it and leaving it dormant and of little use to us or benefit to our children. Intuition is probably like flying in *Peter Pan*—it responds well to being believed in.

2) Fear of Psychological Intensity

When we do plug into our children's emotional states it can be very disorienting and disturbing. If our own psychological bowl is leaky we may be unconsciously avoidant of allowing our child to spill their overwhelming feelings into us. We may be uncomfortable with strong emotions because of the way we were raised (i.e. in a cold or sarcastic environment). We may be insecure about our instincts and mean to protect our children from our hurt or negative feelings but end up seeming distant or uncaring. Fear of emotional intensity may be partly because we are actually a lot more sensitive (i.e. able to read and even transmit energy, if not thoughts, with our kid) than we might have realized. One of the best things we can do for our parenting, psychic or not, is to heal and strengthen the vessel of the self so that we can better calm, contain and love our children at an unspoken, intuitive level.

3) Unhappiness

Jung says that children carry the unsolved problems of their parents. Our own unhappiness is a problem for our children at many levels. At the intuitive level our melancholy threatens to leak into our child's sense of self and mistakenly teach them that it is they who are problematic, uninteresting or depressing. Another issue with unhappiness is that it reflects a past and future orientation where we worry about what will come and lament what has been. Failing to be in the present moment blocks our chances of true happiness, and it also blocks our openness to the feelings, thoughts and energies that our children are experiencing right now. To help our children be happier, as well as to snap out of our own dark moods, we need to have some good, or even painful but *connected*, times right now. Sincerely trying to figure out and feel what may be going on in the inner lives of our children is a way to break out of the self-focus that traps us in loneliness and sorrow.

4) <u>We've Stopped Trusting Our Gut</u>

In our efforts to conform to the world and "succeed" we may have stopped talking about anything that isn't practical and agreed upon by everyone we know as "real." If we are male we may have been taught that it's un-masculine to have strong feelings (other than anger and lust), much less intuition. Rather than waiting until our deathbed to remember the emotional importance of simple pleasures (like Orson Welles' yearning in *Citizen Kane* for "Rosebud"—which turns out to be his childhood sled), we need to become true to ourselves while still in the full bloom of life and parenting.

Our gut instincts tell us when something is off with our child and while all manner of experts may tell us that we are wrong, if our gut says otherwise we must trust it and keep searching until we find a path that feels right. Both our children and the universe are constantly "talking" to us, and if we learn to listen we find that even pain guides us to learn and grow.

5) <u>Family Secrets</u>

While most kids know about the relatives who cured diseases, made great art or fortunes, the relatives who went insane, committed suicide or went to prison are more likely to languish in secrecy at the back of the family closet. Traumas such as war experiences or victimizations may also go undiscussed so as not to burden the children or upset them. Yet if children are naturally psychic, they somehow know everything; only they don't *know* that they know and instead may carry a vague sense of foreboding, loss or melancholy and not understand it. Being aware of our own family's history (or of the fact that a lot of information has been never shared with us) helps us consider the possible impact of our ancestors' experiences on us and our children.

6) Dulled Senses

If we are willing to accept that psychic, or at least intuitive, connection with our children are possible, a potential block to it flowing could relate to the state of our physical bodies. If we want to be able to tune into our kids' subtle thoughts and feelings, we would be wise not to smoke, carry excess weight or eat a lot of artificial foods. Just as well trained actors think of their bodies as their "instrument," it makes intuitive sense to cleanse, purify and condition our bodies, as well as our hearts and minds, via diet, exercise, prayer, meditation, yoga, etc., to better attune to our children.

7) Sexism

Even though there is no more reason that a woman should be psychic or intuitive than that a man should be good at math, it is important to be aware of our own prejudices. Why are cats considered feminine when any given cat is as likely to be male as female? Why is it "feminine intuition" and not "masculine intuition"? From ancient times, women have come to be associated with mystery—probably because of the mystery of birth. The woman of the well, a symbol of fertility and abundance, is an ancient archetype that morphs into the healer with her potions and then veers off into the witch at her cauldron. Patriarchy artificially splits masculine knowledge from feminine wisdom and has tended to assign the sixth sense to women more than men—and then vilified it. The unconscious residue of this is that we may discourage intuition in our daughters as being associated with evil, and in our sons as being negatively associated with being feminine.

Broadening Our Perspective

Wisdom and the Language of the Animals

In the Grimm's fairytale, *The Three Languages,*[1] a ne'er-do-well son is sent off to study for a year and returns having only learned how to bark like a dog. His wealthy, powerful and exasperated father sends him to another teacher and he returns having learned to croak like a frog. In his final chance to redeem himself he merely learns to coo like a dove and his disgusted father orders that he be taken to the forest and killed. His father's henchmen show mercy by abandoning him to wander alone and probably die. When the young man comes to a castle that is overrun by menacing dogs he is able to speak with them and break the curse, securing a treasure for himself. Frogs then tell him to go to Rome where the Bishops have declared that the next person to enter the Vatican will be the Pope. Doves perch on his shoulders and coo the Latin prayers into his ear that he needs to fulfill his role as spiritual leader.

In *The White Snake,*[2] a lowly servant tastes the king's secret food and suddenly knows the language of animals. Now able to hear pleas for help from meager ants, fish and orphaned crows, he is kind to them and they end up returning the favor to help him gain love and treasure. In both of these stories animals may symbolize natural, instinctive and wise, but usually overlooked, aspects of the Self. The moral of these stories is that kindness, respect and sincere attention for the seemingly small (be it our children or the faint voice of our intuition) brings us into harmony with nature, assures success in love, delivers us into material, as well as spiritual, treasure and renders us fit to lead—perhaps even to parent.

Once upon a time we human beings were unselfconscious and part of nature. We were just one sort of animal amongst all the animals. The loss of paradise is also the loss of our unselfconscious connection to nature—and the dimming of our instinctive ability to vibe with children. Noted pediatrician, Dr. Harvey Karp, likens toddlers to Neanderthals and claims that parents need to learn "toddler-ese" to be able to soothe them when upset.[3] When a tantruming child wants a cookie, compassionately saying, "I'm sorry honey but you have to wait until after dinner" may only escalate their rage because the child feels not at all understood. Karp suggests a more primitive style to mirror their level of language: "You want. You want. You want cookie. You say, 'Cookie, now. Cookie now.'" By using our children's words in a simple and repetitive manner we are essentially employing the language of the animals. Children who cry incessantly, whine and do not respond to caregiver soothing are the most vulnerable to child abuse.[4] Anything that helps us understand, respect and soothe our children (especially those most difficult to comfort) is highly worth learning and cultivating in ourselves and in our parenting culture.

Children are generally enchanted with animals, perhaps in part because they recognize them as kindred spirits who are delightfully unsophisticated, authentic and straight-ahead just as they still are. Animals, in being in full possession of their instincts, are good teachers when it comes to psychic parenting. Our pets are very tuned into our energy and pick up on whether we are pleased with them or not. Our children also pick up on whether or not we are pleased with them even if we don't say anything about it. Recognizing that we are constantly sending and receiving many unspoken messages to and from our children may encourage us to purposely make those messages kind and positive, and to consider the possibility that random painful feelings that come over us may be messages from the animal sides of our children, or from long-ignored aspects of our Selves.

Mind-Reading and Micro-Expressions

A rational explanation of psychic phenomenon may be found in Malcolm Gladwell's *Blink*,[5] which explores how we continually take in, and transmit, all sorts of information below the radar of our conscious minds. Very often our first impressions and "snap decisions" are spot-on because our subconscious minds register and evaluate much more information, and much more quickly, than our conscious minds. The shadow side of "thin slicing" the world is where our prejudices influence us to draw knee-jerk, but mistaken, conclusions that we don't even realize are biased (i.e., tending to picture a white male if someone mentions a "doctor" or a "scientist").

A lot of the information we unconsciously give out and take in is right on our faces. The human face is capable of a very wide array of expressions, which are consistent across all cultures and which we are hard-wired to recognize. We sometimes have fleeting "micro-expressions" that pass across our faces so quickly that they go mostly unnoticed, yet potentially reveal our true feelings. To the degree we are able to consciously recognize micro-expressions (and read body language) it might make us appear as "mind-readers" to others who are less gifted in close observation. We may not be *consciously* aware of micro-expressions (i.e., a flicker of eye-rolling contempt) on someone's otherwise respectful face, but we may still get a gut feeling that something is off. Trusting our gut may mean that we are heeding the micro-expressions our subconscious picks up.

We may fail to "mind-read" our children for fear that we cannot handle difficult emotions such as anxiety, depression, anger or disappointment and so see only what we want to see in our child and not what they need us to see and understand. When this happens they must resort to more than micro-expressions, such as tantrums or dangerous acting out—but all along they probably want to be understood so we help them heal, learn and grow.

If we, or our children, are a bit autistic or have Aspergers syndrome (developmental disorders marked by extreme difficulty with social interactions), or if we have been wounded in ways that cause us not to make ready eye-contact, we are at a huge "mind-reading" disadvantage and will generally find social relationships very challenging. Miscommunication, feelings of inadequacy, withdrawal and social isolation all too easily follow from not instinctively knowing how to look for feelings. Deepening empathy for how our children may not naturally read faces might help us better coach them toward positive social relatedness where possible, and to feel better about who they are no matter what limitations they confront; learning to look for feelings in our kids' eyes and to closely watch their faces (especially if this doesn't come naturally for us, or if we tend to be too busy to consistently do it) is essential to improving our attunement with our children.

Whether or not we learn to read micro-expressions, we can ask ourselves if we are paying enough attention to the overt expressions, words and gestures of our children. It has been emphasized throughout this book that paying genuine and patient attention to our children is like an elixir of growth, trust and positive connection. It is said that emotions often actually *begin* on the face; so if we smile gently and serenely, like the Buddha, we can truly make ourselves feel better. The more often we smile, the more authentic our smiles will become—and the more good they will do for our children.

The Mystery of Psychic Phenomena

Jung, in being open to mystical ways of knowing, was ahead of his time. Freud was more interested in making psychology a classical science. He was aware of telepathic phenomena, experienced them and discussed them with certain trusted colleagues, but he argued against publicly acknowledging them because he felt it worked against his cause of establishing psychoanalysis as a legitimate science.[8] Freud was a man of his time, when science was virtually deified. Late in his life he said that he regretted not giving more attention to the realm of telepathic connecting. Freud was more famous, and widely read, than Jung who was also a man of science—just one who happened to be more open to exploring (and writing about) his own intuitive experiences. In the wake of what rational, logical, masculine, Newtonian "science" (absent intuitive, feminine, compassionate spirit) has wrought in the world (i.e. nuclear weapons and global warming), Jung has a lot to offer us in the 21st century. Jung writes about uncanny events such as when he experienced a sudden pain through his skull only to later learn that a patient had committed suicide by a bullet to the head at that very same moment.[9] Jung referred to such mind-blowing occurrences as synchronistic phenomena whereby events not accessible to rational consciousness are somehow perceived by the unconscious.

When synchronicities occur in our lives we may hesitate to believe that the universe could be "talking to us," warning, teaching and guiding us (i.e. if we literally see a "sign" or billboard that seems to appear in answer to a question we have asked ourselves). If we open ourselves to the idea that the world is alive and interacting with us, what could possibly speak more eloquently, or at least urgently, to our souls than our children? Parenting is a convergence of paths, a symbiotic relationship between a child's quest for self and a parent's quest for soul. The fact that our children come into existence and into our care could be seen as synchronicities that mark the crossings of individual threads of consciousness that weave us together in a vast collective web of inter-being.

What We Expect Is What We Get

The psychic abilities we naturally possess are likely to be more apparent if we slow down and pay closer attention to our inner and outer worlds as well as those of our children. By taking consistent time from our busy lives to pay sensitive, non-judgmental attention to messages that mysteriously come to us from our children via body sensations, images, emotions or telepathic communiques we may find that things start to go inexplicably better with our kids.

A logical extension of recognizing that we may be psychically connected with our children is that in addition to being kind with our words and behaviors, we also need to be kind in our *thoughts*. Many families can be read like comics or graphic novels, with angry thought bubbles hanging, all too legibly, above everyone's heads. If we imagine that others, especially our children, actually know our thoughts, we might pause before slipping into hostile mental images or muttering curses in our mind. Since we can't help but be human, and sometimes our worst self rather than our best Self shows up, good intuitive parenting might include mentally apologizing for our angry thoughts and following it up with some validating and loving unspoken sentiments. The possibility that we can consciously offer healing thoughts, and possibly make things better, without having to say or do anything is a big plus if our child is angry, oppositional or has us feeling like everything we say and do ends up misunderstood.

Keeping open to possibility, the following are guidelines for intuitive parenting:

1) Know what we transmit. Try and be aware of how critical or angry thoughts and feelings could cause our children pain if they consciously, or unconsciously, pick up on them with their own psychic abilities. This is all the more reason for us to try and be conscious, calm and happy.

2) Spend more time trying to pick up on our kids' vibes and intuiting their inner feelings. Consider how we might be missing subtle messages. Pay attention to seemingly random thoughts and feelings that could clue us into better understanding and helping our children.

3) Send out good. Take a leap of faith and actively try to communicate understanding, compassion, valida-

tion and undying love to our children with the greater subtlety, grace and diminished misunderstanding we offer when we telepathically "say" things and leave our all-too-often problematic words out of the equation.

Primitive Mental States

As an intern I had a client who, on the surface, appeared to be rather typical: A man in his late twenties seeking psychotherapy for mild depression. Due to his work schedule, he needed to meet at seven in the morning and so I sat bleary-eyed (I had a newborn at home) in a windowless office and listened to this shy but respectful loner dispassionately tell me about his unsatisfying life. While there was nothing unusual about the mundane things he told me, thirty minutes into our session I was gripped by a bizarre feeling: it was as if my client was engulfed in a dark tunnel where he zoomed away from me until he was a tiny figure I could hardly see or hear. I felt like I was under some kind of spell and could barely keep my eyes open. It was oddly frightening, and I feared that I might lose consciousness, not to mention feeling concerned that I would not be able to help him. I endured the experience, figuring it was due to the early hour, my own mental state from sleep-deprivation or that I was coming down with a bad cold. The bad feelings, however, left with the client and then returned along with him in our next session: the tunnel got even longer and darker, my hands and feet grew cold and I felt dizzy and unreal. Time stretched out horribly, and when the session finally ended I was drained and confused.

I explained this surreal experience to my supervisor who listened pensively and then said, "This guy's psychotic." I was baffled because the client didn't say or do anything overtly "crazy." My supervisor instructed me to directly ask the client about hearing voices or having visual hallucinations. I felt uncomfortable about asking, out of the blue, if he happened to be hearing or seeing things, but as the bizarre gloom closed around me in our next session I queried, "Do you ever hear voices?" Without missing a beat the client acknowledged that he did in fact hear voices and had visual hallucinations as well. He was quite open and forthcoming as we explored the nature of his hallucinations, and the history of his illness. We also discussed the importance of a medications consult with a psychiatrist. Once we were directly talking about his actual problem my own weird feelings dissipated—it was as if I had finally heard his unspoken cry for help. As he left I felt relieved and hopeful that we were on the road to really helping him. He never came back to the clinic.

I tried to follow up with him, but his contact information turned out to be false— he had vanished. While he may have fled because he couldn't trust me specifically, or therapy in general or perhaps feared medications, it seems noteworthy that during the sessions when I was literally feeling the fear and confusion of his psychosis he was able to tolerate meeting with me, but once I consciously understood the pain as "his problem" I no longer palpably felt his unbearable anguish— and so he went back to being as alone as ever. At that point in my development I lacked the skills, real understanding and emotional solidity to help him contain and struggle with his illness and the feelings it brought. It was a humbling encounter.

In the wake of this experience I began to notice that there were times when my weeks-old son was agitated or enraged, and I became aware of fleeting, yet similar, feelings of dread and annihilation as I had felt with my client. The parallel was uncanny and made me viscerally realize that the mental state we are born in is analogous to the one we break down into in the face of psychosis or overwhelming trauma. Could I have been extra-open to picking up on my client's psychosis because parenting a newborn had unconsciously opened some sort of natural telepathic channel that we form with our babies? If so, is this "channel" another way that we might pick up on their distress and, because we are so powerfully disturbed by the bad feelings, we are compelled to comfort them and bring relief. Whatever the truth, my more-conscious understanding about what it feels like to be utterly unhinged suggested to me that my baby was able to unconsciously transmit his inner states of fear and chaos into my psyche for containing, understanding and help with structuring. It is arduous to mentally hold such tumult. Intuiting that this was my baby's mental cry for help allowed me to stay present, engaged and not just think that I was going crazy due to sleep deprivation (which may well have been the case).

I began to mentally experiment when these feelings would flood me, typically between midnight and five a.m. when my baby, despite four straight hours of breast-feeding by my wife, was howling and virtually impossible to soothe; I would try to envision a tranquil scene, typically a blanket on some imagined hillside in Scotland with my son fully fed and laying between my wife and I watching clouds drift overhead. As long as I could hold a positive image clear and steady my baby would soothe, as I lost my focus he would slip back into agitation. These bleary-eyed and surreal experiences reinforced my belief that our children need us to hold them in mind, particularly when they are either coming apart from stress, hunger, anger or fear—or feeling these things because they are so young that they have not yet come together in the first place.

As babies we have no bowl of self and so we depend on our caregivers' psyches to contain us. In this primitive mental condition, our bodies are born but our psyches take a while to catch up and realize where we are—and *that* we are. When we are still psychologically unformed, we seek refuge in the borrowed mental spaces of our parents' psyches. As parents, some of our darkest and most infuriating moments come when we are caught unaware, and flooded, by primitive feelings that we may not even recognize as our children's mental experiences. Whether our child is three months, three years or thirteen, when they are swamped they unconsciously broadcast their distress and we may not realize that our uncanny and unpleasant feelings of pain, confusion or fear might be an excellent approximation of what it feels like to be our child at that moment.

It is one thing to read about primitive mental states and quite another to viscerally experience the power of someone else's tumult wash over us uninvited, misunderstood and unrecognized for what it is. My hope is that with a "head's up" we may be better able to consciously field these experiences when they come—perhaps *realizing* that the pain our children evoke in us is sometimes the only way they have of communicating the pain that they themselves do not understand. Primitive mental states can be so excruciating that after a few weeks with a colicky newborn it's not uncommon for us to suddenly have a deeper understanding about how parents could ever cross the line into losing it and abandoning or hurting their own children—and that is a horrifying thing to discover as part of our psyches; hopefully a discovery that brings more compassion, less judgment and a deeper commitment to work together and hold our children lovingly in mind.

Body Memory, Body Wisdom

As we hone our sensitivity to our children's inner thoughts and feelings and strengthen our ability to hold them in our minds, we may discover that we receive key information about our children and our Selves not just with our minds but also with our bodies. As primitive "mental" states hark to a time before our minds have been able to develop, they may be better understood as primitive *bodily* states. We literally have gut minds and heart minds—nets of neurons that surround those organs to independently fear, love and guide us if we will listen. We pick up information from our children's tummies and hearts with our own tummies and hearts. We also unconsciously transmit information from our bodies so we want to pay conscious attention and take loving care of our physical selves in the service of our kids.

We sometimes store non-verbal memories and unprocessed emotions in our bodies. Such "body memories" can be triggered when our children reach ages that brought losses, or traumas, to us when we were that age. For example, there were a couple of weeks early in my first son's life when, after a middle of the night stint trying to calm him, I would hand him back to my wife and be overcome by a need to go out to the living room and discharge intense feelings of rage by punching the middle of the couch. I tried to think of this as a normal release of pent-up frustration built up in the previous hours of *not* yelling back at my howling newborn. My wife thought my behavior was scary and weird—especially because my rage was so intense and I'm not usually prone to angry outbursts. The whole thing left me vaguely ashamed and confused.

Somewhere in this surreal stretch of sleep-deprived couch punching I found myself talking to my mom on the phone and sincerely appreciating, probably for the first time, the mere fact that she parented me. Perhaps validating her contribution as my mom put her in an open mood and out spilled: "I always worried that I permanently damaged you that day I threw you at the couch." She explained how I had also been a very difficult baby who she often could not get to stop crying no matter what she did. At one point she couldn't take it anymore and literally hurled me across the room at the couch. She said I was stunned and went "dead" for a moment, which apparently gave us both a good scare. She had carried that secret moment with her for all the intervening years and I had too—as a body memory.

With my mother's confession, I realized that I had been re-enacting that moment again and again in punching the couch: my newborn son was triggering my own experience as a newborn which, up until that point, I had no way of understanding much less remembering. As the parent of a high-maintenance baby, I was now in a position to better understand how a mother *could* throw a child at a couch. Rather than feeling angry with my mom I felt much better—validated in my feelings of couch-rage. What I felt for my mom was spontaneous forgiveness, love and increased closeness. Since my angry impulses now made sense to me, the urge to punch the couch never again returned. My baby, however, still took nine months to sleep through the night.

Sometimes our bodies can be psychic without our minds' awareness. There have been experiments in which a person is shown pictures of various things, in random order, with equipment measuring their bodies; when the picture that is *about to be shown* is a disturbing image, the person's body unconsciously braces for a shock, but when the next picture up is a flower the body stays tranquil.[11] If our bodies might be psychic this is all the more reason to learn to quiet the mind, be present to our bodies and listen to what they might be saying. Calm and happy bodies may better allow us to convey calm and containing energy to our kids. Finally, loving touch can be a powerful way to communicate directly with our children's body-minds to soothe them when words are of little or no help.

The Third Eye and The Insula

The third eye, or inner eye, is a concept found in Eastern and Western mystical traditions that relates to precognition, clairvoyance and spiritual enlightenment. Buddha, Shiva and various yogis are often depicted as having a third eye or brow chakra (an energy center located just above the center point between the eyebrows); this same region is emphasized in alchemy and Kabbalah and is a focal point in various meditation, religious and spiritual practices. As parents we might wonder if there really is such a thing as a third eye, and if so, how might we open it to better see our children?

An intriguing recent discovery may offer a clue. There is a little-studied area of the brain in the neighborhood of the brow chakra, sitting between the forebrain and the lower brain, which is called the insula. It appears that the insula may help to mediate between our fight/flight response and our intuitive and interpersonally connecting upper, or pre-frontal, brains. Our ability to calm and contain our primitive emotions (and perhaps those that spill psychically or unconsciously over into us from our loved ones) seems to be enhanced by the thickness of our insulas; it is as if greater neurological cushioning in this area dampens our reactivity to cues that normally push us toward impulsive fear or aggression. So while a thicker insula might not, in and of itself, give us mystical visionary ability, it might help us stay calm, clear and leave us better able to use our capacity for higher consciousness, empathy and compassion.

If the bad news about the insula is that size matters, the good news is that we can actually get it to grow (and this goes against what neurologists had previously believed about the adult brain). In a Harvard research study it turned out that people who engaged in yoga or meditation practices had thicker insulas than those whose physical exercise lacked any sort of meditation or "spiritual" aspect.[12] There was a direct correlation between hours spent meditating and thicker insulas—and the effects are *cumulative*; in other words, gains add up and do not reverse; so, every single minute we spend meditating adds to our insulas, our potential Zen and our capacity to be our best Selves as parents.

Meditation is now seen as a scientifically valid treatment for depression, anxiety and a number of other conditions (and this means that we may even now get reimbursed by our health insurance for money we spend on things like mindfulness based stress reduction or MBSR). Of course it takes quite a bit of yoga before enhancement to the insula visibly shows up on a brain scan, but that owes more to the current lack of refinement in our brain-imaging techniques. And if this is not enough to get us to the yoga studio or into a meditation class, these researchers also discovered that meditational practice correlates with maintaining thickness in the outer covering of the brain; this layer naturally thins as we age, and leads to memory loss—but in the brains of long-term yoga practitioners and others who meditate this layer is the same in their fifties and beyond as it would be in brain of someone in their twenties or thirties. So, yoga and the like may also help us be our best Selves as grandparents.

Envision What We Want

In each of the previous chapters there has been a section on envisioning the feelings, behaviors and relationships we want for, and with, our children. In a sense, visualization is akin to "psychic parenting." But before we place "mind over matter," it is important to place heart over mind. If we are clear on what we want for our child, and can consistently picture it, this alone may shift our energy and is likely to have a positive effect.

At the intuitive level, envisioning what we want may boil down to learning how to envision ourselves wanting what we have. By consciously embracing what is, we choose not to envision a better tomorrow, but rather to envision today in a more compassionate, accepting and loving way. Meditating on the beauty of what we have, pain and all, sets us in alignment with the mysterious universe, opens our psychic capabilities, propels us toward becoming our best Self and empowers us to create the right conditions to bring out the best in our children.

Strategies For Helping

The Overriding Case For Compassion

Given that the world contains a lot of cruelty and suffering it would be absurd to *like* everything about it, yet to *love* the world by truly seeing, appreciating and living consciously in it is highly consistent with being compassionate. Psychic phenomena may be best understood as instances when we become *consciously* aware of a pervasive underlying truth, which is that we are connected with everyone, and everything—all the time, whether we realize it or not. To the extent this may be true, compassion is our wisest and most helpful attitude toward everyone, especially our children.

The more we recognize "bad" behavior in others as suffering, the more we learn to not turn away but instead bear kindhearted witness. Whether telepathically or directly accomplished, opening our Selves to receive and lovingly recognize our children's thoughts and feelings is the epitome of compassion and a hugely effective strategy for helping them heal and grow. Seeing clearly and without judgment, neither turning away nor rushing in to make things all better, communicates a love that helps melt anger into sadness and transforms sadness into tranquility and appreciation. Our hearts naturally awaken to compassion when we see without judgment, and that compassion soon finds its way to our children across the strands that link us all to each other.

Make it Possible: Cultivate Intuition

As a psychologist, I have noticed that we are often able to break through fears and achieve goals when we place our efforts *in the service* of something greater than our ego-selves (such as our deep Selves or our children). Our egos may want a promotion, but if our deep Self says it's time, or we recognize that it's really about making more money to feed and clothe our children, our power may be unlocked. By wishing to improve our intuitive or telepathic abilities in the service of our children, we create favorable conditions for inner doors to open and reveal solutions to outer world problems and obstacles.

To enhance intuitive parenting it helps to pay attention to all sorts of random thoughts, feelings and information, even if they come to us in seemingly strange ways. We can also focus our desire for more understanding on one or two key questions, such as: "What's really causing our child distress?"; "What do they truly need from us?"; or, "What unconscious wounds of our own might be interfering with our parenting?" It helps to continually ask ourselves our questions when we are in different moods and at different times of day—especially just before bed in the hopes that we may get an answer in a dream.

Because dreams are like seashells that wash up from the sea of our unconscious, walking along the beach of our morning mind and paying serious attention to what we find there is a great way to enhance our intuitive sensibilities. We may not consciously remember our dreams, but we all dream every night. If we purchase a dream journal and put it beside our beds, we tell the deep Self that we are ready to listen; it can take days, weeks or months, but eventually we will recall a dream. If we spend a little time with that dream we will soon get more. Interpreting dreams is an art, but we can begin by meditating on the images, figures and situations we dream about and begin to learn our personal vocabulary of symbols. One possible approach to dream interpretation is to imagine that everything in them represents aspects of our Selves, such as our Inner Child, our Shadow or our ideal masculine or feminine lover/helper/partner (representatives not of our soul-mates but of our souls themselves); dreams can help us compassionately notice the parts of ourselves that are afraid, unhappy, scared, trapped or abandoned. Dreams may also symbolically represent our outer situations and if we compassionately and non-judgmentally consider what our deep Selves are bringing into consciousness, such as anger, fear or sorrow, we may unlock our best Selves and be freer to love and parent. Sometimes we get so many dreams we cannot sort through them all or begin to figure them out. In these situations it can be helpful to trust our intuition and select one dream, or image and then do active imagination; here we try to place ourselves back in the dream and let it continue to play out. We can imagine asking the figures in our dream for guidance, insights or gifts. If we are playful and patient, our imagination will activate and all sorts of unexpected things may occur in our mind's eye.

While dreams offer valuable information, the real world offers many surrealistic opportunities for guidance. If we walk along our street with a question in mind, and pay careful attention to everything, we may see and hear what the universe is whispering on any given morning; we get clues from our bodies, from trees, birds, clouds and countless coincidences. Music can get our creative minds flowing and since music correlates with psychic ability, it might help our intuition if we listen to more music or play music if we are able. If we learn how to encounter everything as a child once again, the world reveals itself to be fantastically alive, beautiful, sad and continually talking to us. Dusk and dawn are the best times to walk along these sorts of psychological beaches, when treasures glimmer in the half-light between pragmatism and mystery. If we ask our questions day after day, at dusk and at dawn, we will get insights and guidance that, while hard to justify or explain, will help us be better parents—and if our children become happier and lighter in spirit, that's all the "proof" we really need.

Priming

"Priming" is the concept of exposing people to words or images at an unconscious level in order to influence their behavior. For example, people exposed to words like "wrinkle," "old" and "bingo" when doing word puzzles end up leaving the room walking significantly slower than they came in; words like "courteous," "appreciate" and "considerate" leave people much more patient and polite than others exposed to words like "rude" and "aggressively."[13] In *Blink*, Malcolm Gladwell offers important insights about race and gender biases related to priming, but priming might also offer utility for parenting.

If we become more aware of the words and images that unconsciously influence our children, and us, we might deliberately invite our minds, and/or our children's minds, to be more prone to patience and kindness by exposing ourselves to calming and loving words or images. Coming home to the smell of baking brownies primes us differently than the stale smell of cigarettes and unwashed dishes. Just as we might set a romantic mood for a romantic evening, we can set a loving and encouraging mood for a loving and encouraging life with our children. Having interesting magazines, books and music around the house may prime our kids to be more interested in the world and open to it. In a sense we prime our children to feel loved and cared about with nicely made beds, neatly folded clothes, hot cocoa in winter or lemonade in summer; making time to sit down near our child and be available to listen primes them to know that they are loved, lovable and interesting; these messages build self-esteem and the confidence to share ideas and contribute to the group. The more our children are consistently exposed to our patient, gentle and polite love the more prone they may be to exhibit that sort of attitude, mood and behavior themselves. Priming suggests that watching cruel "reality" shows and playing violent games may facilitate negative and rude behavior while more positive programming probably sets them up to be more positive kids.

We can think about what we want to enhance in our parenting, and then do things that prime ourselves to be kind, patient, firm or humorous—whatever we want to be. For example, we might set our computer wallpaper to images that remind us to be our best Self. Consistency is a key to good parenting, so if it helps to send ourselves a daily email of encouragement, to put post-it notes in our car or leave ourselves (or our partners) encouraging and supportive messages this is not only nice, it is priming us to be our best Selves.

Priming may be what accounts for the vast popularity of self-help books, and may contain the secret to their utility: perhaps priming is what helps us do better at whatever we are trying to achieve in the midst of reading about it, and why we drop off our improved behaviors soon after we finish a book, because we are no longer being primed to keep them up. Perhaps reading one page per day of a book, such as this one, will do more to keep us on track as parents than if we read it all at once.

In research dating back to the 1960's Lloyd Silverman used priming to unconsciously expose subjects to the words "Mommy and I are one."[14] Not only did the priming prove effective, the message itself seemed to enhance functioning in a wide array of recipients ranging from schizophrenics who were more stable, neurotics who felt better and university students who were seen to have their math grades go up. As parents, we are in a powerful position to transmit the message of oneness with our children. While the idea may give rise to bad Jewish Mother jokes, if the notion of oneness (subtly transmitted to the unconscious) can help our children feel and function better, we ought not to toss it away out of hand. To the extent that we, as parents, do not feel comfortable with the idea that we are "one with our Mommy," "Mommy" might be understood in a wider sense of ocean, earth, cosmos or whatever transcendent force represents the ultimate, if unknown, source of us. The question of our own relationships to our parents, and to a sense of oneness, has a huge impact on our parenting.

Psychically Individuating from our Parents

When we are very young we either like something or we don't. Since we can't yet see that our parents are both wonderful and infuriating we split them into two different parents. We internalize these two parents, good and bad, and are affected by the way *they* continue to treat us, long after the influence of our actual parents weakens. Depending on how much of the time we were loved and soothed versus yelled at or neglected, our inner "good" mothers (and fathers) end up stronger, weaker or evenly matched with our inner "bad" mothers (and fathers). As adults we may be encouraged or debilitated by these inner figures—we may feel supported by inner parents to be our best Selves or mocked and maligned, which may trickle down to our children (much as it may have trickled into our parents over generations).

As we individuate we can consciously work to grow kind and encouraging inner voices to the point where they can dwarf, and even be nice to, our critical inner voices. Since we are psychically linked with our children, the sorts of relationships we have with our inner parents are likely to have a large impact on our kids. And while having a good relationship with our real parents is a great thing to do for our children as well as ourselves, sometimes that is easier said than done. Parents may have passed away or be impaired in ways that make interacting with them feel like trying to draw water from an empty well. Sometimes the best we can do is to *psychically* individuate from our parents. We can imagine telling our parents how we really feel, and they hearing, acknowledging and apologizing. We can imagine forgiving and feeling loved and connected. If psychically individuating from our parents frees us to love more compassionately, and benefits our children, it is certainly worth a try. So, how do we do this?

Imagine finding ourselves in a tranquil and safe place with our parents (or we can imagine them one at a time). Using our imagination, and trusting that our inner parent will sit and listen to all that we have to say to them, we make a covenant to be kind and compassionate to ourselves *and* to our inner parents. We approach this dialogue in the spirit of love, motivated by our wish to have a better relationship with our parents in the service of our children. We commit to share our true feelings not as a recrimination, but as an authentic offering—a gift, an offering in honor of our children who are also our inner parents' grandchildren, releasing all expectation that the past could be undone and instead striving to respect and acknowledge that our parents have pain of their own and, from their perspective have had, perfectly good reasons for everything they have done.

In our inner conversation we seek to make the following six points:

1) First and foremost, we want a better relationship with our inner parents, and if possible outer parents as well, and this is why we seek to express our pain as well as our love.

2) We love our parents and our hurt does not negate that love.

3) Although we recognize that they did not consciously intend harm (certainly not in the core of their best Selves), we ask that they recognize that we have nevertheless felt hurt by them, even if we may have misconstrued or distorted the facts.

4) We wish to be validated in the truth of our emotional pain and offered a sincere apology to the extent that their thoughts and actions contributed to our suffering, low self-esteem, anxiety, anger or depression.

5) With or without apology, we forgive our parents for hurting us and recognize that our individuated truth is that we love our parents *and* that they have hurt us.

6) Finally, as the duality of our hurt and our love is recognized, accepted and understood by our inner parents, we are free to express our love, gratitude and appreciation so that the past becomes water under the bridge. We commit to having a grown-up to grown-up relationship, enjoying our time together, in spirit if not in outer reality, and loving our kids and each other.

Taking It To the Street, Or At Least Our Parents' Street

If these ideas of psychic individuation inspire us to try and have this type of conversation with our real parents, we must stand forewarned that we risk wrath and rejection, at least at first—but if we are honest, thoughtful and non-defensive, not to mention brave, our parents, like our children, may eventually (perhaps after some months of not speaking with us) recognize that this sort of conversation is not ultimately about blame but about love and healing. People, whether in our inner or outer worlds, who feel good about themselves are generally kind. If we get an earful back from our real parents, we can strive to realize this is their pain and that it did not come from us, that more than likely it came before we entered their lives. Cruelty is born of suffering. We can validate our own sad epiphany that they have probably unconsciously asked us to hold their emotional overflow, and their wounded child selves, and that they may still be unable to recognize and hold our feelings. But at least we might learn that they fail us because they are limited, and not because we are too much for *any* parent or essentially unlovable.

I had an adult woman client who called this painful individuation, "breaking up with my dad." Having personally walked this minefield, and having helped many clients across it, there are a couple of things we can keep in mind: we can semi-psychically intuit our parents' underlying feelings by examining the feelings just thinking about talking honestly to our parents, not to mention actually doing it, brings up in ourselves— particularly fear of abandonment (i.e. that they will stop loving us or talking to us), in other words, it is *our parents* who fear being unloved and abandoned by us and so they attack, manipulate and control to unconsciously avoid being helpless and abandoned for no reason. They *give us* reason to hate them in order to justify their self-fulfilling, shame-infused belief that we will hate them no matter what they do. We can use the bowl of self that we have been building to catch our parents' overflowing feelings of rage and dread, and then tip those messy and unpleasant emotions into mother and father bowls we mentally prepare for just this purpose so as to protect and not absorb these feelings into our sponge-like, pre-bowl, inner-child selves.

At whatever level we make use of these ideas, the hope is that they can serve as healing exercises to make us calmer, stronger and more able to let others, especially our children, know that we love them and are open to hearing their authentic hurt and pain as well as their love. Losing parents is profound and very painful and if they are no longer able to be physically present that needn't stop us from reaching out, in our minds, to see if their spirits might not be available. They may be more available to listen and help, and less defensive, as they come to exist in our hearts, than they were when they were alive. Think about it, if it were even remotely possible to send love and support to our children after we had passed away wouldn't we do that? So we shouldn't rule out the possibility that our ancestors are forever sending love and rooting for us to become our best Selves—whispering love, guidance and encouragement from the far corners of our Selves and from every sacred, spirit-infused being or "thing" that we encounter.

The Individuated Guy

It was a dark and foggy night as the Pacific Ocean pounded the rugged cliffs of Mendocino. My girlfriend (now wife) and I tumbled into the warmth of a cozy pub. As we waited for a table to come open, we noticed a man, well into his forties, who was also waiting for a table along with his parents. The man had a charming manner and a sweet face; his parents were a handsome couple bearing the radiant inner beauty that comes from living a happy life. The three of them were having a quietly marvelous time simply enjoying each other. They spoke, they listened to each other, they laughed together, genuinely interested in each other. My wife and I were enchanted and astounded. We had certainly had nice times with our parents before, but never *that* nice. Where was the irony? Where was the veiled resentment? Where was the neurotic subtext that we expected to be part of any sophisticated person's relationship to their parents? We'd seen starry-eyed parents before, but never a grown-up "child" who, despite our covertly intense scrutiny, appeared authentically confident, happy *and* well-related to his parents. He may have actually been a serial killer for all we knew, but our fantasy was that he truly and actually enjoyed his parents and got along with them. We named him "The Individuated Guy," and in our minds he still roams the rugged coast of Northern California, perhaps appearing out of the mist but a single night every hundred years, and forever enjoying his parents.

These were times, before we had children, when our parents were still to blame for *everything*—days when one's own therapy seemed to turn entirely on what our parents did and didn't do. Over the intervening years, children have arrived, my wife's parents have passed and are terribly missed, while my own parents have aged along with us and are appreciated more than ever. By his quiet and authentic example The Individuated Guy created favorable conditions for my wife and I to grow by allowing us to glimpse a picture of what is possible. I share our sighting of The Individuated Guy in the hopes that his spirit may inspire others, like a psychological Statue of Liberty who welcomes us wounded would-be grown-ups and teaches us that we can love, honor and most of all *enjoy* our parents—even if only in our minds. And meanwhile, we send thanks to an unknown hero, wherever he may be, who once truly enjoyed dinner with his parents.

Hold that Thought—Even if it's not Our Own

With very young and/or highly distraught children, we may be asked to hold some extremely uncomfortable feelings and confusing mental states. Their need for us to be good at mentally containing feelings is all the more important if our child must deal with actual mental illness, the isolation of autism, the exhausting dread of OCD, etc. Perhaps the more we let ourselves feel awful in the service and recognition that *this is psychically helping our child* the more we might find the strength, patience and love to pull their mental sled across the sometimes frozen tundra of child development. When our children suffer we can actively, albeit mentally, *invite* them to give us the feelings that they cannot hold, understand or deal with.

When our children unconsciously and psychically share things like dread, rage and fragmentation (psychologically going to pieces) with us we need a pretty strong bowl to be able to consciously recognize and contain these intrusive emotions and resist rejecting, distancing or retaliating in the face of what can feel like an attack on our own psychological solidity. The best we can do is help them make their own bowl by teaching them how it is done—by holding their psychic baggage for them until they get their sea legs in this world. It is as if they slosh around inside the bowl of us until they begin to slowly form into the bowl of them.

Much as we try not to catch actual vomit with our bare hands when we can help it, it is perfectly defensible to catch our children's chaotic and primitive feeling states with whatever psychic utensils we can muster, envisioning bowls, pots, canoes or other containers as we see fit. If we can hold their little head when they are literally vomiting, we can also hold it when they are psychologically vomiting. If our kids are older than newborns, when they lapse into tantrums and other regressive states (and who doesn't from time to time?), we can strive for compassion and tenderness rather than shaming them that they should grow up already. We can also try to mentally validate and soothe our children, especially if they are not yet talking, or are so upset at any given moment that talking is a bad idea, and notice if they feel any better. Listening usually helps more than talking, even at the psychic level. The deceptively simple and subtle act of intuiting when our pain could be a semblance of our children's pain, and not prematurely giving it back to them, is the essence of psychic holding.

When it comes to psychic holding, our mandate is to *be the bowl*. The more we understand when feelings that threaten to depress, frighten, confuse or enrage us are actually our children's overflow the less we are likely to feel maliciously attacked or out of control. While we need to let our children make use of our psyches in the beginning, and intermittently along the road of their development, we also must be sure to let them have their own minds and not presume that we ever really know what's in theirs. Actively wondering about what our children think and feel lets us hold them in our minds and helps them feel thought about, but thinking that we have them all figured out is a delusion. If we start to imply, or overtly suggest, that we know them better than they know themselves we risk disconfirming their faith in their own perceptions, which lowers confidence. When we psychically hold our children, we must avoid prematurely telling them what they feel; this is like putting the feelings they have just told us are too much for them back into them. This breaks unspoken trust and causes them to put up walls to protect them from us. Because they can barely contain their own feelings we must be extremely conscious about not spilling our own unwanted feelings into our kids.

We should keep in mind that with second and third children the parent's ability to tolerate sustained crying and screaming increases, especially when coming from very little babies, but a second or third baby's ability to tolerate their own feelings is probably no stronger than was the first child's. First kids demand that we learn something about psychic holding, even if we have no name for it. Second kids may benefit from "benign neglect," as we parents are no longer so anxious about every little thing, however, second, third and fourth kids need psychic holding just as badly as first children do. The more we understand that it is "normal" to be terrified and undifferentiated in early life and that it calls for mental TLC, the more we may be able to help our newborns get adjusted to our world as well as more compassionately assist our older children, friends, relatives and even ourselves (if circumstances ever cause us to tumble and fall backward into the psychological soup from which we all come).

Think But Don't Say

Sometimes it's easier to speak from our hearts if we don't actually have to say things out loud—and once we get started, our loving feelings have a way of getting clearer, stronger and more helpful as we talk things out in our heads. Taking some time to spell out the kind things we want to say in our heads, or by writing in our journals, can help us be more effective communicators of our love and support, and also leaves open the possibility that our children will magically improve *as if* they've heard our thoughts.

Whatever age our child is, there are times when we just can't talk to them: moments when they are too young, too proud, too wounded or too enraged. These are good times to *think* but not *say* what we understand about their feelings, or their situation, and continually try to mentally let them know that we love and are with them.

In *Blink*, Malcolm Gladwell discusses how John Gottman, a Princeton psychologist, is able to accurately predict if a marriage is doomed based on short snippets of mundane conversation between couples.[16] What Gottman has learned to look for is *contempt*—eye rolling, sarcasm, dismissing the other's opinion as dumb, etc. Contempt turns out to be deadly to relationships. Given that contempt is poison for marriage, it cannot possibly be good for children. As parents, and especially as intuitive or psychically sensitive parents, it logically follows that we do not want to express contempt for our children overtly, covertly or even mentally.

So, before we think about what to telepathically *say* to our kids it is important that we learn to NOT mentally spew mean, belittling or destructive messages. If we imagine that our children somehow unconsciously know how we actually feel about them, the implication is that they are affected by our cruel words and disparaging remarks even if we merely think them, or say them apart from our child in another room, house or city. If we trust that our kids are psychically connected with us, we need to be kind and thoughtful about everything we say, do and think about them. Our first step is to be mindful about what we think; if we find that we are consistently negative in our minds we need to recognize that we are feeling badly about ourselves.

Imagine our children's words literally forming into letters that hang in the air and drop into a big soup pot; imagine their thoughts and emotions taking shape or color and floating down into the pot. Now imagine making a soup out of all these ingredients, letting it cook long and slow and then eventually offering a taste back to our child—a tiny baby spoon full of everything they have said, felt and unconsciously spilled over into us. We need add little, if anything, to what they give us; we mentally contain them by providing the pot, our love is the low flame that simmers and melds the ingredients and compassion is the patience to wait for everything to cook and come together. By telepathically holding, blending and offering back manageable amounts of what our children could not hold, we psychically mirror them and help them form into solid, loved and lovable selves.

In deciding what to psychically say to our children at any given moment, a good place to start is to imagine being in our children's shoes, and then fantasizing what we might wish would be said to us. Perhaps something like our parents saying, "Of course you feel bad—you have every right to feel hurt and angry. You deserve an apology, and so I offer my most sincere and humble apology. You deserve to be treated with love, respect, patience, encouragement and dignity and I am going to make more of an effort to do this. I fall short because I am limited and because sometimes I feel badly about myself, but that only explains, and does not excuse, my disappointing behavior. Even if I fail to become the parent you wish you had, and who I wish I could be right now, please at least know that you are a great kid and deserve all the best. I will keep trying to do better, and wish that you could know how terrific and lovable you are right now as you are." Now who, when feeling maligned, wouldn't like to hear that?

Even if this sort of thing seems indulgent, or inconsistent with the way we see our children's "bad" behaviors, we can try it as an experiment; if our children mysteriously feel understood, accepted or calmer we might realize that they need this sort of radical, unconditional acceptance, and validation, *in order to* grow to the point where they can look at, and take responsibility for, themselves and their behavior. By listening to these imagined conversations, our own inner children might heal right alongside our actual children; in our inner world there is always plenty of room on the laps of our Great Mothers and Great Fathers.

If we are unsure about what sorts of nice or positive things we could mentally say to our children, an excellent resource for mindfulness and a great spirit is to be found in the works of Thich Nhat Hanh, a Buddhist Monk, poet and peace activist; in his *Teachings on Love*,[17] he offers many loving and healing meditations. A simple and positive thing to mentally say on behalf of our child could be: "May my child be peaceful, happy and light in body and spirit." By selecting a phrase like this, or by making one up that we tailor to our child's current feelings or situation, we set an intention for our child's life becoming happier. By consistently mentally reiterating our blessing, we send good wishes while continually recommitting to being our best Selves. If we mindfully contemplate our affirmation for our child, and remember to do it every day, we may be surprised and delighted at how a change as subtle as daily good wishes can unlock love and happiness in our child.

Exercises To Consider

Given that psychic connections are mysterious and difficult to force, the following exercises focus on cultivating an open mind and a loving heart in the hopes that we might invite greater intuitive understanding in the service of better parenting.

1. Parenting flash cards: If we are exposed to specific sorts of words and images, we are more likely to feel and behave in ways consistent with those words and images; this is called "priming." We could deliberately prime ourselves toward good parenting by clipping out pictures from magazines that suggest intuitive connecting, loving patience, fun with kids, etc. or we could lovingly write down words on index cards such as "Intuitive," "Sensitive," "Wise," "Patient," "Helpful," "Effective," "Consistent," "Loving," "Kind," "Spiritual," "Enlightened," or any other words we sense would encourage us to be our best Selves. We can flip through our parenting flash cards every morning, in the car, when we are feeling frustrated with our children, etc., and

see if it helps. Reading inspiring books, even just one page per day—but every day, may also prime us to stay on our path.

2. Parenting film festival: For periodic bigger boosts to the priming process, consider programming your own personal parenting film festival. Rent your favorite inspiring or uplifting movies about parenting or consider the following picks: *Mary Poppins* for an idealized Great Mother in mythic action. *To Kill a Mockingbird* for an archetypal Great Father at his human best. *Babette's Feast* for a mother figure who brings food and love to change the mood. *Lorenzo's Oil* for parents working together against all odds to heal their child. *Mr. Mom, Parenthood, Baby Boom,* or *Mother* to laugh instead of crying. *The Diving Bell and the Butterfly* for realizing the importance of appreciation for what we have, especially our children.

3. Sleuthing for family secrets in service of love: Make a list of family secrets: anything disgraceful, embarrassing or tragic that you have overheard, been told in secrecy or merely suspect may have happened. Casually get parents and relatives talking by expressing general interest in the family's history, and then digging deeper about the relatives that don't get talked about; express readiness to know some of the less proud moments in the family history—based on the notion that we, and our children, are less likely to reenact the past if we are conscious of it. Perhaps no secrets come to light, but you suspect they're there; in this case,

imagine making up a "family secret" to possibly account for the troubling behaviors of your parents, yourself or your child. For example, if your mother is cold and withholding, imagine making up a story in which she was raised in a harsh orphanage and never properly socialized. Even though it is fantasy, there may be emotional truth embedded in, and revealed by, the fabricated stories we create (i.e. that mother probably feels like she was treated the way your fantasy suggests).

Finally, imagine that your child already unconsciously knows about the suicides, madness, crimes, betrayals, etc. and subconsciously fears that this is who they are destined to become; would that help explain any of their interpersonal problems, self-defeating behaviors or painful feelings? Work to telepathically, but honestly, explain what has happened in the past and how your ancestors may have made mistakes or had bad fortune, but this is not your child's destiny; use words or thoughts to consistently reinforce the idea that your child is kind, honest, capable, deserving of good self-esteem and destined for a happy and successful life.

4. Meditate on your child's face: Everything has soul—from pebbles to wind to children. Being "psychic" is about tuning into what the soul of the world is whispering to us. Sit quietly and contemplate your child's face as they play, do homework or talk to you about whatever's on their mind. Breathe and softly allow yourself to see everything you possibly can about their energy,

thoughts and emotions—from fleeting micro-expressions that the subconscious can read (but only if we are looking) to seeing the edges of their luminous soul. Notice how this sort of mindfulness brings tranquility and opens your heart like a flower. When we see the beauty of our child as a sacred light, the seeing is its own reward—and we are at least partway there to psychically connecting with them, sensing what they need and intuiting how to provide it.

5. Have you psychically hugged your kid today? Commit yourself to at least one moment each day where you mentally visualize hugging your child and picturing love flowing from you into them (or you can literally hug them if they are good with it); during this real or imagined hug, think, and internally say, something like, "I send you love and wish for you to be happy, peaceful and know that you are a sacred, beautiful and wonderful kid." Refine your message as you see fit, but send it every day for at least a week, better yet several weeks, and make note if this correlates with any change in your child's, or your own, moods or behaviors.

6. Love to the past, love from the future: Using creative visualization, do a time travel exercise. Go as your current self to past situations where you could have used love and understanding and picture enshrouding your former self in love and compassion. Imagine telepathically transmitting empathy, encouragement and guidance,

steeped in the absolute trust that they (your self as you were in the past) will, at the very least, survive and arrive one day into being the self that we are now as we send back love to them. Next, imagine a wiser and more compassionate version of your future Self coming to you now and enshrouding you in their love, compassion and encouragement. Open your heart, mind and soul to your future Self's warmth, affection, understanding and to their absolute confidence that you will one day evolve into being your future Self.

7. Yoga (and/or meditation) builds and thickens a part of the brain that can help us better modulate our reactions to emotional provocation (i.e. mouthy and oppositional kids) and be able to tolerate intense emotions without drowning in them and becoming depressed or anxious. Such tranquility benefits us and supports us in our efforts to be better parents by improving our ability to practice psychic holding. If you practice yoga and seek to specifically enhance intuition, particular poses to consider might include shoulder stand, headstand, child's pose (where third eye presses to the earth) and lotus, which is a classic pose for contemplation. Savasana (corpse pose) is also an essential final pose for any yoga practice; it is the time in which we absorb the benefits of the poses that came before, where our minds may drift back to the intention we set at the start of the practice (i.e. to be a more intuitive parent) and where we can open ourselves to guidance from the deep Self.

Chapter 9

Spiritual Parenting

Parenting and the Art of Loving What Just Is
"The Great Way knows no difficulties, if we refrain from picking and choosing."

Sansho Kanchi Zenji

Love your life and your kids exactly as they are and you have instant happiness and enlightenment. Got it? Great— you're the Buddha! And as for the rest of us who would just appreciate a little balance and a better mood some of the time (much less enlightenment or Oneness with God), for those of us who are *trying* to be here now, but for whom the demands of life keep interfering, leaving us wondering if things *have* to be so hard and so unfair, this chapter strives to help us feel happier, and more successful, by realizing that in trying to be our best Selves as parents we have *already* taken a critical and essential step on our path to enlightenment. All that remains is to realize in our *conscious* minds that by parenting with heart and soul we are on a spiritual path, aligning with and serving the deep Self, the world and God (or whatever you prefer to call our cosmic situation).

If we go on a spiritual retreat and the master tells us to pick up grains of rice, this apparent busy work opens to reveal deeper resonance. If we don't have time for a week of meditation, but the universe asks us to pick up the kids from soccer, clean and fold their clothes or read *Hop on Pop* yet again, we might deliberately embrace these tasks as spiritual practice which, if done with enough presence or over enough time, invite enlightenment to arise spontaneously within us.

According to a Harvard study[1], when a group of maids working in a hotel were informed about how many calories it burns to clean rooms all day—it's like constantly exercising—they were found to spontaneously lose weight and become more healthy compared to an equally hard-working group of maids who were not given this perspective. By logical extension, if we consciously realize that parenting is a spiritual endeavor—a living expression of Christianity, Torah, Islam, Buddhism, Taoism and yoga—consistent with all paths and faiths, it seems possible, even likely, that merely armed with this awareness we parents will naturally become more compassionate, wise, happy and enlightened.

Clouds of Glory

Our birth is but a sleep and a forgetting:
The Soul that rises with us, our life's Star,
Hath had elsewhere its setting,
And cometh from afar:

Not in entire forgetfulness,
And not in utter nakedness,
But trailing clouds of glory do we come
From God, who is our home:
Heaven lies about us in our infancy!

-William Wordsworth

From a spiritual perspective we can re-think the frustrations and burdens of care-giving to discover that our children, even at their most difficult, still trail if not "clouds of glory" at least threads of glory. By mindfully parenting we find and follow these threads to better relationships with our children and to greater harmony with our deep Selves and our lives. Parenting is a spiritual discipline, a potential teacher of selfless love and full presence to the moment.

In parenting, the believer and the atheist find common ground: We all love our children. For those with strong faith, parenting is a field ripe for epiphanies; and for those who prefer to leave God out of it, parenting brings an earthy and direct opportunity to find meaning, purpose and freedom by loving and serving a mystery that we *can* see, touch and believe in: our children.

With or without God, if we stop believing in love we are lost. While we all need love, parenting teaches us that by *giving* love, particularly the quiet and compassionate recognition of soul, spirit or essence in the other, particularly in our children, we find joy and tranquility. If this moment of reading finds you in some dark night of the soul, the intention of these words is to bring whatever faint love they can carry as an offering, meant to re-kindle the natural process of growing and healing that comes from seeing without judgment. They are meant to help you relinquish shame, guilt, resentment and despair and try again to simply gaze upon your child as an act of love; to keep an open heart to the possibility that your own deep Self, God or the universe may open back up to you the way it once did, long before you can most likely remember.

Children are born enlightened, at least in the sense of being utterly natural and free of any particular religiosity—quite open to whatever those who love them will later choose to teach them (as well as open to whatever cruel lessons may break their trust or compassion). Babies are in direct relationship with what actually is, call it God or Godless "reality." This Buddha-like existence doesn't "work" on being present to the moment—for in the eyes of a dreamy newborn there is nothing but the eternal moment. As we acclimate to the world our bodies and brains become dominant while our spirits tend to dim and recede. We slowly forget our true (and arguably eternal) natures and fall prey to a life of getting and losing, always dimly yearning to return to a paradise of just being (hence our pervasive fantasies of perfect holidays, perfect relationships and also the fantasy of perfect children—instead of the realization that we, and our children, are in our own ways, already perfect). Parenting can help us remember, and return to, a more natural way of being—a happiness that comes from honoring and inhabiting our authentic Selves.

When Thinking "Happy Thoughts" Doesn't Cut It

Many spiritual teachings encourage us to recognize the transience of our ego-selves, our short-lived bodies and our material circumstances and discover that we are, at heart, spirit, energy or light—part of an eternal Oneness. This is all well and good, but for many of us the notion that life, with its sorrows and worries, is an illusion does not free us from our troubles, does not pay our bills and does not heal our children—even if so-called reality is all an illusion we must admit that, for the majority of us, it is an extremely convincing one.

My intention is to welcome you into this chapter and its ideas wherever you are, with no agenda to convert you to anything other than a believer in your own deep Self—which contains both light and dark aspects. While I naturally wish to offer comfort and encouragement, as a therapist I have learned that non-judgmental understanding and recognition of what a person truly thinks and feels facilitates healing. Individuation, becoming our full and authentic Self, rests upon the integration of opposites. When taken as a dialectic of opposites, parenting becomes a path to individuation.

While sages across time counsel love and compassion, it's not that we *don't* want to practice love and compassion, it's just that it's so damned hard to consistently do it.

The "Great Teachers" often don't have kids (and when they do, like Gandhi, they aren't always the best parents). We parents are busy, we fall short, we wrestle with darkness and cynicism and lament missed moments. While we would love some help that actually works, we sure don't want to be negated, shamed or shushed for our authentic outrage and pain at the way the world is sometimes. There is no way around it—spiritual growth is a painful business. If you've had no pain and no struggle as a parent then you are probably not reading this book.

Dark and difficult situations relate to the Shadow side of parenting—the times when forces beyond us bring us to our knees. The strange beauty of the dark, the tragic and the overwhelming is that they offer opportunities to look for something more within our Selves—to help us realize our interconnection with each other and to deepen our capacity to care. As parents we must sometimes play God, and whether or not we believe in God, parenting quickly teaches us that we are not God.

The Empty Bed

When it comes to taking care of our children, we struggle both individually and as a society. One particularly haunting experience as a group home psychologist illustrates the collective Shadow of parenting.

This particular incident occurred after Laurence had a psychotic break and was sent off to a locked ward, leaving us with an empty bed. In the past, "admissions" assigned new kids to my house whenever a bed opened up, but this time the phone rang and my supervisor told me that I had to go to "Mac" and pick a kid. My throat tightened. McClaren Hall (now closed down) was a notorious hell-hole where kids were housed by the juvenile court pending placement in foster care, group homes or psychiatric hospitals—placements that more often than not never came, and if they did, they didn't stick. As visions of Meryl Streep having to choose which of her two children to save in *Sophie's Choice*[2] flashed through my head, I asked my supervisor for some guidelines about what to look for when "picking a kid" and was bluntly told, "No fire-setters, no violent kids, no drug addicts."

"Mac" was meant to be a place where no one stayed for more than sixty days but was, in fact, a brutal Dickensian-type orphanage where victims of bad luck were thrown together with young criminals, sexual predators, gangsters, drug addicts and the mentally ill and left stewing together in the bitterness of neglect. Mac was a dangerous place for all involved. Disinterest, poorly utilized funding, systemic dysfunction and turf battles between warring agencies mixed into a cocktail of kids continuously attacking each other and staff. Mac was a place that kids with no place else to go still ran away from; broken bones were commonplace; staff beatings of children alleged; it was a place where kids had died.

I nervously drove my crumbling Honda Civic into the bleak outskirts of Los Angeles County looking for an Oliver

Twist and hoping not to inadvertently bring home a young serial killer. I parked in the baking hot parking lot and entered a non-descript cinderblock building. The empty foyer of sorry linoleum, scratched glass and dusty cases exuded melancholy; smiling celebrities faded from yellowing photos like Chesire Cats while a vacant Plexiglas reception booth greeted me with mute indifference.

I had expected outright Bedlam, but everything was enigmatically muffled. Joyless shouts came from somewhere deep in the bowels of the place. Although not officially a "locked" facility, the vibe was of a prison abandoned by guards. I made my way along a corridor and met a ghostly administrator who led me to a "library"—more sorry linoleum, chipped Formica tables and endless rows of grey metal file shelves. A thick stack of files were dropped with an echoing thud onto a table and then another stack—all the males currently residing at Mac between the ages of fourteen and eighteen. The official shuffled away and I sat down to read under gloomy fluorescent light.

The more I read, the taller the "rule out" pile grew: "Allegations of sexual assault resulted in discharge from previous placement." "Repeatedly exhibited fire setting behavior." "Denies problems with substances despite history of drug abuse and dependence as well as arrests for possession and suspicion of dealing." "Beat mom severely with a vacuum." It was hard to fully grasp that these terrible chronicles reflected the lives of children, that every one had once been some mother's baby. The weight of all those I could not help weighed heavily as the choice about the one child I could offer a hand out of this place began to take shape.

I managed to find four or five possibilities—thinner files telling hard luck stories of dysfunctional parents unable to care for their children because drugs, poverty and/or the criminal justice system had rendered them unavailable. Perhaps these were the softer kids who couldn't find placements because they were too old (foster families typically wanted little kids). I was particularly looking for a kid who could benefit from a therapeutic environment and make use of what it offered, a kid who was more emotionally disturbed than anti-social.

I wended my way down Kafkaesque hallways, holding my selected files. The administrator didn't bother to escort me to the boy's cottages, but merely roughed out the directions and disappeared. The facility spread over ten acres and I had to pass through the nursery on the way. The children themselves were out playing or at lunch, but the mere sight of bassinets, cribs and ragged teddy bears in this horrid place stopped me in my tracks and I had to fight back tears, pushing away images of my own kids, then one and three, ending up here.

I wandered, half lost, amongst kids and staff who eyed me warily; everyone was moving slowly in the heat. *Everything* was bolted down to prevent their use as weapons. A counselor who had been arbitrating a dispute when I walked into the cottage stopped to offer frank assessments about who on my list was more or less trouble. It was hard to know whether their recommendations were slanted toward the kids they most wanted to help or be rid of.

A buzz spread through the ranks that I was there from a group home and several boys came up to me and pleaded, "Take me! Please...?" I met each boy on my list, asking them questions meant to gauge their readiness and ability to "work their program." I tried, by looking into their eyes, to ascertain their kindness and sincerity, ridiculously hoping to see who they really were—and trying to be fair about who was most deserving and likely to succeed in our setting.

Each kid made his pitch, and every kid seemed like they deserved a shot. The kids who I didn't have on my list also made impromptu bids to be chosen, but with a clowning defensiveness that recognized they had no chance. Without the tattling files, I had no clue which one beat mom with the vacuum or which one was the sexual predator; they were just a bunch of kids—moping, laughing, rough-housing—living the life fate had dealt them. I can't say I was personally eager to take care of them all, but I sure wished none of them had to be there. How was I supposed to pick one and reject the others?

And then there was Justin. Reddish blonde hair, freckles, soft blue eyes—he seemed like just what we were looking for: a fish out of water amongst all these rougher teens, a skinny kid who was, like me, new to the system and in obvious need of protection. Justin had to push back tears when talking with me in contrast to the rough and tumble kids who had been in and out of many placements. Justin was convincing as a kid who truly wanted to work his program and make a life for himself, intelligent and demure, with beguiling touches of vulnerability he seemed like a case that I could really work with in therapy and make a difference.

As I drove away a fantasy formed in my head as a hedge against the darkness: perhaps Justin and I would one day arrive at some *Ordinary People* or *Good Will Hunting*[3] moment of rage-tattered realization, of breakthrough tears and the release of shame—a beginning of a positive manhood. But this was quickly engulfed and blotted out by the bewildering enormity of the situation facing the hundreds of children at Mac, and the thousands more in "Juvee," Youth Authority, locked mental wards and fighting for survival on the streets. This was not a problem for one therapist to address by selecting one kid, this was a problem for a society to solve, a symptom of a society that wasn't well, that didn't take care of its children. I felt ashamed at my ignorance. I had thought I knew what was going on in "the system" because I had been working with such difficult kids, but now realized that I had the relatively easy ones, and so few of them at that. To actually visit Mac and *feel* what it was like, and then savor the guilty relief of getting back in my car and driving away had deepened my world view to the next layer down.

I reported at the admissions committee meeting and "presented" Justin. They seemed to trust me, or maybe they needed to answer the gap in funding that comes with an empty bed, but they said that if I liked him he was now my kid. We called Mac and the next day Justin was delivered to my group home. It was so strange and so personal to pick a human being and then to overnight become their therapist and de-facto parent. Some years later when we rescued a dog from a shelter it was a more involved process of meetings, screenings, home-visits and a trial period before we were allowed to have her.

The other boys in the group home liked Justin well enough. He and I took some walks to the taco stand. While kids who had already been in the home when I first arrived had been slow to open up, Justin was ready to talk from the start. He opened up about his dad not being in his life and about his mom being more involved with his younger stepsiblings than with him; he spoke of life around gangs—white neo-Nazis and their rivalries with black and Latino gangs. He told harrowing stories of violence witnessed, of a boy's mouth jammed onto a curb and a boot stomped to the back of his head to break out all his teeth. (Justin did not, however, admit to being violent himself). He was bright and got off to a good start in the special needs school.

The staff was less keen on Justin and soon stories of his being "sneaky" began to surface. He became more defiant, evasive and markedly less charming. That was to be expected as the honeymoon period always gave way to the real problems and issues. His drug tests started coming back positive. But we were there to help him with his problems—and his behavior could even be understood as trusting us enough to show us what he needed help with.

And then it turned out that Justin was indeed sneaking out of the group home at night. The kicker was that he had been robbing people in the neighborhood. One of the other kids in the home who felt frightened, and who had been threatened by Justin, trusted staff enough to tell on him. Staff found stolen items and a black ski-mask hidden in Justin's belongings. Given that the neighbors did not want a group home in their neighborhood in the first place (we had recently worked hard to convince several families that a dead cat thrown into a yard was the work of *other* disturbed kids in the area and not our kids), the clinic administrators were clear and adamant that Justin had to go.

Justin's Department of Mental Health case-worker arrived the next day to take him back to Mac. The social worker planned to recommend a locked facility in Utah that he felt got results. I had heard from kids who'd been there that they locked you in freezing rooms and broke you down until you complied; some kids came back with discipline and self-esteem but as often as not they soon fell apart again without the structure of a place like that; some kids never came back at all. As we sat chatting in his car, the social worker told me that Justin was a sociopath and that there was no point to doing therapy with a sociopath—that he had worked many years with these kinds of kids and that there was a line that a person crossed and after that there was no rehabilitating them. I had heard this idea along the way in my training, but I still couldn't totally believe that Justin was a "sociopath." I had looked into his eyes and I had seen feelings, soul and humanity. Some said that this was nothing but a clever act.

However "bad" Justin may or may not have been, and although we never had our breakthrough moment, he nevertheless lives on in my heart and I hope the best for him— and for all the Justins I don't know by name—and especially for all the Justins who may be trying to overcome their Shadow selves now in order to parent and be there for their kids in a way that no one was for them. The story of Justin raises more questions than it answers and this is why I tell it here. Parenting, and helping kids in general, be it as a teacher, therapist or grandparent, puts us in positions of power and decision-making, in a sense asks us to play God only to humble us and continually remind us that our ego selves alone are no match for the task of collectively parenting our children.

In the face of questions that are beyond our capacity we can at least admit our limitations and, perhaps, turn to our deeper Selves for guidance and answers. In this way parenting, by raising the need for greater wisdom than our ego-selves can generally muster, is a natural call to deepening spirituality. Caring for others is enlightened Self-interest, but my experiences with Justin taught me that we don't have to rescue everyone so much as we must compassionately recognize ourselves *in everyone*.

Why Aren't We Happy and Enlightened?

Life is like improvisational comedy—we are tagged into an often absurd or painful scene, but in order to have fun (and be funny) it is absolutely essential that we completely embrace and go along with the situation in which we find ourselves no matter what it is. Our delight in watching skilled comedians do great improv comes from their fearlessness in radically accepting whatever is thrown at them.

The selfless love that parenting calls forth is a key that can be used to unlock the mystery of our existence. Loving our children, and the world, as they are unlocks happiness, yet straining or forcing ourselves to love the world is folly. We are better off to meditate without judgment on all that we find hard to love. If we manage to actually see, rather than criticize, what we don't like, we will discover our own Self in everything we had thought was alien, other or wrong. We never really understand something *until* we have loved it; this is true with regard to our children, our deep Selves and even our God-given or cosmically indifferent unhappiness.

What's In Our Child's Way?

1) <u>Our Failure to see them as Spiritual Beings</u>

All kids are sacred and all are potentially happy in their own selves. We can view our children's confusion, or unhappiness, as a result of fading consciousness of their transcendent spirit as they learn to see themselves in the mirror of our judgment, criticism or materialism.

2) <u>Our Failure to see Ourselves and our Children as Connected</u>

At the heart of our spiritual situation is the fact of our interconnection with each other and with everything, what Thich Nhat Hanh calls, "Inter-being." Our children know this in their souls when they are very young, but they also desperately want our love, and so they will slowly disavow the mystical connection they have with the ants, the trees and the homeless people in the park if that's what it takes to stay in our good graces. If we deride our children's compassion for the living world as weak or naive, we inadvertently teach them to stop caring and connecting with everything. This is the beginning of our disconnection with them, and the birth of our mutual unhappiness.

3) <u>We Fail to Understand Them</u>

This is related to not understanding our interconnectedness with our children and the world. When we fail to understand our children's feelings and arrogantly "correct" or negate their perceptions (be it their so-called "imaginary" friends, or their intuitive realization of our anger or sorrow) they lose faith in their own senses and in the validity of their feelings and intuition, which is their best guide to happiness and to their right-path.

4) <u>Shame</u>

Shame is when a child comes to believe that it is not just their behavior that is bad but that their core essence and character is wrong. It is much easier to crush spirit in someone who loves and depends on us than it is to cultivate and protect it. If we are to serve the spirit in our children as the driving engine of their happiness and wisdom, we must actively endorse, see and reflect their luminous and eternally lovable Selves.

What's In Our Way?

Our children are fantastic potential teachers of spirituality and happiness. Whatever has transpired in our lives, none
of it is more important than loving our children right now.

1) <u>Arrogance</u>

Certainly, as a therapist, this is one of my greatest potential
downfalls; if I think I'm getting pretty good at understanding people I may start to see what I expect to see, rather than
what really is. This is the end of sacred relating and the demise
of growth and healing. As soon as we start placing people in
boxes and labeling them we limit them, ourselves and our
potential happiness. As parents we may think we know our
kids, but they are always changing and growing. Our children
are prone to please us if they can, even to the point of agreeing with us or changing their opinions to match our own, yet
that does not mean we are "right"; later they may relentlessly
oppose us as they form their identities as emerging adults, but
this doesn't necessarily mean we are "wrong." If we manage to
be a little more playful and free, we may appreciate the beauty
of their turbulent process. If we want our children to feel loved,
respected and understood we are wise to listen to their perspectives and opinions—and we may also learn something about
becoming humbler, happier and more authentic.

2) <u>Refusing to Heed the Messages of Our Pain</u>

When pain, misfortune or bad luck seem to block us from
our desired goals, we might re-consider whether these seeming obstacles are in fact redirecting us toward what the deep
Self really wants for us. If we try to learn and grow, even
from pain and gloom, we may figure out some things about
where we got off our true path and about what is wanted
from us rather than what our ego-selves wanted *for* us. If our

children are unhappy, ill, excluded or struggle with differences or disabilities it is worth asking what the situation at hand could be offering to teach *us*. Maybe we are supposed to learn patience, non-judgment, advocacy or unconditional love—or just to be inspired by the intrepid spirit of our children.

3) <u>Lack of Gratitude</u>

Gratitude is an essential spiritual tenant. As soon as we want what we have, for better and for worse, we are free— our former stuckness and suffering is transformed into happiness while our situation, having been recognized and accepted, perhaps with lessons learned, is suddenly free to change.

4) <u>Chronic Restlessness</u>

If we are always rushing off to the next activity instead of being fully present to the one at hand we are not happy because happiness can only really be had in the present moment. By projecting happiness onto something that may happen in the future, we actually block ourselves from being content right now. Our children are great reasons to slow down and smell the roses, to see the world as they see it. When we are too busy to find time for our children because we are trying so hard to give them more things in the future, we miss the point of it all. Yes, most of us have to work, but we can be fully at work when we work—which will make us generally more "successful" as a person (and probably more materially successful as well), but when we are home, even if just for one hour with our kids, we can try to actually be there in mind and spirit as well as in body. I fail at this over and over, but when I do succeed, I am at my happiest.

5) <u>Anger</u>

Anger is a natural human emotion. It can be appropriate and a powerful motivator at times; but when we get stuck in our anger, in blame, bitterness and feelings of powerlessness, it eats us up and corrodes our relationships with our children and the world. We all have anger within us, but none of us are fully or accurately defined as "an angry person." We can evolve to a point of consciousness where we recognize our Shadow and yet choose to act with compassion and gentleness. Denial of anger only makes things worse, but venting it onto others doesn't release anger, it only makes it grow stronger. If we unleash our wrath onto our children it particularly deepens our feelings of shame and isolation.

6) <u>Apathy and Indifference</u>

Another detrimental issue is pervasive apathy—the indifferent parent not bothering to look up from their computer, the depressed and drinking parent who cannot find joy in anything at all, not even their children, is sure to spread a mantle of low-self esteem like a muffling cloak over the family.

I have had many parents call me up, meaning to drop off their child for therapy. Some allowed me to persuade them to do the work themselves in honor of their children. These parents became more conscious, responsible and loving and saw great "improvement" in their children.

While our love for our children represents a higher purpose, our *ability* to "recover" (i.e. return to our natural state of loving and being loved) typically hinges on us turning things over to a "higher power." The deep Self *is* our personal higher power and our conduit to the even higher power of the collective SELF or God. Parental addiction, whether to drugs or to working, ruins kids' lives. Any clinician or AA sponsor will readily confirm that giving up drinking is only a part of true recovery; people resist going to AA, but getting better means joining the group, accepting help and collectively realizing that we are powerless over our "diseases" of the ego-self (our lack of a bowl and mistaken attempts to fill a colander-like self with good feelings that run right through and call for more and more of whatever our drug of choice happens to be). Caring and being cared for in the group—at AA, in therapy and in our families—heals the colander to form it into a bowl, which can then be used to contain our children.

What's In God's Way?

1) <u>Nothing</u>

If we are to believe in an omniscient, omnipotent and all-encompassing God, then our conceit would have to be that nothing could possibly be in God's way. This view is consistent with seeing the world as perfect and ourselves as blessed; this puts the responsibility squarely on ourselves to work like mad, especially if our lives are frustrating or painful, to figure out how even pain could be perfect for teaching us an attitude of love and appreciation. What we thought was misfortune could then be re-envisioned as an awe-inspiring opportunity to live consciously in God's immanent dialectic of the opposites of love and loss (a.k.a. the world as it is).

2) <u>Not Existing</u>

No matter how spiritual we are, we need to account for the fact that many people do not believe in God or may have doubts, and others hate the very idea of God and religion as something that causes way more harm than good. A philosophically complete God would have to *not* exist as well as exist (and neither exist nor not exist). The faithful could love those for whom God does not exist as representing a legitimate and divinely manifest expression of the God of infinite possibility. An inspired position leaves nothing held so tightly that we couldn't find common ground with every possible view.

Even if there really is no God, the *concept* of God is at least very much alive and, if not well, certainly talked about. If we are so bold or disillusioned to declare God dead or non-existent, then we must at the same moment take up the mantle of responsibility— to deal with *being* part of whatever "God" the world has at its disposal. In this way, God not existing becomes a rallying cry to either invent God or to step up and be, if not God, at least truly our best Selves as parents.

3) Our Participation

To educate means to draw out. Parenting educates us by drawing our loving Selves into active service. Parenting can help us relate to, and better understand, the suffering God, the misunderstood God and the tempestuous, short-tempered, irrational God; parenting gives us a chance to personally experience the God that lives and breathes within us by bringing the living God into our sacred and eternal relationships with our children.

To participate is to recognize our place in the group and the cosmos. If we sit around waiting for God we might wait forever, yet if we love the world as if it were our child and love our children as if they were a microcosm of our world, we make the living God manifest in our shared existence.

Privilege of Parenting

Broadening Our Perspective

Parenting is a Spiritual Dependency

When a parent significantly fails or hurts a child it is extremely sad for that child, but *spiritually* the child is still free to heal and grow; but *for the parent* such a failure marks a truly tragic situation, a spiritual catastrophe that brings unspeakable misery to the deepest core. Thus, as parents, our happiness and spiritual well-being utterly depend on us loving our children with sincerity and a semblance of nobility (then the ultimate outcome is up to forces beyond us, but we have played our role admirably); this spiritual obligation helps ensure that kids are, at least most of the time, nurtured and protected, but the symbiotic nature of parenting also naturally facilitates our own awakening relationship between the deep Self and the collective SELF (or God).

Bound to Love

As parents we are bound to our children in every way imaginable: physically, emotionally, economically, mentally, developmentally and spiritually.

Few stories in the Old Testament carry as much dread and pathos as "The Binding" of Isaac to be sacrificed by his own father, Abraham, at the command of God— the primordial "cliff-hanger" of a child on the cusp of death at the hands of a parent who must act as agent of a God-Father who makes offers that cannot be refused. Whether we hear it as a child or as a parent, "The Binding" is a troubling and perplexing story that seems to create a love triangle (platonic but passionate) between parent, child and God. But then, what does it mean? Why would a God who forbids murder ask a father to murder a child? And wouldn't an omniscient God *already know* that Abraham's faith could be trusted and not need to test it?

Perhaps this tale tells us something about how things are between us, our kids and God; maybe it is better understood as a poetic representation of the relationship between the child-like ego, the hero-like deep Self and the God-like collective SELF. Abraham serves as a hero of whom more is asked than any human parent should be expected to give—and in return Abraham becomes the father of western spiritual consciousness. "The Binding" demonstrates that it is ultimately God who gives and takes away, while the confusing and gut-wrenching near-tragedy of the sacrifice drives home the point that the "whys" of who lives and who dies, of love, gain and loss are beyond human comprehension.

At the very roots of Judeo, Christian and Islamic faiths we find the exhortation to bind ourselves to God, to serve and love that all-encompassing force, power or higher consciousness with all our hearts and souls—and to do this *for our own good*. These faiths all suggest that we should love God unconditionally and also that we should fear God. Yet it is often hard enough to *find* God in the first place, much less bind ourselves to a mystery that we cannot see or touch. Our children, to whom we are bound in a tangible way, are ambassadors of the Divine. In our children we glimpse the generally unseen God in their glimmering "clouds of glory," in the sacred spark in their smiles and in the dark fury they occasionally unleash in us.

The word "yoga" literally means to bind. Yoga as a path to enlightenment is also based on the concept of binding the body, mind and spirit to God. Like Ulysses bound to the mast, our binding ourselves to God in the service of our children helps us stay the course, and not be diverted from giving love, patience and compassion no matter what obstacles may befall us.

Ulysses, tied to the mast in honor of a larger purpose, anticipates another variation on binding: Christ nailed to the cross—fixed inexorably to a spiritual situation. Christ symbolizes an integration of opposites, God *and* man; the crucifixion itself can be understood as the binding of the living God (the body as human container of sacred and eternal spirit, the same one we all contain) *to* the cross, which is itself an immensely ancient symbol of the intersection of space and time (and thus a portal to transcendent consciousness). The pathos of the crucifixion is that now God doesn't ask man to sacrifice his son, but instead He sacrifices His own Son. The idea of Christ consciousness is that in it we can awaken and realize that all children are not just God's children but *our* children—and at this point it becomes utterly unacceptable for us humans to sacrifice any of them for any reason.

There is no more universal path to God than parenting. Pagan parents loved their children, as do primitive peoples who have never heard of our religions but have still met gods and spirits in their fast disappearing forests. Perhaps in the crucifixion we can also see an archetypal binding of Apollo (the sun god) *to* Dionysus (the dark vegetation god often represented as a tree pillar—and who was known to evoke both loving ecstasy and cause women to go mad and kill their children).

Some of the most disturbing (and not uncommon) nightmares we have involve our children being hurt or killed. Given that our deep Selves are the architects of our dreams, such horrible scenarios might be understood as symbolic sacrifices of our inner children. They might also be viewed as the confrontation of our worst fears coming into consciousness—a terror that evokes the dread of God and thus God's dark presence in our conscious minds. Painful as this is, such Shadow work (at least psychologically, and who is to say not also magically) might even help us avert lived disaster and bring into being deeper and more fully realized loving relationships.

Parenting is tantamount to being bound to, and loving, the God of all opposites. In this sense religion and yoga can help us be better parents, but parenting can also help us be better yogis, Christians, Jews, Muslims, Buddhists or atheists. It can also just help us be better humans. As to ultimate Truth, it is said that while a lie requires a liar, the truth just is. When I ask a parent, who is struggling and confused, to tell me one thing, anything, that they are absolutely sure of, the response is almost always, "That I love my child." This is a truth that we are already bound by; this chapter is written in the service of making that binding conscious—to bring the busy ego-mind into harmony with God (or spirit), yoking it to the deep Self by serving whoever the universe has placed in our care, most typically, our children.

Relating to Spirit

"Wisdom that a wise man tries to communicate always sounds foolish... We can find it, we can live it, we can be carried by it, we can work wonders with it, but we cannot utter it or teach it." -Herman Hesse, *Siddhartha*[4]

As parents we, hopefully, transition from unconscious children of nature into conscious participants *with* spirit in the great cycle of nature. Spirit, spirituality and religion are not the same thing. If religion speaks to us it may prove a path to spirit, but if we're disenchanted with religion that does not preclude spirituality. Our personal spirituality can be conventional or utterly unique, but some sort of spirituality lies at the heart of optimal parenting (as well as at the core of a well-lived life).

Spirit tends to manifest in the context of particular sorts of relationships—those marked by authentic seeing and appreciating as opposed to relationships where others are "of use" or give us "things." When we get beyond getting and using, and enter into relating free of all use and purpose, we encounter the sacred spirit in the other; through this sort of relating, which Martin Buber[5] calls "the essential deed," we come truly to life and touch the eternal. It is in parenting, above all other relationships, where we most readily and deeply discover that the purpose of relating is the relating itself. Parenting potentially teaches us how to relate to the sacred in a selfless way, revealing the unifying spirit that pulses at the subtle heart of everything. It is by virtue of our ability to *relate* that we are able to live in spirit and, hopefully, even parent with it.

God May Be Our Parent, But Not Just Our Parent

God (or even the mere concept of God) may enter into one's consciousness as a Father or Mother figure, but God (even as an idea) is infinitely more than our parent. "Mother" and "Father" are constructs we can understand, while an eternal all-encompassing spirit is beyond images, words or conscious understanding. The Great Mother or Father is *of* God, but to think that such an archetype *is* God creates more problems than it solves. As children, the image of God as a heavenly parent is something we can grasp, but as a child develops and must confront an unfair world, they might naturally ask, "What sort of Divine Parent allows this sort of world?"

As parents we know better than to equate being a parent with being any sort of God. Whether God creates us in His/Her image or we create God in our image, as our consciousness expands toward the infinite so does our need for an imageless and infinite God. An infinite God certainly can be, amongst many things, our Divine parent, but never solely our parent. James Hillman writes about "The Parental Fallacy,"[6] by which we blame everything that goes wrong on our parents. Hillman suggests that we each have a guiding spirit that transcends our parents. He equates this with a sense of "calling" and believes that parents must follow the calling of their true Selves while staying out of the way of the callings of their children.

If we, as parents, have a calling to write or to arrange flowers, we might have to do this while our children are in the sling, napping or texting. When it comes to a calling, we never are given the time—we basically have to steal it. But if we don't, our souls start to wither just as they will if we fail our children. In this way, God is also a child tugging at our sleeve, demanding that we take photographs, go back to school or fix up old cars. Parenting nourishes our souls, but following our passions do too—and this sets the example for our children that they too must find, and follow, the deepest callings of their souls.

Gita, Marcel and Jonathan

The casket began to lower and Gita threw herself onto it with an unspeakable wail that pierced my soul, jolting me back into the full reality of the moment. I was forty yards away, half shielded by an open car door with my mother's protective arm angled across my chest. My mind struggled to reconcile how the body of my best friend, in his favorite jeans and Puma sneakers, mangled by the motorcycle that hit him while he was on his bike, could be locked in that descending coffin.

Jonathan was a soul-friend—we had been inseparable since early childhood. As I staggered backward into our car I heard a passing grown-up say, somberly but with smug conviction, "God has His reasons." What kind of God makes it a brilliant sunny day in June for a funeral of a young boy? Or, for that matter chooses *my* fourteenth birthday for the occasion?

Until that point I had held a cynical but scarcely examined view of religion as an occasion for boredom and hypocrisy, a time when adults dressed up, preened and showed little honest spirituality. Yet I had been willing to accept my grandmother's assertion that, "God is everywhere" with its implicit implication that God is real and exists (even if He might be boring). As my family chewed on lunch at a highway overpass restaurant, the surreal gave way to the real: THERE WAS NO GOD!

All at once I lost my fear of God, my faith in God and my belief that being alive was a good thing. Although I was very interested in the idea of no longer being here, I was terrified about the alternative. I had nightmares about rehearsing for my own funeral and would wake in a panic as the coffin lid was closed over me. My rage at God for probably not existing, or worse, not doing anything to prevent Jon's death, went beyond my personal sense of loss and dread and seemed exponentially magnified by the plight of Jonathan's parents.

Gita and Marcel were originally from Prague and had survived the holocaust to forge a life of comfort and safety in Chicago only to have the veneer of happiness cruelly ripped away. Gita was an elegant beauty who brought a cultured charm and old world resonance to her Midwestern situation while Marcel was like a spirit-father to me; I had always loved his Czech accent and found him exotic, sophisticated and enchanting. He was a caring doctor, a gifted painter and he could play Gershwin flawlessly on the piano; like his departed son, Marcel was tall, athletic and rugged, and yet gentle and erudite. While their kids wanted to be all-American, I wanted nothing more than to be European. Marcel would entertain my philosophical questions with respect and was the first person in my life to mention Jung. I fondly recall sitting in his study leafing through photographs of Prague and yearning to be there—to commune with the city of Kafka.

Jon's younger brother, Michael, had been deeply shaken to see his imposing father uncontrollably sobbing face down on his bed the morning of the funeral—a man who had never been known to cry. Neither Gita nor Marcel were the sorts to talk about their traumatic pasts, but as Jon's brothers and I tried to make sense of the arbitrary puzzle of life and death I learned fragments of what they had been through before they lost their child and the beautiful life they had built toppled like children's blocks.

As a teenager, Marcel had hidden out in an attic and had to swim the Danube alone at night to escape the Nazis. Gita had been fleeing the Gestapo, hand in hand with her best friend who stepped on a landmine and all that was left of her splattered across Gita's dress. Gita had then been put up against a wall to be shot when the sound of approaching allied troops made them hurry off, neglecting to shoot her. Gita and Marcel were alive by strange twists of fate, but to what end? To face the worst loss imaginable...? To my fourteen-year-old mind it was simply too much to believe that God could possibly have a "reason" for taking their son. Yet Gita and Marcel endured.

I stayed close with them throughout the decades after Jon's death; they came to my wedding and, with the passing of years, I came to realize that, like Jon and I, Marcel and I too were kindred spirits—"Anam Cara" or soul-friends. In the intervening years I have also had my own epiphanies and have come to believe in God again—a God of subtle light and whispering leaves; and I have come to appreciate that for me at least, a good long time of not believing in, and even hating, God was, if not necessary, at least part of my journey.

Losing a best friend shaped my entire life, fuelled my rebellion and my search for meaning—and yet this wound pales compared to the loss of a child. Now that I am a parent it is clear that the death of a child is the worst thing imaginable to a parent, it is our deepest fear and we have no way of denying that it could happen—and yet this underscores the profundity of the gift that our children are to us. Wishing to address the parent who might face the prospect of this horror, but unequipped (thank God) by experience to directly address the issue, I called Marcel recently and asked him directly about how he managed to survive the holocaust and then the death of his son and to endure?

In his elegant Czech inflection Marcel laconically acknowledged that it was tough. They are now in their eighties; Gita's been feeling ill and Marcel's eyesight is failing, which makes reading and painting impossible. He paused and then said, "I was contemplating suicide but instead I'm going to have dental implants."

So while the Christian spirit may bring redemption and the Buddhist spirit enlightenment, the Jewish spirit perhaps brings dark humor—a very important element for enduring, and transforming, suffering.

Darkness is Part of the Divine

In speaking of God as awesome and infinite, we also must speak of the issue of evil within the totality of the Self and the way it is so often split off and projected onto others. Denying evil in ourselves while projecting it onto others fatefully binds us to the objects of our hatred. No psychologist sums this up better than the novelist Herman Melville who, in *Moby Dick*, writes: "Small reason was there to doubt, then, that ever since that almost fatal encounter, Ahab had cherished a wild vindictiveness against the whale... came to identify with him, not only all his bodily woes, but all his intellectual and spiritual exasperations. The White Whale swam before him as the monomaniac incarnation of all those malicious agencies which some deep men feel eating in them, till they are left living on with half a heart and half a lung. That intangible malignity which has been from the beginning; to whose dominion even the modern Christians ascribe one-half of the worlds; which the ancient Ophites of the east reverenced in their statue devil;—Ahab did not fall down and worship it like them; but deliriously transferring its idea to the abhorred white whale, he pitted himself, all mutilated, against it. All that most maddens and torments; all that stirs up the lees of things; all truth with malice in it; all that cracks the sinews and cakes the brain; all the subtle demonisms

379

of life and thought; all evil, to crazy Ahab, were visibly personified, and made practically assailable in Moby Dick."[7]

While ostensibly a story about a whale, *Moby Dick* could well be a metaphor (at least in our darker moments) of parent-child, and especially parent-teen, relationships. Parenting and great art are both about our relationship to God in all of the dark, light, eastern, western, good, evil, religious and pagan multiplicity that the Divine contains. *Moby Dick* offers insight into parenting which, like the quest for the White Whale or the Holy Grail, is ultimately a quest for God (even if parenting typically plays out on a seemingly more pedestrian stage of kitchens and malls). In keeping with our theme of binding, it is also noteworthy that the book's narrator begins with, "Call me Ishmael" and Ishmael is also the name of the Biblical Abraham's other son—born by his wife's maid at his wife's request and then chased away, along with his mother at Sarah's insistence. When we think about the rifts in our world, it seems not insignificant that Islam traces its roots to Abraham by way of Ishmael.

A hundred years after Melville, C.G. Jung, in trying to come to terms with an ambivalent God who could allow the Third Reich, the holocaust and Hiroshima states, "I had to wrench myself free of God, so to speak, in order to find that unity in myself which God seeks through man."[8] In *Answer to Job*, he writes that the recognition that God "fills us with evil as well as good... involves man in a new responsibility. He can no longer wriggle out of it on the plea of his littleness and nothingness, for the dark God has slipped the atom bomb and chemical weapons into his hands and given him the power to empty out the apocalyptic vials of wrath on his fellow creatures. Since he has been granted an almost godlike power, he can no longer remain blind and unconscious. He must know something of God's nature and of metaphysical processes if he is to understand himself and thereby achieve gnosis of the Divine."[9]

Jung makes the case for full awareness, for consciousness of our own darkness as well as light *in order to avert disaster.* The milieu of parenting is as important an arena as any other in which we might recognize our Shadows and, through consciously loving our children in full awareness of our power to destroy them and the world that they stand to inherit, achieve both personal and collective salvation, redemption and transcendence—by participating *with* God in the world and all its opposites.

Redemption

Jung, also in *Answer to Job* writes, "All opposites are of God, therefore man must bend to this burden; and in so doing he finds that God in his 'oppositeness' has taken possession of him, incarnated himself in him. He becomes a vessel filled with divine conflict. We rightly associate the idea of suffering with a state in which the opposites violently collide with one another, and we hesitate to describe such a painful experience as being 'redeemed.'"[10]

If life is a school for our souls, at the level of the deep Self we are more like classmates with our children than we are their teachers. Parenting in the context of a God who is, in part, dark, suffering and conflicted is no mean feat. As wanna-be-best-Self parents we would rather not think about our hypocrisies, not be shaken out of our complacent and pseudo-harmonious relationship to an all-good God of peace and light. But as understandable as this desire is, it does not bring forth our best Self as a parent but rather an incomplete self that unconsciously calls forth the dark in the other, typically the troubled child. Our failure or refusal to integrate the Shadow into our psyche leaves it to our children to pay the price for our shoddy and *unconscious* care of the world. As parents we must do more than "find God," we must *represent*— we must meet the dark/light Divine in our children by mirroring them in their service to us as ambassadors of Divine spirit—shielding them from the darker aspects as best as we can, while not denying evil in us or them, and instead working to consciously contain our natural portion of it and the overflow from our still-developing children. But *how* can we contain such volatile forces?

Soul is our Ultimate Bowl

In childhood, hopefully with our parents' help, we must make the bowl of our ego-selves (or perhaps do so later on in therapy), while in parenting we are tasked with making our soul-Selves. Soul is our ultimate vessel, a sacred capacity to hold and live consciously in something of God's Love *and* its opposite. Such enhanced ability to contain is true grown-up work and can be extremely painful.

While the ego-self is formed largely by *getting* (i.e. attention, support and encouragement) the soul-Self is formed by *giving* (i.e. attention, compassion, non-judgment) which is organically called into action by the demands of parenting. A growing soul-Self deepens our capacity to contain the unwanted feelings of our children.

Often our so-called "fears of intimacy" might be better understood as fear of emotional intensity, or more precisely as the fear that our ego-selves will go to pieces in the face of too much feeling, be it love *or* dread. Sexual acting out, drug and alcohol abuse, overspending and over-working may all, at heart, be understood as defenses against slowing down and feeling the full brunt of our emotions. Truly being present and loving our children is an exceptionally intense mode of experiencing, often as much agony as ecstasy. In order to withstand such intensity it helps to be fairly well individuated. The bowl of self must grow solid and then be placed in the service of the deep Self, which becomes our penultimate parenting tool—the ability to hold, to bear compassionate witness and to simply *be* with our children.

Amazing Grace

Life surprises us sometimes.

I had done a lot of work with kids who would "go off" and break windows, chairs, even a piano, and with children who would try to harm themselves; I bore witness to "take downs" where kids kicked, writhed, spat and swore as two or three (or four) staff held them down. I crouched numerous times in "QA" (quiet area) where amidst the smell of urine, burnt carpet and sweat, terrified children murmured the horror of their lives to me; countless heartbreaking stories, all sad and shocking in their particular way. I am haunted by a harrowing litany of the walking wounded: a boy who was conceived in a mental institution by a mother who was raped there; a boy whose psychotic mother would give her son tips on masturbation ("use your left hand, it will feel like a stranger"); an incorrigible thief who had been abandoned at age four in the lobby of a flea-bag hotel with nothing but his underwear; a child whose early childhood was lived with a homeless mother in empty lots and abandoned buildings;

a fire-setting boy who had been taken along by his father on arson sprees, and many others as well. Yet these kids were always much more than their stories of woe—they were children that despite it all still lived, fought, tried, cried, desired and dreamed. And no less could be said of Joseph who stands oddly apart from all the others, and who was probably my most personally transforming case.

Joseph was a mentally retarded child who had been in a special needs school of low-functioning autism, Downs Syndrome and other developmentally delayed children like himself for twelve of his seventeen years. He was a relatively easy case who had, as a consequence of his being low-maintenance *and* a sweetheart, been usually assigned to inexperienced interns. Year after year he had repeatedly said good-bye to his therapists as they finished their internships. When I was assigned to Joseph for his final year of high school, I had risen to the level of supervisor at the clinic and my specialty was the "bad" kids. I liked the challenge of complex kids who were hard to figure out and nearly impossible to reach. I had once "baby-sat" Joseph's case for a week when his regular therapist had been away and it was Joseph who had personally requested me for his last year when his latest therapist left the clinic. Although he was a nice kid, it just didn't seem like a good use of my time and abilities. Still, I couldn't say no.

Joseph was like a four-year-old in a seventeen-year-old body. I could watch him shoot baskets and we could just manage a checkers game, but there was nothing for me as therapist to work on—no angst, no anger, no real "problems" to speak of. Joseph was limited to a degree where he would never be able to live on his own, but he lived with a loving family who raised him and for the most part he was happy and joyful albeit exceedingly simple. He was just smart enough to know that he was a little different, and sometimes he might even get mildly frustrated about it, but he was not blessed with enough cognitive endowment to compensate for, surmount or in any significant manner change his situation. It was sad that he would not grow and progress, and it was scary to think what would happen to him in the future after his parents could no longer care for him, but there was little to be done about these things. Nevertheless our work together plodded along, hours passed slowly and I was often bored.

Week by week Joseph was teaching me patience, teaching me that sometimes change, improvement or growth isn't the point. But then what *was* the point? After many months of trudging down to Joseph's basement classroom and getting to know his wonderful teacher and the rest of the students, none of whom could aspire to much more than filling ketchup bottles at Wendy's, something happened. After weeks of riding the bus with them to Costco so they could learn how to pay a fare and not inappropriately talk to strangers, after celebrating the coming and going of Joseph's eighteenth birthday, after endless checkers games and basketball free-throws I happened into Joseph's classroom one morning when they were practicing a song for graduation—a graduation that would not lead to college and promising futures, not even to the hope of independent living. But there they stood, swaying and singing with heart, soul and spirit, learning "Amazing Grace." And in the dreary basement of a special needs school, the angels sang to me. Joseph and his friends' own amazing grace lovingly bludgeoned my blind and lost self. Their off-key voices enshrouded me in soft wonder, and I stood transfixed, moved, sad, happy, inspired and alive. Words cannot capture the essence and impact of this moment for me, but suffice it to say that it was one of those epiphanies where time stands still as these splendidly angelic human beings sang, if not to me directly, to a world that at least included me.

I had experienced many moving, powerful and keenly felt moments in my years working with troubled children, but this one snuck up on me with its subtlety, its humility, its authentic grace. I had heard this song many times, but the words had never penetrated my soul, "...how sweet the sound that saved a wretch like me. I once was lost but now I'm found, was blind but now I see." Tears welled in my eyes that day, and again as I write about it—a resonant experience that still echoes in my soul.

As we all got ready for graduation, something about my work with Joseph fell into place: even if I didn't much help him, he was a gift to me. I felt proud of Joseph— hopeful and scared for him; he wasn't my kid and yet he *was* my kid. He was, in his own way, launching—it was Joseph who was doing the leaving and it was my turn to be left by someone I had attached to. I knew that one day I too would leave this clinic to move on and contribute in different ways, and that getting to know Joseph was an honor; learning from someone who was closer to their own true nature than I was gave me a Grail that I wasn't seeking, dropped it right in my lap. It blessed me with some moments of authentic relating, which clued me in on our essential task as human beings: loving presence to the moment and all it contains.

On many days I'm glad those years of struggle are behind me, yet they've only been traded for new and different struggles; without those years I could not possibly be, for better or worse, the therapist, the parent or the man I am now. The pain and joy of it all seems to get easier and harder, lighter and heavier, to make more sense and less sense. Whatever your current challenges as a parent (or otherwise) open yourself to the beautiful, sometimes terribly beautiful, guiding, teaching and unifying spirit that resides in every apparent obstacle or problem, and in the gift of children. Parenting is a path that comes from, and leads to, a universal and unifying force that has been called "God," but whose real name cannot be expressed with human language. It can be lived though, in the deceptively simple act of loving.

Envision What We Already Have

When we fantasize or envision a "better life" for ourselves we train the mind to see and believe in new possibilities. And while this can be a good strategy for improving our situations, ironically, it can also block happiness by trapping us in the mistaken message that what we have and where we are right now is not good enough. By radically and lovingly embracing our situations as they are, we unlock a door to enlightenment.

Perhaps our sorrows, fears and suffering are part of what the universe has wisely crafted for us; they cause us to slow down and reconsider things. In *Man's Search For Meaning*,[11] Victor Frankl writes about finding happiness in the midst of Aushwitz. He had been a successful doctor and could not believe that this was happening to *him*. His wife was killed right away and he was on the brink of death when he had a sort of epiphany. He had been a non-spiritual and non-religious man, but on a forced march to dig frozen earth with scant clothes and tattered shoes he saw a bird and all at once somehow knew that it carried the spirit of his wife. A feeling of transcendence, love, happiness and freedom enveloped him—in the worst place imaginable! While others around him strategized to survive yet perished, Frankl helped who he could and let fate do as it wished. He was one of just a very few to live. He wrote about his experiences and that, more than any of his scholarly texts as a scientist, touched millions of people's lives.

So if Victor Frankl could find meaning and transcendent love in a concentration camp, we could certainly find as much in our own lives. If we are unhappy, perhaps this is a sign that we have not yet seen the meaning or the beauty in our lives as they are— especially if we have not yet truly seen, or have lost sight of, the magical and eternal spirit that is our children.

Strategies For Helping

Love the World

"All I hope to say in books, all that I ever hope to say, is that I love the world."

-E.B. White, author of *Charlotte's Web*

Spiritual parenting is the art of being and appreciating instead of getting, spending and achieving—of perceiving the sacred, particularly in our children. When we learn to tend the world as if it were our child we are abundant and happy. When we love our children from a place of true happiness, our role-modeling is convincing and inspiring.

Pause

In moments of non-action at least we are not doing the *wrong* action. Pausing quiets our mind and lets our soul speak up to calm and guide us.

The Tibetans have a concept they call "all accomplishing wisdom."[12] It is about cultivating the tranquil Self who can get everything done without rushing; this calls for actually doing what we are doing and not being preoccupied with all the tasks that are waiting for our attention. Pausing helps unlock our all-accomplishing inner tortoise and not exhaust ourselves playing the frenetic hare. When we pause we can consider our children's words and actions in a non-defensive manner; and we can accept criticism as guidance on how to get things right, and as encouragement for us to be happier and more present to those who love us the most.

Be Present For Each Thing You Do

Every task is an opportunity for transformation and happiness. Read when you are reading, kiss your child when you are kissing them and really hear their pain when they are suffering; if we can somehow *want* to fold laundry, resolve conflicts or make dinner, we experience the unexpected happiness that can come from any activity so long as we are present to it.

Solve for Perfect

Life could be written as the following equation: what is = perfection.

If, for example, $3 + x = 5$, we can "solve" for x and find that it must be 2. If we take our lives as perfect, our challenge is to "solve" or reconcile our pain, sorrow, losses and frustrations as being somehow just right—perhaps as teachers of lessons that go deeper than our conscious minds can readily fathom. (Some things make spiritual sense only after a very long time has passed.)

If *how* we go about things is, arguably, more important than what we actually do, we can let go of an over-focus on right decisions in favor of a great attitude. Radical and loving acceptance of what is has a mystical way of opening doors that we have been pushing against for years, never realizing they opened *in*. The more we see that our lives are perfect, the more perfect they feel; suffering yields its messages and, having served its purpose, subsides.

Although this idea can have an awful way of inadvertently suggesting that victims "deserve" or are responsible for their victimization (i.e. "I was raped because I needed to grow"); this is not what I wish to imply by "solving for perfect," rather that the transcendence of the human spirit allows us to re-frame such traumas as, "I learned that one can violate my body and yet my spirit is beyond the touch of such ignorant, wounded, pathetic, tortured and ultimately weak brutality." If Victor Frankl could "solve for perfect" in a Nazi concentration camp, we can probably do as much in our lives no matter how challenging they may be at the moment. In this way we learn that we are truly free, no matter what befalls us.

Thank You As Our Ultimate Prayer

"If the only prayer you say in your whole life is 'thank you,' that would suffice." -Meister Eckhart, 13th-Century Dominican Mystic[13]

Giving is a cure for not having—it sends a message to the self that we do have. No matter what other obstacles we face, we can always give love and we can always give thanks. Saying, "Thank you" to the universe affirms our well-being, our abundance and our deep Selves as *givers* of love, charity and gratitude. To say an unqualified "thank you" for all that is present, even in the midst of darkness, loneliness and despair, is a triumph of spirit. If we can manage to live in our gratitude no matter what, our consciousness rises to meet, and align with, the God of what IS. There begins our optimal parenting and our good feelings that last.

Put a Lid On It

Sometimes it's a good idea *not* to let out our feelings. We all have Pandora's Box within us, but as parents we are wise not to open it around our kids. While we do not serve our children by denying darkness, we *do* need to put our chaos and confusion in proper places (i.e., journals, therapy or channeled to creative work).

Embrace the Tiger

While I was writing this chapter, I came across the following anecdote in an article in *The New Yorker* by Caroline Alexander titled, "Tigerland, A Journey Through the Mangrove Forest of Bengal."[14] A scene where a man is collecting wood and is attacked by a tiger stunned me with its compelling, horrifying summation of Zen wisdom: "As the tiger gripped him with its paws, its head hung over his shoulder, drenching his shirt with saliva. 'I knew I was going to die. So I embraced the tiger. He was soft. The tiger was soft. Like a sponge.' Somehow, this surrender freed him—the tiger released him and turned on one of his companions. Taking the companion by the throat, the tiger headed back into the forest."

The man who survived was badly scared and carried the terrible guilt of surviving at the expense of his companion, yet it also underscores how embracing the dark aspects that leap out at us can be a life-affirming, if not life-saving, strategy. The story is really another way of saying, "love the world," and illustrates the almost mystical wisdom of embracing even the most terrifying, unwanted and painful situations. If our children are vexing, bewildering or just breaking our hearts we can softly accept the situation as it is and see if this frees them, or ourselves, to do better.

Soul Tending

Every child may not be Mozart, but every child has a profound meaning, purpose and gift that may enrich the world in spectacular or quietly profound ways. As far as the daimons of our children go, we do not "parent" them; we shape the self and help it develop, but when it comes to soul our main task as parents is mostly to just stay out of the way and maybe pay for music lessons, buy their first chemistry set or sign them up for soccer. Children are gifts from God, on loan from the eternal. Our overriding spiritual obligation is to love our children's souls by seeing and appreciating them as clearly as we can—and not for a second believing we need to change them.

Sacrifice

If we think of sacrifice as what we lose or give up, we gain nothing from it and might as well keep what we have (God doesn't *need* it and even the poor don't need begrudging negativity loaded onto their assistance). But if we learn how giving (resources, time, love) is in our most enlightened Self-interest, then "sacrifice" takes on a different meaning; we discover and enhance our good fortune and abundance *by* giving freely. Whatever parenting asks of us, if we give it generously, and without expectation of thanks, we unlock our most patient, compassionate and effective parenting.

Another aspect of sacrifice is that as parents we also *receive* sacrificial offerings from our children; they may be easily overlooked, but the pieces of lint they pick off the floor and hand to us, scribbled drawings, pencil cups and the like they make for us in preschool are like ritual gifts meant to help them be closer with us. The more we can receive our children and their words, gestures and creations as Divine offerings, the more profoundly we help them trust that they have a lot to give, and that their love will be received, and make a difference, in the world. When our children grasp that this is true, they are spared bitterness, despairing isolation and low self-esteem.

Love Thy Neighbor As Thy Child

A core Christian teaching is to love thy neighbor as thyself. Yet if deep down we are unable to love ourselves, loving our neighbors as ourselves falls short of the ideal. Perhaps loving the other (and ourselves) *as we love our children* brings us closer to the Christian ideal—and to a better world.

Mentors-in-Spirit

Imagine your ancestors or anyone living or dead who you admire. Using imagination, ask these figures to bless and guide your parenting. Visualize, hear or intuit how they might support, guide, encourage and teach you. By conjuring mentors in our minds their spirit comes to life in us.

Let Go Of the Outcome

The ultimate results of our actions are often beyond our control. What we can do is parent with sincerity, nobility and compassion. A conscious approach to life helps us choose loving actions, and even loving non-action where appropriate. Simply doing our best, and not focusing too much on the outcome (i.e. how everything will turn out in some future time), helps us be present to our children and our lives right now. This is our best chance at happiness—and it teaches our children how to be happy over the course of their lives.

The Yoga of Parenting

Yoga supports us to let go of ego, power struggles, materialism, judgment and anger. This aligns us with spirit, which puts us in the ideal frame of mind in which to parent. The poses we commonly think of as "yoga" are merely a technique of quieting the mind in preparation for meditation; what makes it "yoga" is our conscious spiritual intention. Since the crux of yoga is the yoking of body, mind and spirit to something bigger than ourselves, doing the dishes is potentially "yoga" if we dedicate it, for example, to being better parents.

"Namaste" (pron. Nah-mah-stay) means, "The light in me recognizes the light in you." This is a traditional greeting amongst yogis, but no matter what words we use, respect for, and recognition of, the sacred in the other and in ourselves, particularly in the parent-child relationship, potentially transforms all of life, and particularly parenting, into "yoga."

Let God

When my mother-in-law was languishing for weeks in intensive care, desperately trying to recover from heart surgery, I walked blithely past numerous post-cards, pamphlets and pictures of Jesus, Mary and other saints for more than eight weeks until it became clear that she was not going to recover. Facing the inevitable death of this beloved mother-figure, I found myself gathering up these materials despite the fact that they were not from my own tradition. Yet I was too exhausted to actually read them and so they lay at the side of my bed through the awful days of Ellie's dying, and my wife losing her second parent. A pall of numb confusion hung over what was left of the family.

I found myself in bed, depleted and morose, and the forgotten pamphlets quietly beckoned from the nightstand. That night I drank them in, finding that they did not ask me to convert to anything, but rather offered love, compassion and understanding for just what I was feeling (and for just what my wife was feeling, but who was even less inclined at that moment to read about it). One of them, titled, "Let God" carried just that simple message—with love, anecdotes and faith—and I found hope and comfort in it. The God who was in those pamphlets, felt to me like the same God who had been in my Bubby's temple, and in my yoga classes, and in my consulting room and in my children's eyes: the God that unites us all in our faiths, and non-faiths, in our love and losses. "Let God" is another way of saying surrender our limited ego-consciousness to the beautiful and sad mystery of what just is. When we have truly done all that we can do, what other choice do we have left?

The End of Words

Thanks to the human heart by which we live, Thanks to its tenderness, its joys, and fears, To me the meanest flower that blows can give Thoughts that do often lie too deep for tears.

-William Wordsworth

Through natural and fateful development, through the creative process, through the grace of love, through psychotherapy, through becoming of use and helping others, through the blessing of my own children, through yoga, prayer, and heeding messages of spirit that my ego-self did not at first want to hear I find myself gratefully living in a world alive with spirit. This book is a post-it from my soul in support of us all to keep trying our best. Writing has been an honor and a pleasure, and it has been painful, haunting and sometimes akin to torture. I have written about God with great trepidation. I hope that I have not offended, and that my love of God and of the world has been enough to compensate for my limitations in struggling to put things into words that are destined to remain beyond them.

I find myself writing these final words on my forty-eighth birthday, thirty-four years to the day after my best friend, Jonathan's, funeral. I spoke with Gita and Marcel this morning and they are happy with their six grand-children and are doing much better than even the last time I had spoken with them. As I turn forty-eight, my older son is fourteen, the age I turned when Jon died. And I realize that my mother lost her father when she was fourteen, and he was forty-eight. We live and parent in the swirl of the living God and it is an agony that we are powerless against, but which, when we love and embrace it, spills us into the ongoing eternal moment.

Exercises To Consider

1. Write your own parenting book: I noticed that the process of writing this book seemed to help me be a better parent on a day-to-day basis. By writing down what you would advise (and it doesn't have to be a book—a post-it note is fine), it may help you clarify your own thinking and perhaps encourage you to more consistently follow your own good advice.

2. CPR for the spirit: When you feel scared, frustrated, sad or angry—or when you just want to feel calm and happy, consider this exercise that John O'Donohue speaks of in his book, *Anam Cara*: Breathe in Love. Breathe out fear and desire. That's it. The deeper our in-breath the more we are physically, psychically and spiritually nourished; the more completely and consciously we breathe out the more fully we relinquish sorrow and anxiety. Imagine your soul as a container, purifier and spirit-support for your child. Picture their distress as a dark cloud and consciously breathe in their pain, fear, sorrow, etc. Mingle their gloom with the love you simultaneously breathe in, then breathe out their fear, desire and unhappiness.

3. Read spiritual books, or read any book spiritually: Reading books that nourish the soul primes us to be more compassionate, mindful and spiritually awake. Reading even a sentence or two of a spiritually inspiring book every day is good

practice that supports spiritual growth, and better parenting. The obvious, but venerable classics include the Torah, the New Testament, the Koran, the Bagavad Gita and the Tao Te Ching.[15] A few others that I find particularly worthwhile include any works by Thich Nhat Hahn such as *Being Peace* or *Teachings on Love*[16], *Anam Cara* by John O'Donohue[17], *I and Thou* by Martin Buber and *Answer to Job* by C.G. Jung. Some of these books can be difficult, but then parenting is not easy either. Any book we read, if we dedicate it to our children, infuses the experience with spiritual resonance. If we ask a question of the world, and then read any book at all (but with sixth sense open) we might be amazed by the seeming coincidences of relevant messages that often occur.

4. Mirror work: Spend some time before the mirror. Watch, gaze, look softly, not to see if you are attractive or adequate, but to see you as you are, as nature and your experiences/environment have rendered you –look deeply, meditate on yourself in the hopes that you might be able to see the spirit, divine spark and essence that you really are. Gaze softly into your own eyes and ask them to reveal the eternal You, the Self that unlocks love, faith, gratitude and illuminates our interconnection with everyone and everything. Take this gaze to your child.

5. Take a walk in gratitude to the universe: The universe is always talking to us, guiding and

teaching us at the soul level; our best Selves are keen to walk through it with appreciation. Walk, in whatever mood and with whatever troubles you carry, and appreciate the tree, the light, the garbage and the flowers to discover that you are free and that things are as they must be— perfect, full of love and guidance and infinitely open to change.

6. Plan for not being here: Be sure to make a will, be sure you have life insurance. Being responsible for our lives includes being responsible to those who depend on us. Fear might block us from confronting these tasks, but they are actually liberating and consistent with freeing ourselves to prosper and to live more fully. When we bring along a book there's rarely a line at the bank; when we bring an umbrella it doesn't rain (well sometimes it does, but then it's good to have an umbrella).

7. Set a working intention (every day): Select one thing you wish to improve about your parenting. Keep it simple and write it down (i.e. "be more positive," "be less sarcastic," or "listen more"). Place your intention in your wallet, car, computer or someplace else where you will frequently see it. When you feel you are consistently achieving your intention, set another intention.

8. Do yoga and dedicate it to being a better parent: If you're only going to do one thing out of all the things in this book, consider yoga. Try

the following pose: lay on the floor, eyes closed and breathing naturally while thinking of nothing. This is one of the most important poses in yoga, Savasana (or corpse pose); it is the proper last pose of every class. By just laying down, if you dedicate it to your children's well-being, you are on your way to being a yogi.

As far as the physical practice of yoga, it doesn't matter if you can touch your toes, or even see your toes; if you try with sincerity you are unlikely to regret it. If you are a beginner, find a teacher who has a kind and welcoming energy, and don't just go to one class. Do it for a month and then another; do it for a year and see what happens. Set an intention each time and dedicate your yoga to it. After yoga (or doing the dishes with a yogic attitude) come back to your intention (i.e. to love God in the service of our children); you will probably be calmer and you will very likely be more patient and attuned as a parent. If you are more advanced in your practice, consider increasing emphasis on intention, on breath and on keeping in mind that all of the poses are essentially preparation for meditation; whether in lotus, headstand or Savasana, quiet the mind and open the heart.

Notes

Introduction
[1] If the reader is interested to learn more about yoga, an excellent choice is: B. K. S. Iyengar, *Light on Yoga*, (1979; Paperback revised edition, New York: Pantheon/Random House; First published by Schocken Books, George Allen & Unwin [publishers] Ltd., 1966).

Chapter 1
[1] Note that in all case examples names and identifying details have been changed to protect the privacy of those involved.

Chapter 2
[1] C. G. Jung, *Memories, Dreams, Reflections* (recorded and edited by Aniela Jaffé, translated from the German by Richard and Clara Winston; originally published under the title, *Erinnerungen Träume Gedanken*; 1989, Vintage Books Edition; originally published New York: Pantheon Books/Random House, 1963).
[2] The notion of parents' declining influence over children as they develop was popularized in the media following the release of Judith Rich Harris' *The Nurture Assumption* (Free Press, 1998). A number of counter-arguments to this position are noted in an article by Beth Azar, "How do parents matter? Let us count the ways," *Monitor on Psychology,* (31 no. 7, July/August, 2000).
[3] *Mary Poppins* (Film), Disney, 1964.

[4] *The Andy Griffith Show* (TV Series), CBS, 1960-68. *Marcus Welby, M.D.* (TV Series), Universal Television, 1969-76. *Mr. Rogers' Neighborhood* (TV Series), Family Communications/WQED, 1968-2001.

[5] *Barney & Friends* (TV Series), Connecticut Public Television, 1992-????.

[6] *The Cosby Show* (TV Series), Bill Cosby/Carsey-Werner/NBC, 1984-92.

[7] Harper Lee, *To Kill a Mockingbird*, (New York: HarperCollins, 1960).

[8] *To Kill a Mockingbird* (Film), Universal Pictures, 1962.

[9] Heidi Murkoff and Susan Mazel, *What to Expect When You're Expecting* (New York: Workman Publishing 1984).

Chapter 3
[1] Dr. Seuss (pseudonym for Theodore Seuss Geisel), *Yertle the Turtle and Other Stories*, (New York: Random House, 1950).

[2] *The Tramp* (Film), 1915; *The Gold Rush* (Film), 1926; *City Lights* (Film), 1931 and numerous other films by Charlie Chaplin/Charlie Chaplin Productions. *A Charlie Brown Christmas* (TV Special), Lee Mendelson/Bill Melendez Production/CBS, 1965. *Napoleon Dynamite* (Film) Access Films/Fox Searchlight/MTV Films/Paramount Pictures, 2004.

[3] "To look at a thing is very different from seeing a thing. One does not see anything until one sees its beauty." Oscar Wilde, playwright, poet and novelist, 1854-1900.

Chapter 4
[1] Jakob and Wilhelm Grimm, *Grimms' Tales for Young and Old*, (translated by Ralph Manheim. New York: Anchor/Double-

day, 1977; Translated from the Winkler-Verlag [Munich] edition of the Complete Kinder-und HausmŠrchen by Jakob and Wilhelm Grimm, as first published in 1819).

Chapter 5
[1] A. A. Milne, *Winnie-the-Pooh*, illustrated by Ernest H. Shepard, (New York: Dutton Children's Books, 80th Anniversary edition, 2006; originally published in London by Methuen, 1926).

[2] Christopher Layne, "Painful truths about depressives cognitions," *Journal of Clinical Psychology*, 39, no. 6 (published online 21 Feb. 2006): 848-853.

Chapter 6
[1] Yakov Leib haKohain references this Jewish mystical creation story, attributed to Rabbi Isaac Luria, a 16th century Kabbalist, in an online article, "Sabbatianism, Tikkun and the Big Bang Theory," (posted October 1999, modified 12 July 2004) (www.kheber.net/essays/Tikkun_and_Big_Bang_Theory.html).

[2] Bruno Bettelheim, *The Uses of Enchantment: The Meaning and Importance of Fairy Tales*, (1989, Vintage Books Edition/Random House; first published New York: Alfred A. Knopf, 1976).

[3] Kate Dicamillo (Author), Bagran Ibatoulline (Illustrator), *The Miraculous Journey of Edward Tulane*, (Candlewick Press, 2006). Kate Dicamillo, *Because of Winn-Dixie*, (Candlewick Press, 2001).

[4] Beverly Cleary, *Dear Mr. Henshaw* (New York: Harper Classics, 1983).

[5] *Crimes and Misdemeanors* (Film), Woody Allen, 1989.

[6] *Mr. Bean* (TV Series), Tiger Aspect Productions, 1990-95. *Sherlock Jr.* (Film), Buster Keaton Productions, 1924; and *The General* (Film), Buster Keaton Productions, 1927 are particularly fun for kids. *School of Rock* (Film), Paramount Pictures, 2003.

Chapter 7
[1] Lewis Carroll, *Alice's Adventures in Wonderland* (London: Penguin Classics, 1998, originally published in England, 1865).
[2] Article by J. Daw Holloway referencing research by June Tangney, Ph.D. of George Mason University, in "Monitor on Psychology," November, 2005.

Chapter 8
[1] Grimm's Tales, "The Three Languages."
[2] Grimm's Tales, "The White Snake."
[3] Harvey Karp, *The Happiest Toddler on the Block: How to Eliminate Tantrums and Raise a Patient, Respectful, and Cooperative One-to Four-Year-Old*, (New York: Bantam/Random House, 2004). Referenced in an article by Tara Parker-Pope, "Coping with the Caveman in the Crib" *The New York Times*, February 5, 2008.
[4] Tara Parker Pope, *The New York Times*, February 5, 2008: "'The No. 1 precipitant to child abuse is the kid who cries and gets upset and doesn't settle down and whines and whines,' says Robert Fox, professor of psychology at Marquette University and director of the behavior clinic at Penfield Children's Center in Milwaukee. 'It's a real vulnerable situation for abuse.'"

[5] Malcom Gladwell, *Blink—The Power of Thinking Without Thinking* (2005; reprint, New York: Back Bay Books/Little, Brown and Company, 2007).

[6] Elizabeth A. Rauscher and Russell Targ, "The Speed of Thought: Investigation of a Complex Space-Time Metric to Describe Psychic Phenomena," *Journal of Scientific Exploration*, 15, No.3. (Fall, 2001): 331-354.

[7] Elizabeth Lloyd Mayer, *Extraordinary Knowing: Science, Skepticism, and the Inexplicable Powers of the Human Mind*, (2007; reprint, New York: Bantam/Random House, 2008).

[8] Elizabeth Mayer discusses this, citing Eva Brabant, Ernst Falzeder, Patrizia Giampier-Deutsch, *The Correspondence of Sigmund Freud and Sandor Ferenczi* (Cambridge, MA: Harvard University Press, 1993).

[9] C. G. Jung, *Memories, Dreams, Reflections* (recorded and edited by Aniela Jaffé, translated from the German by Richard and Clara Winston; originally published under the title, *Erinnerungen Träume Gedanken*; 1989, Vintage Books Edition; originally published New York: Pantheon Books/Random House, 1963) p. 137.

[10] Rauscher & Targ, "The Speed of Thought: Investigation of a Complex Space-Time Metric to Describe Psychic Phenomena."

[11] Dean Radin, *The Conscious Universe: The Scientific Truth of Psychic Phenomena*, (San Francisco: Harper Edge/Harper Collins, 1997).

[12] As presented by Harvard researcher Sara Lazar on the neurobiology of meditation, at a conference on Psychology and Mindfulness at UCLA, September, 2007.

[13] Based on research conducted by John Bargh, Mark Chen and Lara Burrows at New York University, as referenced in Gladwell's *Blink*.

[14] Based on research done by Lloyd H. Silverman, F.M. Lachman, and R.H. Milich, *The Search for Oneness* (New York; International Universities Press, 1982); Lloyd H. Silverman and K.K. Silverman, "A Clinical-Experimental Approach to the Study of Subliminal Stimulation: The Effects of a Drive-Related Stimulus Upon Rorschach Responses" Journal of Abnormal and Social Psychology 69, no. 2 (1964): 158-172; Lloyd H. Silverman, "'Mommy and I Are One': Implications for Psychotherapy," American Psychologist 40, no 12 (1985): 1296-1308. Silverman's work is referenced by Mayer in *Extraordinary Knowing*.

[15] Eileen J. Garrett, *Adventures in the Supernormal* (1949; reprinted New York: Helix Press, 2002), 116-117. Referenced by Mayer in *Extraordinary Knowing*.

[16] Gladwell, *Blink*.

[17] Thich Nhat Hanh, *Teachings on Love*, (Berkeley: Parallax Press, 2007).

[18] *Mary Poppins* and *To Kill a Mockingbird* were referenced in Chapter 2. *Babbette's Feast*; original Danish title: *Babettes Gæstebud* (Film), Panorama Film, 1987. *Lorenzo's Oil* (Film), Universal Pictures, 1992. *Mr. Mom* (Film), Sherwood Productions/Twentieth Century Fox, 1983. *Parenthood* (Film), Imagine Entertainment, 1989. *Baby Boom* (Film), Myers/Shyer, 1987. *Mother* (Film), Albert Brooks/Paramount, 1996. *The Diving Bell and the Butterfly*; original title in French: *Le Scaphandre et Le Papillon* (Film), Pathé Rene Productions, 2007.

Chapter 9

[1] As noted in an article by Christopher Shea, "Mindful Exercise" in the *The New York Times*, December 7, 2007: "Simply by telling 44 hotel maids that what they did each day involved some serious exercise, the Harvard psychologist Ellen Langer and Alia J. Crum, a student, were apparently able to lower the women's blood pressure, shave pounds off their bodies and improve their body-fat and "waist to hip" ratios. Self-awareness, it seems, was the women's elliptical trainer."

[2] *Sophie's Choice* (Film) Incorporated Television Company, 1982.

[3] *Ordinary People* (Film) Paramount Pictures, 1980. *Good Will Hunting* (Film) Be Gentlemen Limited Partnership/Miramax, 1997.

[4] Herman Hesse, *Siddartha: An Indian Tale* (New York: Penguin, translated from German by Joachim Neugroschel, 1999; originally published in German, 1922) p. 124.

[5] Martin Buber, *I And Thou* (A new translation by Walter Kaufmann, 1996, First Touchstone Edition/Simon & Schuster; translation copyright, New York: Charles Scribner's Sons, 1970) pp. 60, 162.

[6] James Hillman, *The Soul's Code: In Search Of Character And Calling*, (New York: Warner/Random House, 1996) p. 63.

[7] Herman Melville, *Moby Dick*, (1984, reprint, 5th printing, New York: Bantam; first published, 1851) p. 175.

[8] Quote from a letter Jung wrote to H. Schär of Nov. 16, 1951, from *C. G. Jung: Letters*, selected and edited by Gerhard Adler in collaboration with Aniela Jaffé (2 vols., Princeton and London, 1973-74) referenced in the Editorial Note by

Gerhard Adler in *Answer to Job*,p *v*. C. G. Jung, *Answer to Job,* (2002, Fiftieth Anniversary Edition, Bollingen/Princeton University Press; originally published as part of *Psychology and Religion: West and East*, New York: Meridian Books, 1960).

[9] Jung, *Answer to Job*, p. 99.

[10] Jung, *Answer to Job*, pp. 54-55.

[11] Viktor E. Frankl, *Man's Search For Meaning: An Introduction to Logotherapy* (1984, Third Edition, Touchstone/Simon & Schuster; originally published Boston: Beacon Press, 1959; first published in Austria under the title *Ein Psycholog erlebt das Konzentrationslager*, 1946).

[12] Lama Anagarika Govinda, *Foundations of Tibetan Mysticism* (First American Edition, York Beach, Maine: Samuel Weiser, Inc., 1969) p. 86.

[13] Meister Eckhart lived from 1260-1327.

[14] Caroline Alexander, "Tigerland, A journey through the mangrove forest of Bengal," *New Yorker*, April 22, 2008.

[15] Good translations of the *Tao Te Ching* and the *Bhagavad Gita* can be found in: Lao Tzu, *The Tao Te Ching* (A New Translation by Brian Browne Walker, New York: St. Martin's/Griffin, 1995). Stephen Mitchell, *Bhagavad Gita: A New Translation. Stephen Mitchell* (Three Rivers/Crown/Random House, 2000).

[16] Thich Nhat Hanh, *Being Peace* (Berkeley: Parallax Press, 1987). Thich Nhat Hanh, *Teachings on Love* (Berkeley: Parallax Press, 2007).

[17] John O'Donohue, *Anam Cara: A Book of Celtic Wisdom* (2004 reprint Perennial; New York: Harper Collins, 1997).

References/Bibliography

Bruno Bettelheim, *The Uses of Enchantment: The Meaning and Importance of Fairy Tales*, (1989, Vintage Books Edition/ Random House; first published New York: Alfred A. Knopf, 1976).

D. Bohm & B. J. Hiley, *The Undivided Universe*, (New York: Routledge, 1993).

Paul Bowles, *The Sheltering Sky* (1990, New York: First Vintage International Edition/Random House; originally published by The Ecco Press, 1949).

Jean de Brunhoff, *The Story of Babar,* (translated from the French by Merle S. Haas; New York: Random House, 1933).

Martin Buber, *I And Thou* (A new translation by Walter Kaufmann, 1996, First Touchstone Edition/Simon & Schuster; translation copyright, New York: Charles Scribner's Sons, 1970).

Kate Dicamillo, *Because of Winn-Dixie*, (Candlewick Press, 2001).

Kate Dicamillo (Author), Bagran Ibatoulline (Illustrator), *The Miraculous Journey of Edward Tulane*, (Candlewick Press, 2006).

Kate Dicamillo (Author), Timothy Basil Ering (Illustrator), *The Tale of Despereaux*, (Candlewick Press, 2006).

Charles Dickens, *Oliver Twist*, (1999, Oxford University Press; originally published in Bentley's Miscellany as a serial in monthly installments, 1837-38, then by Richard Bentley, 1838).

P. D. Eastman, *Go, Dog. Go!* (New York: Beginner Books/ Random House, 1961).

Edward F. Edinger, *The Mystery of The Coniunctio: Alchemical Images of Individuation*, (Toronto: Inner City Books, 1994; based on material first presented as lectures at the C. G. Jung Institute of San Francisco, October 19-20, 1984).

Mircea Eliade, *Shamanism: Archaic Techniques of Ecstasy*, (translated from the French by Willard R. Trask. 1974, second paperback printing, Princeton University Press/Bollingen; Originally published in French as *Le Chamanisme et les techniques archaïques de l'extase* by Librairie Payot, Paris, 1951).

Mircea Eliade, *Yoga: Immortality and Freedom*, (translated from the French by Willard R. Trask. 1990, Ninth Printing, Princeton University Press/Bollingen; Originally published in French as *Le Yoga. Immortalité et Liberté*, Librairie Payot, Paris, 1954).

Viktor E. Frankl, *Man's Search For Meaning: An Introduction to Logotherapy*, (1984, Third Edition, Touchstone/Simon & Schuster; originally published Boston: Beacon Press,

1959; first published in Austria under the title *Ein Psycholog erlebt das Konzentrationslager*, 1946).

Sir James George Frazer, *The Golden Bough*, (New York: Collier/Macmillan, 1922).

Malcom Gladwell, *Blink – The Power of Thinking Without Thinking* (2005; reprint, New York: Back Bay Books/ Little, Brown and Company, 2007).

Lama Anagarika Govinda, *Foundations of Tibetan Mysticism*, (First American Edition, York Beach, Maine: Samuel Weiser, Inc., 1969).

Jakob and Wilhelm Grimm, *Grimms' Tales for Young and Old*, (translated by Ralph Manheim. New York: Anchor/Doubleday, 1977; Translated from the Winkler-Verlag [Munich] edition of the Complete Kinder-und Hausmärchen by Jakob and Wilhelm Grimm, as first published in 1819).

Thich Nhat Hanh, *Teachings on Love*, (Berkeley: Parallax Press, 2007).

James Hillman, *The Soul's Code: In Search Of Character And Calling*, (New York: Warner/Random House, 1996).

S. E. Hinton, *The Outsiders*, (New York: Viking Penguin, 1967).

Victor Hugo, *The Hunchback of Notre Dame*, (New York: Signet Classic/Penguin, 1964; originally published in French, 1831).

Lewis Hyde, *Trickster Makes This World: Mischief, Myth, and Art*, (New York: North Point Press/Farrar, Straus and Giroux, 1998).

B. K. S. Iyengar, *Light on Yoga*, (1979; Paperback revised edition, New York: Pantheon/Random House; First published by Schocken Books, George Allen & Unwin [publishers] Ltd., 1966).

C. G. Jung, *Answer to Job,* (2002, Fiftieth Anniversary Edition, Bollingen/Princeton University Press; originally published as part of *Psychology and Religion: West and East*, New York: Meridian Books, 1960).

C. G. Jung, *Memories, Dreams, Reflections* (recorded and edited by Aniela Jaffé, translated from the German by Richard and Clara Winston; originally published under the title, *Erinnerungen Träume Gedanken*; 1989, Vintage Books Edition; originally published New York: Pantheon Books/Random House, 1963).

Jon Kabat-Zinn, *Coming To Our Senses*, (New York: Hyperion, 2005).

Harvey Karp, *The Happiest Toddler on the Block: How to Eliminate Tantrums and Raise a Patient, Respectful, and Cooperative One-to Four-Year-Old*, (New York: Bantam/Random House, 2004).

Harper Lee, *To Kill a Mockingbird*, (New York: HarperCollins, 1960).

Elizabeth Lloyd Mayer, *Extraordinary Knowing: Science, Skepticism, and the Inexplicable Powers of the Human Mind*, (2007; reprint, New York: Bantam/Random House, 2008).

Herman Melville, *Moby Dick*, (1984, reprint, 5th printing, New York: Bantam; first published, 1851).

A. A. Milne, *Winnie-the-Pooh*, illustrated by Ernest H. Shepard, (New York: Dutton Children's Books, 80th Anniversary edition, 2006; originally published in London by Methuen, 1926).

Stephen Mitchell, *Bhagavad Gita: A New Translation. Stephen Mitchell*, (Three Rivers/Crown/Random House, 2000).

John O'Donohue, *Anam Cara: A Book of Celtic Wisdom* (2004 reprint Perennial; New York: Harper Collins, 1997).

John O'Donohue, *To Bless the Space Between Us: A Book of Blessings* (New York: Doubleday, 2008).

Tara Parker-Pope, "Coping with the Caveman in the Crib" New York Times, February 5, 2008.

Dean Radin, *The Conscious Universe: The Scientific Truth of Psychic Phenomena*, (San Francisco: Harper Edge/Harper Collins, 1997).

Carl R. Rogers, *A Way Of Being* (Boston: Houghton Mifflin, 1980).

Elizabeth A. Rauscher and Russell Targ, "The Speed of Thought: Investigation of a Complex Space-Time Metric to Describe Psychic Phenomena," *Journal of Scientific Exploration*, 15, No.3. (Fall, 2001): 331-354.

J. K. Rowling, *Harry Potter and the Sorcerer's Stone*, (New York: Schoolastic, 1998; originally published in London by Bloomsbury as *Harry Potter and the Philosopher's Stone*, 1997).

J. D. Salinger, *The Catcher in the Rye*, (Boston: Little, Brown, 1951).

Dr. Seuss (pseudonym for Theodore Seuss Geisel), *Yertle the Turtle and Other Stories*, (New York: Random House, 1950).

Lemony Snicket (pseudonym for Daniel Handler) *A Series of Unfortunate Events by Lemony Snicket, Book the First, The Bad Beginning*, (New York: HarperCollins, 1999).

D. T. Suzuki, *Zen Buddhism*, (1996 reprint Image/Bantam/Doubleday Dell; originally published by Anchor Books, 1956).

Eckhart Tolle, *The Power of Now*, (1999 First U.S. printing Novato, CA: New World Library; originally published in Canada by Namaste Publishing, 1997).

P. L. Travers, *Mary Poppins*, Harcourt Brace & Co, 1934.

Daniel J. Siegel, *Mindsight: The New Science of Transformation* (Random House, 2010).

Lao Tzu, *The Tao Te Ching* (A New Translation by Brian Browne Walker, New York: St. Martin's/Griffin, 1995).

Gerhard Wehr, *Jung: A Biography*, (translated from German by David M. Weeks; 2001, Boston: Shambhala; originally published Munich: Kösel-Verlag GmbH & Co, 1985).

Richard Wilhelm (translation), *The I Ching or Book of Changes*, (1981, eighteenth printing, Bollingen/Princeton University Press; first edition in two volumes, 1950).

Marianne Williamson, *A Return To Love: Reflections on the Principles of A Course in Miracles*, (New York: Harper Collins, 1992).

William Wordsworth, "Intimations of Immortality from Recollections of Early Childhood" originally published in *Poems in Two Volumes (1807)*.

Connie Zweig & Jeremiah Abrams, *Meeting The Shadow: The Hidden Power of the Dark Side of Human Nature*, (edited by Zweig & Abrams; New York: Tarcher/Putnam, 1991).

* * *

Filmography and Television Shows Referenced

The Adventures of Ozzie & Harriet (TV Series) Stage Five/ABC, 1952-1966.

The Andy Griffith Show (TV Series), CBS, 1960-68.

Babbette's Feast; original Danish title: *Babettes Gæstebud* (Film), Panorama Film, 1987.

Baby Boom (Film), Myers/Shyer, 1987.

Bambi (Film), Disney, 1942.

Barney & Friends (TV Series), Connecticut Public Television, 1992-????.

A Charlie Brown Christmas (TV Special), Lee Mendelson/Bill Melendez Production/CBS, 1965.

The Cosby Show (TV Series), Bill Cosby/Carsey-Werner/NBC, 1984-92.

Crimes and Misdemeanors (Film), Woody Allen, 1989.

The Diving Bell and the Butterfly; original title in French: *Le Scaphandre et Le Papillon* (Film), Pathé Rene Productions, 2007.

It's the Great Pumpkin, Charlie Brown (TV Special), Lee Mendelson/Bill Melendez Production/CBS, 1966.

How the Grinch Stole Christmas! (TV Special), MGM, 1966.

To Kill a Mockingbird (Film), Universal Pictures, 1962.

Lorenzo's Oil, (Film), Universal Pictures, 1992.

Marcus Welby, M.D. (TV Series), Universal Television, 1969-76.

Mary Poppins (Film), Disney, 1964.

Mary Poppins (Musical), opened on West End, 2004.

Mr. Mom (Film), Sherwood Productions/Twentieth Century Fox, 1983.

Mother (Film), Albert Brooks/Paramount, 1996.

Parenthood (Film), Imagine Entertainment, 1989.

Peter Pan (Film), Disney, 1953.

Mr. Rogers' Neighborhood (TV Series), Family Communications/WQED, 1968-2001.

Shrek (Film), Dreamworks, 2001.

Sicko (Documentary Film), Michael Moore/Dog Eat Dog Films/The Weinstein Company, 2007.

The Sopranos (TV Series), HBO, 1999-2007.

Made in the USA
Lexington, KY
22 December 2011